Mastering SIMD with Java Vector API

Unlocking Single-Core Performance Through SIMD Optimization

Roman Snytsar

Mastering SIMD with Java Vector API: Unlocking Single-Core Performance Through SIMD Optimization

Roman Snytsar
Sammamish, WA, USA

ISBN-13 (pbk): 979-8-8688-2675-7   ISBN-13 (electronic): 979-8-8688-2676-4
https://doi.org/10.1007/979-8-8688-2676-4

Managing Director, Apress Media LLC: Welmoed Spahr
Acquisitions Editor: Melissa Duffy
Editorial Assistant: Gryffin Winkler

Cover designed by eStudioCalamar

Cover image designed by Pexels

Distributed to the book trade worldwide by Springer Science+Business Media New York, 1 New York Plaza, New York, NY 10004. Phone 1-800-SPRINGER, fax (201) 348-4505, e-mail orders-ny@springer-sbm.com, or visit www.springeronline.com. Apress Media, LLC is a Delaware LLC and the sole member (owner) is Springer Science + Business Media Finance Inc (SSBM Finance Inc). SSBM Finance Inc is a **Delaware** corporation.

For information on translations, please e-mail booktranslations@springernature.com; for reprint, paperback, or audio rights, please e-mail bookpermissions@springernature.com.

Apress titles may be purchased in bulk for academic, corporate, or promotional use. eBook versions and licenses are also available for most titles. For more information, reference our Print and eBook Bulk Sales web page at http://www.apress.com/bulk-sales.

Any source code or other supplementary material referenced by the author in this book is available to readers on GitHub. For more detailed information, please visit https://www.apress.com/gp/services/source-code.

If disposing of this product, please recycle the paper

To my wife: my first reader, my best critic, and my biggest fan.

Table of Contents

About the Author xix

About the Technical Reviewer xiii

Introduction xv

Chapter 1: Programming Vector Hardware 1

In This Chapter 1

x86 Architecture: Intel and AMD 1

ARM Architecture 3

RISC-V Architecture 3

Choosing Vector Length 3

Performance Testing: Intel and AMD 7

Performance Testing: ARM Processors 8

What's Next 8

Chapter 2: Vector Addition 9

In This Chapter 10

Sequential Addition 10

Pairwise Addition 13

Rounding During Addition 15

Kahan's Algorithm 18

What's Next 21

Chapter 3: A Taste of Statistics 23

In This Chapter 23

Two-Pass Algorithm 23

Single-Pass Algorithm 25

Vector Approach 29

Benchmarks 35

What's Next 40

Chapter 4: Multiples of Three or Five **41**

Problem Statement 41

In This Chapter 41

Scalar Solution 41

Vector Loop 58

Arithmetic Progression 73

Benchmarks 75

What's Next 76

Chapter 5: Removing Duplicates **77**

In This Chapter 77

Two-Pointer Method 77

Vector Compression 78

Extra Memory Access 82

Benchmarks 84

What's Next 85

Chapter 6: Prefix Sum **87**

In This Chapter 88

Scalar Solution 88

Vector Solution 89

Benchmarks 94

What's Next 96

Chapter 7: Finding the Unique Element **97**

Problem Statement 97

In This Chapter 97

Scalar Solution 98

Vector Solution 99

Two Unique Elements 100

Vector Solution 101

Finding Among Triples 103

Vector Solution 105

Practical Applications 107

Benchmarks 108

What's Next 109

Chapter 8: Even Fibonacci Numbers 111

In This Chapter 111

Scalar Algorithm 111

Vector Algorithm 113

Scalar Hopping 116

Vector Hopping 117

Benchmarks 119

What's Next 121

Chapter 9: Random Number Generator 123

In This Chapter 123

java.util.Random 124

Vector Acceleration 128

Practical Applications 135

Benchmarks 136

What's Next 137

Chapter 10: Trapping Rainwater 139

In This Chapter 139

Interview Solution 140

Vector Scan 141

Unrolled Vector Scan 144

Optimal Vector Scan 148

Accelerating Optimal Scan 158

Memoization 177

Mini Algorithm 190

Benchmarks 202

What's Next 203

Chapter 11: Convergents of e 205

In This Chapter 206

Scalar Solution 206

Horizontal Vector Solution 209

Vertical Vector Solution 213

Strassen Algorithm 215

Karatsuba Algorithm 219

The Billionaire Algorithm 223

Short Vectors 227

Benchmarks 230

What's Next 232

Chapter 12: Merging Arrays 233

In This Chapter 233

Three-Pointer Method 233

Merge Path 235

Bitonic Sorting 236

Unrolled Loop 240

Asymmetric Loop 244

Ranking Elements 248

Benchmarks 252

What's Next 253

Chapter 13: Largest Product in a Series **255**

In This Chapter 256

Naive Algorithm 256

Sliding Algorithm 258

Element-Wise Vector Algorithm 260

Two-Scan Algorithm 263

Vertical Algorithm 267

Universal Algorithm 272

Benchmarks 276

What's Next 278

Chapter 14: Maximum Subarray Sum **279**

In This Chapter 279

Kadane's Algorithm 280

Reformulating the Problem 281

Vector Solution 283

Lightweight Algorithm 288

Benchmarks 294

Practical Applications 295

What's Next 296

Chapter 15: The Collatz Conjecture **297**

In This Chapter 297

Problem Statement 297

    Example Orbits 298

Straightforward Solution 298

Divergent Execution 300

Finding Patterns 302

Multi-step Lookahead 305

Combined Approach 309

Work Piling 317

Memoization 324

Over-optimization 329

Result 337

Benchmarks 337

Conclusion **341**

Index **343**

About the Author

Roman Snytsar is a researcher and software engineer with 20 years of experience at Microsoft Research. His work spans performance optimization, computer science theory, and practical algorithm implementation. He has published multiple patents and articles focused on explaining complex technical concepts in accessible ways. With deep expertise in both theoretical foundations and real-world performance-critical code, Roman brings a unique perspective to making advanced programming techniques accessible to working developers. His research background, combined with hands-on engineering experience, makes him uniquely qualified to bridge the gap between academic SIMD theory and practical Java development.

About the Technical Reviewer

Daniel Lemire is a computer science professor at the Université du Québec (TÉLUQ), where he specializes in high-performance programming, software optimization, and data indexing techniques, with a particular emphasis on vectorization and SIMD instructions to accelerate computational tasks. Ranked among the top 2% of scientists worldwide by Stanford University and Elsevier, he has authored over 100 peer-reviewed papers and contributed performance-enhancing code to major libraries and web browsers, including innovations in JSON parsing that earned him the University of Quebec's 2020 Award of Excellence in Research. As one of GitHub's top 1000 developers with over 100 million users on the platform, Lemire frequently explores vector programming in languages through his influential blog and open source projects.

Introduction

Speed changes everything. A program that runs ten times faster is not merely more convenient—it becomes capable of tasks previously impossible. Real-time becomes truly real. Overnight batch jobs finish before lunch. Simulations that once demanded clusters now run on laptops. This book is about achieving that kind of speed: not through exotic hardware or architectural overhauls, but by unlocking the vector processing power that already lies dormant in your CPU. Modern processors can execute the same operation on 8, 16, or even 64 data elements simultaneously—yet most Java code touches none of this capability. You will learn to change that. By mastering the techniques in these pages, you will write programs that fully exploit the silicon you already own, transforming performance from a constraint into a competitive advantage.

The Parallelism Hierarchy

Modern applications—from real-time analytics to machine learning and scientific modeling—demand ever-increasing computational performance. To meet these demands, developers of complex systems must exploit several hierarchical levels of parallelism, ranging from distributed clusters down to parallel acceleration within a single processor core.

At the highest level, parallel processing algorithms distribute computations across multiple systems or nodes, often organized into clusters or deployed in cloud environments. This model proves essential for analyzing large datasets and supporting fault-tolerant, scalable architectures. Platforms like Hadoop and Spark abstract away the complexity of distributed systems, enabling developers to implement parallel solutions through various abstractions: the map-reduce paradigm, resilient distributed datasets (RDD), and dataflow graphs. These platforms handle task scheduling, data partitioning, and inter-node communication, freeing developers to concentrate on application logic.

Within a single system, multi-threading enables parallel code execution across multiple CPU cores. Application and library developers readily access this model through high-level languages. Multi-threading works well for decomposing tasks into independent units, such as processing multiple client requests, parallelizing loops, or performing asynchronous I/O. Java developers use constructs like Thread, ExecutorService, ForkJoinPool, and parallel streams to express multi-threaded parallelism.

Despite the prevalence of distributed and thread-level models, real-world performance often hinges on single-core execution efficiency. This level of parallelism is less visible to most developers, but is crucial for optimizing compute-intensive workloads. Acceleration is achieved through two mechanisms:

- **Data-level parallelism (DLP)** allows a single core to process multiple data elements simultaneously using vector registers. This is the domain of SIMD (Single Instruction, Multiple Data) operations, where one instruction operates on a vector of values.

- **Instruction-level parallelism (ILP)** allows multiple machine instructions to execute simultaneously within a single core through pipelining, superscalar execution, and out-of-order execution. Hardware implements these techniques to boost performance substantially, yet they remain invisible to most developers.

Traditionally, exploiting single-core parallelism required low-level programming in assembly language or using C/C++ intrinsics—cumbersome, error-prone, and difficult to maintain. This additional complexity creates a barrier that limits most Java developers' access to performance-critical optimizations.

What This Book Is About

The Java Vector API changes this equation. Introduced as an incubating feature in JDK 16 and progressing toward standardization, it provides a platform-independent abstraction over SIMD instructions. For the first time, Java developers can explicitly express vector operations without leaving the safety and portability of the JVM ecosystem.

The Vector API opens data-level parallelism to a broader range of developers by

- Providing a platform-independent abstraction over SIMD instructions

- Using familiar object-oriented Java constructs to express vector operations

- Enabling both automatic vectorization and explicit vector programming in the JVM

With the Vector API, developers can write high-performance code that leverages hardware acceleration without leaving the Java ecosystem. This fundamentally changes performance optimization in Java, especially in domains like finance, scientific computing, and machine learning.

Yet data-level parallelism tells only half the story. This book also explores instruction-level parallelism: the art of structuring code so that multiple operations execute simultaneously within a single core. Through techniques like loop unrolling, asymmetric loop construction, and careful attention to structural hazards, we learn to exploit the full capabilities of modern superscalar processors. The interplay between SIMD vectorization and instruction-level optimization often determines whether a solution achieves modest gains or dramatic speedups.

Mastering these techniques, however, requires more than memorizing APIs and patterns. The deeper challenge lies in recognizing which problems yield to vectorization, understanding why certain approaches succeed while others fail, and developing the intuition to make sound performance decisions. This book addresses all three.

A Different Way of Thinking

While Java developers are well-versed in high-level parallelism abstractions, exploiting single-core parallelism requires fundamentally different thinking. Unlocking the full potential of the Vector API demands a paradigm shift in how developers reason about performance, data, and control flow.

This book invites you on a journey through familiar problems, viewed with fresh eyes. Many of the problems examined here are known to anyone who has prepared for technical interviews or studied computer science fundamentals. These problems were deliberately chosen for their simplicity and applicability.

However, this book's goal is not to rehash well-worn solutions. Instead, we present a new way of thinking about these problems: one based on low-level parallelism, with particular emphasis on data-level and instruction-level optimization. By viewing these problems through the lens of vectorization, we discover acceleration opportunities often hidden beneath layers of abstraction.

We invite readers to move beyond traditional algorithmic reasoning and embrace a performance-oriented approach:

- Recognizing program patterns that lend themselves to parallel execution

- Understanding how modern processors execute code at the microarchitectural level

- Learning to explicitly express parallelism using the Java Vector API

The book's ultimate goal is to equip developers with the intuition and practical skills needed to apply this knowledge to real-world software projects. Whether optimizing a numerical kernel, accelerating a data pipeline, or improving the responsiveness of a user-facing application, the techniques covered here can help push systems to new levels of efficiency and scalability.

By bridging the gap between algorithmic clarity and hardware-oriented optimization, this book hopes to inspire a new generation of developers to write code that is not only correct and elegant but also fast.

Who This Book Is For

This book is written for Java developers who want to push the performance boundaries of their applications. You should be comfortable with Java syntax and have some familiarity with algorithms and data structures. Prior experience with low-level optimization or assembly language is not required—indeed, one of this book's goals is to make these concepts accessible without requiring such background.

You will benefit most from this book if you

- Work on performance-critical applications in domains such as scientific computing, financial analysis, machine learning, or data processing

- Want to understand how modern processors execute code at the microarchitectural level

- Seek practical techniques that can be applied immediately to real-world problems

- Appreciate both the elegance of algorithms and the pragmatism of benchmarks

This book is not an exhaustive API reference. The official documentation serves that purpose admirably. Instead, we focus on the reasoning behind vectorization decisions, the patterns that recur across diverse problems, and the pitfalls that await the unwary.

How This Book Is Organized

Rather than grouping all chapters of similar type together, we have deliberately interspersed three thematic threads throughout the book: foundational techniques that build your vector programming vocabulary, classic algorithmic problems reimagined through the lens of parallelism, and mathematical explorations drawn from Project Euler. This arrangement serves a practical purpose: after grappling with abstract concepts like prefix sums or horizontal operations, you encounter a concrete problem that puts those concepts to work. The alternation between theory and application, between building blocks and complete solutions, aims to keep the material engaging while reinforcing understanding through varied repetition.

The threads are loosely categorized below, though in practice, they weave together throughout the chapters.

Thread I: Foundations

Chapter 1: Programming Vector Hardware surveys the landscape of vector-capable processors. We examine x86 architectures (SSE, AVX, AVX-512), ARM implementations (NEON, SVE), and the emerging RISC-V vector extension. The chapter introduces the concept of vector species and explains how to write code that adapts gracefully to different hardware capabilities. We also describe the diverse test platforms used throughout this book.

Chapter 2: Vector Addition begins with the deceptively simple problem of summing an array. This chapter introduces lanewise operations, explores the subtleties of floating-point arithmetic under IEEE 754, and presents Kahan's compensated summation algorithm as a remedy for rounding errors.

Chapter 3: A Taste of Statistics applies our growing toolkit to computing mean and standard deviation. The chapter introduces the crucial distinction between horizontal and vertical vector operations, explains cache-oblivious algorithms, and demonstrates how to minimize expensive horizontal operations by restructuring computations.

Chapter 6: Prefix Sum tackles the fundamental building block of many parallel algorithms. We examine the tension between theoretical elegance and practical performance, discovering that vector scan operations face inherent challenges from sequential dependencies.

Chapter 9: Random Number Generator reveals the mathematical structure behind `java.util.Random` and shows how to vectorize the Linear Congruential Generator. The chapter uses the prefix sum algorithm and demonstrates the **compress** operation for rejection sampling.

Thread II: Classic Problems Reimagined

Chapter 5: Removing Duplicates introduces the powerful **compress** operation, which selectively writes vector elements based on a mask. We compare multiple implementation strategies, including the classic two-pointer method and its vectorized counterparts.

Chapter 7: Finding the Unique Element explores bit manipulation and mask operations through problems involving XOR reduction. The chapter introduces trit arithmetic and examines how branch misprediction influences performance decisions.

Chapter 10: Trapping Rainwater showcases the most sophisticated optimization journey in the book. Starting from a standard interview solution, we progress through vector scans, Blelloch's work-optimal algorithm, vector transposition, and memoization. This chapter demonstrates how multiple techniques combine to achieve substantial speedups.

Chapter 12: Merging Arrays presents the merge path algorithm and bitonic sorting—techniques that transform the familiar merge operation into a parallel-friendly form. The chapter also discusses structural hazards and demonstrates an asymmetric loop optimization that improves instruction-level parallelism.

Chapter 14: Maximum Subarray Sum revisits Kadane's celebrated algorithm through the lens of vectorization. We reformulate the problem using prefix sums, revealing connections between seemingly different algorithmic approaches.

Thread III: Project Euler Explorations

The final thread applies our techniques to problems from Project Euler, a collection of mathematical puzzles that has challenged programmers since 2001. These chapters demonstrate that vectorization can illuminate even well-studied problems.

Chapter 4: Multiples of Three or Five (Project Euler 1) provides a deep dive into JIT compilation, examining the assembly code generated by the C1 and C2 compilers. We encounter Lemire's divisibility test and explore how masked operations enable branch-free conditional logic.

Chapter 8: Even Fibonacci Numbers (Project Euler 2) introduces matrix exponentiation as a vectorization strategy and contrasts Array of Structures with Structure of Arrays data layouts.

Chapter 11: Convergents of e (Project Euler 65) ventures into arbitrary-precision arithmetic, applying Strassen's and Karatsuba's algorithms to accelerate BigInteger operations. The chapter introduces the creative "billionaire" algorithm using a gigenary number system.

Chapter 13: Largest Product in a Series (Project Euler 8) develops a novel sliding window algorithm using suffix and prefix products. The chapter introduces the **gather** operation for indexed memory access.

Chapter 15: The Collatz Conjecture (Project Euler 14) confronts the challenge of divergent execution paths. We introduce the **expand** operation, work piling strategies, and comprehensive memoization. This chapter also delivers a cautionary tale about over-optimization.

Reading the Code

The code in this book prioritizes clarity of vectorization concepts over production-ready style. You will notice:

- **Minimal abstraction**: Methods are often long and repetitive rather than factored into helper functions. This is deliberate. Function call overhead, while usually negligible, can obscure performance characteristics in microbenchmarks. More importantly, seeing the complete algorithm in one place aids comprehension.

- **Explicit unrolling**: Many algorithms appear in both basic and unrolled variants. Unrolling exposes instruction-level parallelism opportunities that the JIT compiler might otherwise miss.

- **Platform-specific variants**: Some chapters include implementations optimized for specific vector lengths. While the book emphasizes vector-length-agnostic programming, there are occasions when targeting a known platform yields worthwhile gains.

All source code is available in the accompanying repository. We encourage you to run the benchmarks on your own hardware—results may differ from those reported here, and understanding why is itself instructive.

What This Book Does Not Cover

To maintain focus, we have deliberately excluded several related topics:

- **GPU programming**: While GPUs excel at data-parallel workloads, they require different APIs and programming models. The Java Vector API targets CPU vector units.

- **Automatic vectorization**: Modern JIT compilers can sometimes vectorize scalar loops automatically. We focus on explicit vectorization, where the programmer controls the transformation.

- **Multi-threading**: Combining SIMD with multi-core parallelism offers additional speedups, but introduces complexity orthogonal to our focus. Each chapter's benchmarks measure single-core performance.

- **API completeness**: We cover the operations most relevant to our examples rather than exhaustively documenting every method. The official Javadoc remains the authoritative reference.

Getting Started

To run the examples in this book, you will need

- JDK 25 or later (the Vector API remains in incubator/preview status; check current documentation for the appropriate module flags)

- A processor with vector capabilities (virtually all modern x86 and ARM processors qualify)

- Familiarity with your IDE's configuration for enabling preview features

The journey ahead will challenge your assumptions about what constitutes "fast" code. Problems you thought you understood will reveal hidden depths. Algorithms you considered optimal will yield to parallel reformulation. And occasionally, despite your best efforts, the scalar baseline will win—a humbling reminder that optimization is empirical, not ideological.

A Word of Caution

On a lighter note: do not try to show off knowledge gleaned from this book at technical interviews.

First, there is a good chance you will run into a wall of complete incomprehension from your interviewer. Not every professional conducting interviews possesses sufficient knowledge in this specific area. Rather than impressing them, you may encounter bewilderment and even skepticism.

Second, creating quality vectorized code requires far greater time and brainpower than typically allotted in interviews. Attempting to squeeze an ambitious solution into a limited timeframe may create the impression that you lack basic programming skills.

We wish you well on this journey.

CHAPTER 1

Programming Vector Hardware

We begin writing every vector program with a deceptively simple question: What is the length of the vectors we would like to use? After all, vector registers come in various sizes. We survey the vector extensions and their evolution across different hardware platforms.

In This Chapter

1. The evolution of vector extensions across x86 (SSE, AVX, AVX-512) and ARM (NEON, SVE) architectures

2. How to select appropriate vector species for your target platforms

3. The concept of vector-length-agnostic programming and graceful degradation

4. The test platforms used throughout this book and their vector capabilities

x86 Architecture: Intel and AMD

Intel pioneered personal vector computing by introducing Streaming SIMD Extensions (SSE architecture). First appearing in the Pentium III era, SSE provided 128-bit vector registers, enabling simultaneous operation on four 32-bit floating-point values. This marked a significant leap in performance for multimedia and gaming applications.

As hardware capabilities improved, Intel increased vector width to 256 bits with Advanced Vector Extensions (AVX) and AVX2.

1

© Roman Snytsar 2026

R. Snytsar, *Mastering SIMD with Java Vector API*, https://doi.org/10.1007/979-8-8688-2676-4_1

The next step in evolution was AVX-512, a powerful and sophisticated architecture with 512-bit vector registers and a rich instruction set for masking, broadcasting, conflict detection, and much more. AVX-512 provides fine-grained control over vector operations and is particularly useful in scientific computing, cryptography, and artificial intelligence tasks.

Nevertheless, due to power and thermal constraints, AVX-512 has been mostly reserved for server-grade processors, while desktop and mobile chips continue to rely on AVX2. This division reflects the trade-off between performance and energy efficiency in consumer devices.

Initially, AMD lagged behind Intel in vector ISA evolution, but new chips starting with Zen 4 began adopting AVX-512 in their product lines. Unlike Intel, AMD is deploying AVX-512 widely, offering broader support on both desktop and server platforms. This strategic move positions AMD as a high-performance alternative for vector-heavy workloads.

Table 1-1. *x86 vector extensions at a glance*

Extension	Width	Year	Intel Support	AMD Support
SSE	128-bit	1999	All modern CPUs	All modern CPUs
AVX	256-bit	2011	Sandy Bridge+	Bulldozer+
AVX2	256-bit	2013	Haswell+	Excavator+
AVX-512	512-bit	2016	Server: Skylake-X+ Desktop: removed Mobile: Ice Lake only	Zen 4+ (all segments)

Table 1-1 reveals the divergent strategies: Intel introduced AVX-512 first but has since restricted it to server platforms due to thermal and power constraints, even removing support from newer desktop chips. AMD, arriving later to AVX-512, chose to deploy it uniformly across all product lines. For developers targeting diverse hardware, this fragmentation means AVX2 (256-bit) remains the most reliable common denominator on x86 platforms.

ARM Architecture

ARM's vector architecture began with NEON, a 128-bit SIMD extension integrated into ARMv7 and ARMv8 architectures. NEON is widely used in mobile and embedded systems for tasks like image processing and signal filtering. However, its fixed vector width and limited instruction set made it difficult to scale code across devices with varying performance requirements.

To address this, ARM introduced Scalable Vector Extension (SVE) in ARMv8.2-A. Unlike traditional vector instruction sets, SVE is vector-length agnostic: it supports vector registers of any power-of-two multiple of 128 bits (e.g., 128, 256, 512, 1024 bits). Instructions are designed to work correctly regardless of the underlying vector width, allowing the same code to run on devices with different vector widths.

This design allows embedded devices to save die area and power consumption by implementing narrower pipelines, while high-performance cores can use wider vectors for maximum throughput. SVE also provides advanced features like predication and gather/scatter operations, making it suitable for high-performance computing and AI workloads.

RISC-V Architecture

The open source RISC-V architecture adopts a similar philosophy in its RISC-V Vector Extension (RVV). Like SVE, RVV is vector-length agnostic, supporting scalable vector width and a flexible programming model. This approach aligns with RISC-V's modular structure, allowing designers to tailor vector capabilities to specific application domains—from low-power IoT devices to data center accelerators.

Choosing Vector Length

The Java Vector API allows requesting vectors of any length—128, 256, or 512 bits, with the final decision left to the runtime environment, specifically the Just-In-Time (JIT) compiler.

When developers write vectorized code using the Java Vector API, they specify the desired vector species, typically using one of the predefined constants like SP_128, SP_256, or SP_512. This species determines the number of bits in the vector. Bit width divided by element size determines the number of lanes (i.e., elements) the vector will process in parallel.

Nevertheless, this specification isn't a hard guarantee. Instead, it serves as a hint to the JIT compiler, which performs dynamic capability checking of the host CPU at runtime. The JIT compiler follows a two-stage process:

1. Hardware capability verification

    - On an Intel processor with AVX2 support, a 256-bit vector may be accepted.

    - On a mobile ARM processor with NEON, only 128-bit vectors may be supported.

    - Currently, the RISC-V vector extension is not supported by the Java Vector JIT.

2. Code generation decision

    - **If the requested vector length is supported**: The JIT generates hardware-specific SIMD instructions (e.g., AVX2, SVE) that operate directly on vector registers.

    - **If not supported**: The JIT gracefully falls back to scalar code, compiling vector operations as a sequence of scalar element-wise computations.

This fallback process ensures portability and correctness even on platforms lacking advanced SIMD support. The benefits of this sophisticated vector length query process:

- **Hardware agnosticism**: Developers can write high-performance code without hard-coding hardware architecture specifics.

- **Graceful degradation**: Code remains functional and semantically correct even when vector acceleration is unavailable.

- **Performance portability**: The same source code scales across a wide range of devices—from mobile phones to high-performance servers.

So what vector length should we request? There are several approaches.

1. Request SPECIES_128—maximum portability

```
var SP = FloatVector.SPECIES_128;
```

- Advantages

  - **High portability**: Code executes uniformly on desktops, servers, mobile devices, and embedded platforms.

  - **Simplified testing and debugging**: Uniform behavior across platforms reduces surprises.

- Limitations

  - **Lower performance ceiling**: You may leave significant hardware capabilities unused on systems supporting wider vectors (e.g., AVX2, AVX-512, SVE).

  - **Not future-proof**: As hardware evolves, using 128-bit vectors may become a bottleneck.

2. Match current hardware—maximum efficiency

```
var SP = FloatVector.SPECIES_256; // or 512
```

- Advantages

  - **Peak performance**: Code tightly couples with hardware SIMD capabilities.

  - **Predictable behavior**: You know exactly which instructions will be generated.

- Limitations

  - **Fragile portability**: Code may not vectorize or may fall back to scalar execution on other platforms.

  - **Maintenance burden**: Upgrading to new hardware with a different vector width may require complete rewriting or retuning of vector logic.

3. Request SPECIES_PREFERRED—adaptive and future-proof

```
var SP = FloatVector.SPECIES_PREFERRED;
```

- Advantages

  - **Performance portability**: Code dynamically adapts to hardware capabilities.

  - **Future-proofing**: As processors evolve, your code automatically benefits from wider vectors and new architectures.

- Limitations

  - **Increased complexity**: You will need to write vector-length-agnostic code—logic that works regardless of the number of vector elements.

  - **Higher cognitive load**: Requires a deeper understanding of vector programming patterns and abstraction techniques.

Table 1-2. *Decision table for required vector length*

	SPECIES_128	Hardware (256)	PREFERRED
Portability	High	Low	High
Performance	Moderate	High	High
Maintainability	High	Low	High
Complexity	Low	Moderate	High

In practice, the choice of vector length is shaped by factors beyond Table 1-2. Consider the ARM ecosystem: the vast majority of existing vector code targets NEON, so porting these algorithms to Java naturally leads to 128-bit vectors. Given the current hardware landscape, SPECIES_128 remains the most portable and maintainable choice for projects that must run everywhere.

For x86 compute instances, the calculus shifts. Targeting 512-bit vectors is a safe bet for peak performance. Should your code land on a machine with only 256-bit support, it will not crash but will simply experience graceful degradation, trading some speed for continued correctness.

I confess that for many years, I wrote vector code tightly coupled to specific x86 widths. The emergence of vector-length-agnostic (VLA) instruction sets brought the familiar curse and blessing of the software engineer: the need to unlearn tricks I had honed to perfection and embrace an unfamiliar discipline.

Yet the VLA approach has made me a better programmer. I now strive to make all my vector code VLA, which renders the code foundational and future-proof. Throughout this book, I have endeavored to follow the same principle. Where vector-length agnosticism proves impractical or suboptimal, I try to remain honest and note the exception. Ultimately, there is only one way to discover what works best for your situation: write the code, run the benchmarks, and let the hardware render its verdict.

Performance Testing: Intel and AMD

For performance testing, we assembled a veritable zoo of processors—from power-efficient devices with minimal vector support to modern supercomputer-class chips. This spread is intentional: it allows us to see how the same vector code behaves across different hardware generations and understand whether the upgrade to wider vectors is worth the effort.

- **Intel Gemini Lake (GL):** We found this specimen in the depths of a home lab to test vector code on a processor supporting up to SSE4.2 instructions with 128-bit vector width.

- **AMD Rome (Z2):** Still impressive server CPU with AVX2 architecture and 256-bit vectors.

- **Intel Ice Lake (IL):** The first generation of processors with full AVX512 support. Our test lab includes earlier samples like Knights Landing and the exotic Cannon Lake, but all code for this book was written and debugged on a laptop with an Ice Lake processor. Unfortunately, this is also the last generation of Intel mobile processors with AVX512 support. When the time comes to upgrade, we will likely turn to a different manufacturer.

- **Intel Sapphire Rapids (SR):** A modern server processor with extensive out-of-order execution capabilities.

- **AMD Turin (Z5):** An excellent server processor with full AVX512 support and an improved pipeline for out-of-order execution.

An important characteristic of server processors is core count, but this is not particularly relevant for us since we are optimizing code within a single core.

Performance Testing: ARM Processors

- **Apple M4 (M4):** A widely deployed ARM processor that does not expose SVE instructions to the JVM and is limited to NEON

- **CIX CD8180 (O6):** A power-efficient processor supporting SVE with 128-bit vector width

- **Microsoft Cobalt (CO):** A server processor supporting SVE with 128-bit vector width

- **Nvidia Grace (NV):** SVE with only 128-bit vector width, but an advanced pipeline capable of executing up to four vector instructions simultaneously

- **Amazon Graviton 3 (G3):** A server processor supporting SVE with 256-bit vector width

All benchmarks use JMH (Java Microbenchmark Harness) with sufficient warmup iterations to ensure stable JIT compilation. We report single-core speedups relative to scalar baselines, isolating the algorithmic benefits of vectorization from other factors such as multi-threading or I/O optimization.

Benchmark tables use abbreviations for test platforms (GL, Z2, IL, etc.) as defined above. Speedup values greater than 1.0 indicate improvement over the scalar baseline; values less than 1.0 indicate slowdown.

What's Next

With our understanding of vector hardware established, we are ready to write our first vector program. In the next chapter, we tackle the deceptively simple problem of adding arrays element-wise. Along the way, we will encounter the subtleties of floating-point arithmetic, learn about IEEE 754 rounding behavior, and discover Kahan's compensated summation algorithm—our first taste of how vectorization intersects with numerical accuracy.

CHAPTER 2

Vector Addition

Consider five four-element floating-point arrays. The task is to add the arrays element-wise—that is, create a new array of four elements where the zeroth element equals the sum of the zeroth elements from all five arrays, the first element equals the sum of the first elements from all five arrays, and so on.

Table 2-1. *Source data*

33554432.0f	33554432.0f	33554432.0f	33554432.0f
2.0f	-1.0f	-33554432.0f	2.0f
0.0f	0.0f	0.0f	-33554432.0f
-1.0f	2.0f	2.0f	0.0f
-33554432.0f	-33554432.0f	-1.0f	-1.0f

It is easy to verify that each column in Table 2-1 contains the same numbers, just in a different order. The numbers are conveniently chosen as powers of two. The multi-digit number equals 2 to the power of 25. It is also straightforward to perform the necessary additions mentally. Take the second column (as Java programmers, we know that the leftmost column is zeroth). The long number minus the same long number gives zero, two minus one equals one, so the sum of five numbers in the second column equals one. Adding the same numbers in a different order gives one in the zeroth column, the first column, and the third column as well.

Since the operations required to compute each column are identical, this problem is ideally suited for solution using Single-Instruction-Multiple-Data (SIMD) extensions available in all modern processors.

© Roman Snytsar 2026
R. Snytsar, *Mastering SIMD with Java Vector API*, https://doi.org/10.1007/979-8-8688-2676-4_2

In This Chapter

1. How to perform basic lanewise vector operations using the Java Vector API

2. The difference between sequential and pairwise addition strategies

3. How IEEE 754 floating-point representation affects computation accuracy

4. Kahan's compensated summation algorithm for minimizing rounding errors

Sequential Addition

For our first program, we will start with a straightforward approach. A float variable occupies 32 bits. Four variables fit into 128 bits, so for our purposes, it is safe to stick with a 128-bit vector length.

```
1    package com.nonpareilcoder.floatingpoint;
2
3    import jdk.incubator.vector.*;
4
5    public class SimpleSummationLanewise {
6      static final VectorSpecies<Float> SP =
7        FloatVector.SPECIES_128;
8
9      static float[] f0 = new float[]{
10        33554432.0f, 33554432.0f, 33554432.0f, 33554432.0f};
11
12      static float[] f1 = new float[]{
13        2.0f, -1.0f, -33554432.0f, 2.0f};
14
15      static float[] f2 = new float[]{
16        0.0f, 0.0f, 0.0f, -33554432.0f};
17
```

```
18    static float[] f3 = new float[]{
19       -1.0f, 2.0f, 2.0f, 0.0f};
20
21    static float[] f4 = new float[]{
22       -33554432.0f, -33554432.0f, -1.0f, -1.0f};
23
24    public static float[] add() {
25      FloatVector _f0 = FloatVector.fromArray(SP, f0, 0);
26      FloatVector _f1 = FloatVector.fromArray(SP, f1, 0);
27      FloatVector _f2 = FloatVector.fromArray(SP, f2, 0);
28      FloatVector _f3 = FloatVector.fromArray(SP, f3, 0);
29      FloatVector _f4 = FloatVector.fromArray(SP, f4, 0);
30
31      FloatVector _sum = _f0.lanewise(VectorOperators.ADD, _f1);
32
33      _sum = _sum.lanewise(VectorOperators.ADD, _f2);
34      _sum = _sum.lanewise(VectorOperators.ADD, _f3);
35      _sum = _sum.lanewise(VectorOperators.ADD, _f4);
36
37      float[] result = new float[4];
38      _sum.intoArray(result, 0);
39
40      return result;
41    }
42  }
```

- The program is very compact and begins with five instructions
  loading data from arrays in lines 25–29. Since vector registers operate
  like arrays, all data transfer between vectors and Java code occurs
  through arrays. In fact, throughout this book, you will encounter
  no data structure more complex than arrays—unusual for a
  programming book, but appropriate for low-level optimization.

- Line 31 calls the element-wise operation method on two vectors;
  in Java, it is named **lanewise**. A *lane* is a position within a vector
  register—think of it as a placeholder—while an *element* is the value

stored in that lane. Although we naturally think in terms of elements, vector hardware is designed around lanes, and Java's Vector API follows this hardware-oriented terminology. The first argument specifies the operation, an addition in our case.

- The addition operation repeats three more times in lines 33–35.

- Line 38 stores the result into a new array, completing the vector portion of the program.

For vector addition, there is also a specialized method that allows us to write all the vector arithmetic in our program in one object-oriented line:

```
FloatVector _sum = _f0.add(_f1).add(_f2).add(_f3).add(_f4);
```

We will use the abbreviated form of the lanewise operators throughout this book whenever possible. The program represents an ideal example of data-level parallelism. Operations in each lane are independent of each other. A vectorizer's dream.

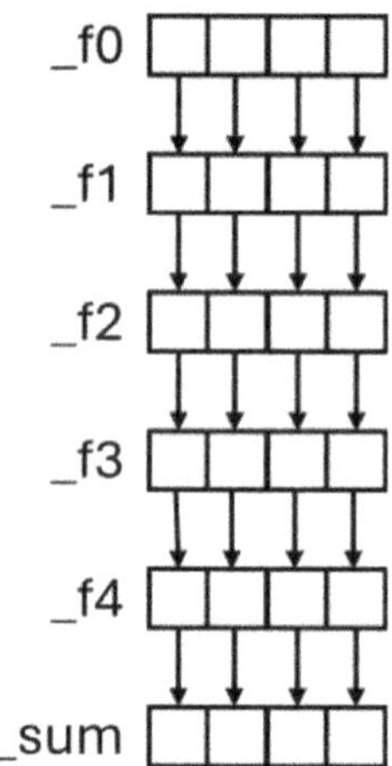

Figure 2-1. *Serial summation*

As illustrated in Figure 2-1, instruction-level parallelism is absent. Each addition operation depends on the result of the previous one and must wait for its completion. Out-of-order instruction execution is impossible. This is called a sequential data dependency: each instruction waits for the previous one, forming a dependency chain.

Pairwise Addition

Suppose we try to "spoil" our elegant program. Accumulative addition, as in our program, is a classic example of a data aggregation operation called **reduce**.

```
1    package com.nonpareilcoder.floatingpoint;
2
3    import jdk.incubator.vector.*;
4
5    public class SimpleSummationReduce {
6      static final VectorSpecies<Float> SP =
7        FloatVector.SPECIES_128;
8
9      static float[] f0 = new float[] {
10       33554432.0f, 33554432.0f, 33554432.0f, 33554432.0f };
11
12     static float[] f1 = new float[] {
13       2.0f, -1.0f, -33554432.0f, 2.0f };
14
15     static float[] f2 = new float[] {
16       0.0f, 0.0f, 0.0f, -33554432.0f };
17
18     static float[] f3 = new float[] {
19       -1.0f, 2.0f, 2.0f, 0.0f };
20
21     static float[] f4 = new float[] {
22       -33554432.0f, -33554432.0f, -1.0f, -1.0f };
23
24     public static float[] add() {
25       FloatVector _f0 = FloatVector.fromArray(SP, f0, 0);
26       FloatVector _f1 = FloatVector.fromArray(SP, f1, 0);
27       FloatVector _f2 = FloatVector.fromArray(SP, f2, 0);
28       FloatVector _f3 = FloatVector.fromArray(SP, f3, 0);
29       FloatVector _f4 = FloatVector.fromArray(SP, f4, 0);
30
31       FloatVector _part1 = _f0.add(_f1);
```

```
32
33        FloatVector _part2 = _f3.add(_f4);
34
35        _part1 = _part1.add(_f2);
36
37        _part1 = _part1.add(_part2);
38
39        float[] result = new float[4];
40        _part1.intoArray(result, 0);
41
42        return result;
43    }
44  }
```

We can represent our required computations as a tree (see Figure 2-2).

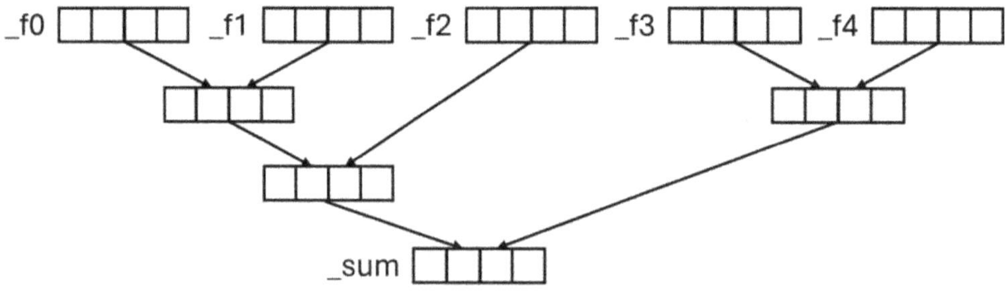

Figure 2-2. *Pairwise summation*

Note that the first two additions—the two upper ones in the diagram—are independent of each other and can execute in parallel. Once the load instructions in lines 25 and 26 complete, the processor can schedule the addition in line 31 without waiting for the other loads to complete. Similarly, once the loads in lines 28 and 29 complete, the addition in line 33 can be scheduled even if the result from line 31 is not ready yet. That is all the parallelism we can extract, and the remaining instructions will execute sequentially. But the right branch of the operation tree is executed in parallel with the left.

Running both programs produces the surprising results shown in Table 2-2.

Table 2-2. *Addition results*

Algorithm	Result			
Sequential addition	0.0	0.0	1.0	-1.0
Pairwise addition	0.0	2.0	1.0	-1.0

First, contrary to the commutative property taught in basic mathematics, changing the order of operands changes the result. This anomaly is specific to floating-point arithmetic; integer addition remains truly commutative, though integers have their own pitfall: overflow and underflow errors that require equal vigilance. Second, in both cases, three of four columns gave incorrect results. The expected result for all four columns should have been 1.0, as we calculated manually earlier. However, we got: first column 0.0 (error!), second column 0.0 or 2.0 depending on order (error!), third column 1.0 (correct!), and fourth column -1.0 (error!). The cause of the discrepancies is rounding errors in floating-point operations. What happened?

Rounding During Addition

The root of the problem lies in the peculiarity of binary floating-point representation in IEEE 754 format. Here is how 2 to the power of 25 is represented in memory under this standard:

0	10011000	00000000000000000000000

The most significant bit stores the sign, 0 for positive numbers. Then, according to the standard, comes the exponent of the power of two of this number plus 127. 25 plus 127 equals 152. Next comes the number's mantissa. As we see, in this case, it consists entirely of zeros. The thing is, according to the IEEE 754 standard, a normal floating-point number's mantissa always has the form 1.xxxxxx. And since the mantissa always starts with one, this one is not stored in memory but is implicit. When a number is loaded into the ALU, this implicit leading one is restored to its position in the mantissa. The mantissa is also extended by several bits. Most often by eight.

0	10011000	1	00000000000000000000000	00000000

Consider how addition works when we add 2 to the 25th power and 2.

0	10011000	00000000000000000000000
0	10000000	00000000000000000000000

We load both operands into the ALU.

0	10011000	1	00000000000000000000000	00000000
0	10000000	1	00000000000000000000000	00000000

Different exponents prevent us from immediately adding the two mantissas. Therefore, we will shift the second operand's mantissa right while simultaneously increasing the exponent. To obtain equal exponents, we need to shift the mantissa by 24 positions.

0	10011000	1	00000000000000000000000	00000000
0	10011000	0	00000000000000000000000	10000000

After this, we can perform the addition operation.

0	10011000	1	00000000000000000000000	10000000

And unload the number back into the register, discarding the extra mantissa bits.

0	10011000	00000000000000000000000

As we see, the resulting number is no different from the original first operand. Whether we added or did not add, a rounding error occurred. Now examine what happens when adding the negative number $-(2^{25})$ with two.

1	10011000	1	00000000000000000000000	00000000
0	10000000	1	00000000000000000000000	00000000

The first operand differs from the number in the previous example only in the sign bit being set to one, showing the number is negative. Just as in the previous example, the second operand's mantissa is shifted right by 24 positions to obtain the same exponent.

| 1 | 10011000 | 1 | 00000000000000000000000 | 00000000 |
| 0 | 10011000 | 0 | 00000000000000000000000 | 10000000 |

But addition cannot proceed yet. The second operand needs to be converted to two's complement form. So all mantissa bits are inverted.

| 1 | 10011000 | 1 | 00000000000000000000000 | 00000000 |
| 0 | 10011000 | 1 | 11111111111111111111111 | 01111111 |

Then a one is added to the mantissa.

| 1 | 10011000 | 1 | 00000000000000000000000 | 00000000 |
| 1 | 10011000 | 1 | 11111111111111111111111 | 10000000 |

Now we are ready to perform the addition.

| 1 | 10011000 | 0 | 11111111111111111111111 | 10000000 |

But the resulting floating-point number is not normalized. The most significant mantissa bit turned out to be zero, not one. Therefore, the number must be normalized by shifting the mantissa left until the most significant bit equals one, while simultaneously decreasing the exponent.

| 1 | 10010111 | 1 | 11111111111111111111111 | 00000000 |

After normalization, we unload the number back into the register, again discarding the extra mantissa bits.

| 1 | 10010111 | 11111111111111111111111 |

But the result is exact—no rounding occurred. In this case, the extra bits in the ALU representation saved the situation. Thus, choosing pairs of arithmetic operation arguments leads to different rounding errors, which produce different results when computing the sum of the same numbers.

Applying this knowledge to our data reveals the issue. In the first column, sequential addition starts with $2^{25} + 2$, which gives 2^{25} due to rounding. Then 0 is added to this result, then -1, then -2^{25}, ultimately yielding -1 instead of the expected 1. Similar precision loss occurs in the fourth column. Pairwise addition in some cases changes the operation order, so numbers that should cancel each other (like 2^{25} and -2^{25}) are added before precision is lost when adding small numbers. But this does not help in all columns.

Kahan's Algorithm

How do we address rounding errors? Pairwise addition often helps reduce overall error, but not in our case; the example was chosen specifically to demonstrate that half-measures are insufficient. Kahan's algorithm (Kahan, 1965) helps compensate for errors, at least partially.

The idea of Kahan's algorithm is based on the fact that when adding two numbers a and b in computer arithmetic, the result of a floating-point addition $s = fl(a + b)$ differs from the mathematically exact value by a rounding error e. This error can be estimated as $e = (a - s) + b$. Indeed, if s exactly equals $a + b$, then $(a - s) + b = 0$. But due to rounding $s \neq a + b$, and the expression $(a - s) + b$ gives an approximate estimate of the magnitude lost in rounding. By accumulating these errors and compensating for them at the end, we get a much more accurate result.

Here is the implementation:

```
1   package com.nonpareilcoder.floatingpoint;
2
3   import jdk.incubator.vector.*;
4
5   public class SimpleSummationCorrected {
6     static final VectorSpecies<Float> SP =
7       FloatVector.SPECIES_128;
8
9     static float[] f0 = new float[] {
10       33554432.0f, 33554432.0f, 33554432.0f, 33554432.0f };
11
12    static float[] f1 = new float[] {
13      2.0f, -1.0f, -33554432.0f, 2.0f };
14
15    static float[] f2 = new float[] {
16      0.0f, 0.0f, 0.0f, -33554432.0f };
```

```
17
18    static float[] f3 = new float[] {
19      -1.0f, 2.0f, 2.0f, 0.0f };
20
21    static float[] f4 = new float[] {
22      -33554432.0f, -33554432.0f, -1.0f, -1.0f };
23
24    public static float[] add() {
25      FloatVector _f0 = FloatVector.fromArray(SP, f0, 0);
26      FloatVector _f1 = FloatVector.fromArray(SP, f1, 0);
27      FloatVector _f2 = FloatVector.fromArray(SP, f2, 0);
28      FloatVector _f3 = FloatVector.fromArray(SP, f3, 0);
29      FloatVector _f4 = FloatVector.fromArray(SP, f4, 0);
30
31      FloatVector _part1 = _f0.add(_f1);
32      FloatVector _c1 = _f0.sub(_part1).add(_f1);
33
34      FloatVector _part2 = _f3.add(_f4);
35      FloatVector _c2 = _f4.sub(_part2).add(_f3);
36
37      FloatVector _t = _part1.add(_f2);
38      _c1 = _f2.sub(_t).add(_part1).add(_c1);
39      _part1 = _t;
40
41      _part1 = _part1.add(_part2);
42      _c1 = _c1.add(_c2);
43
44      _part1 = _part1.add(_c1);
45
46      float[] result = new float[4];
47      _part1.intoArray(result, 0);
48
49      return result;
50    }
51  }
```

- Line 31 adds the first pair of numbers.

- Line 32 computes the possible rounding error. Note that from the standpoint of ordinary mathematics, the result of executing line 32 is identically zero. An aggressive optimizing compiler may recognize this and eliminate the computation in line 32. Make sure it does not do this, and check the generated machine code.

- Lines 34 and 35 add the second pair of numbers from the right branch of the operation tree.

- Lines 37, 38, and 39 perform another addition and recalculate the accumulated error.

- Finally, line 41 performs the final addition, and the result is corrected by adding both accumulated errors.

We run the JUnit test of this code and see that now the result matches expectations. We have compensated for computational error by tripling the number of required arithmetic operations: 13 vs. the original 4. It is no surprise that in the pursuit of maximum performance, measured in "useful" operations per second, none of the accelerators I know of implement Kahan correction. Rapid error growth is facilitated by reducing source data precision and poor choice of "short" number formats. The IEEE 754 standard defines a 16-bit floating-point number (FP16) with five exponent bits and ten mantissa bits. The remaining 16th bit is used for the number's sign. But in machine learning algorithms, the BrainFloat16 format is widely used (though not natively supported in Java), obtained from a 32-bit number by simply truncating the lower 16 mantissa bits. Converting between formats is simple, but the number now still has eight exponent bits and only seven mantissa bits. And as demonstrated earlier, mantissa length determines susceptibility to rounding errors. Of course, it helps somewhat that the running sum is often stored as a 32-bit number, but that is not a panacea, as we have seen in the above example.

Table 2-3. *Algorithm comparison*

Criterion	Sequential	Pairwise	Kahan
Number of operations	4	4	13
Instruction-level parallelism	No	Partial	Partial
Result accuracy	Low	Medium	High
Implementation complexity	Low	Medium	High

As summarized in Table 2-3, the choice of algorithm depends on priorities: if accuracy is critical, use Kahan's algorithm; if maximum performance is important and errors are acceptable, pairwise addition may be a compromise; sequential addition is simplest but least accurate and slowest.

In summary, floating-point arithmetic requires careful attention if accurate results are important.

What's Next

Having mastered basic vector addition and compensated summation, we are ready to apply these techniques to a more substantial problem. In the next chapter, we compute mean and standard deviation: fundamental statistical measures that require accumulating sums across large datasets. We will encounter the crucial distinction between horizontal and vertical vector operations and learn how cache-oblivious algorithms can further improve performance.

CHAPTER 3

A Taste of Statistics

Given an array containing samples of a random variable, our task is to perform basic statistical processing: compute the arithmetic mean and standard deviation of this data.

In This Chapter

1. The distinction between horizontal and vertical vector operations

2. How to minimize expensive horizontal operations by restructuring computations

3. Cache-oblivious algorithm design for memory-bound workloads

4. Applying Kahan's correction to vectorized accumulation

Two-Pass Algorithm

Statistics textbooks give us these formulas:

$$\bar{x} = \frac{1}{N}\sum x_i \,;\, \sigma = \sqrt{\frac{\left(x_i - \bar{x}\right)^2}{N}}$$

It is up for debate whether the denominator for the standard deviation should read N or $N - 1$, but that discussion lies beyond the scope of this book. We program the formulas as written.

```
1    package com.nonpareilcoder.floatingpoint;
2
3    public class MeanDeviationSinglePrecision {
4       static public float[] compute(float[] input) {
```


© Roman Snytsar 2026
R. Snytsar, *Mastering SIMD with Java Vector API*, https://doi.org/10.1007/979-8-8688-2676-4_3

```java
 5          int N = input.length;
 6
 7          float mean = 0.0f;
 8          for (int i = N; i-- > 0; ) mean += input[i];
 9          mean /= N;
10
11          float dev = 0.0f;
12          for (float v : input) dev += (v - mean) * (v - mean);
13          dev = (float) StrictMath.sqrt(dev / N);
14
15          return new float[]{mean, dev};
16      }
17   }
18
```

- Computing from the classical formulas requires two passes through the array.

- The first loop in lines 7–9 calculates the arithmetic mean of the sample.

- The second loop in lines 11–13 computes the standard deviation.

Note that the first loop runs with decreasing indices, the second with increasing indices. If the array fits entirely in the processor cache, both passes use cached data. If the array exceeds cache size, the first pass (from end to beginning) evicts old data while loading new. The last elements loaded—those at the array's beginning—remain in cache. The second pass (from beginning to end) starts with precisely these cached elements, benefiting from the cache for at least the initial portion of the array. Such algorithms that work to optimize cache usage regardless of processor cache sizes are called **cache-oblivious**.

Since vectorized code typically bottlenecks on memory accesses, any tricks that speed up memory fetches significantly improve performance.

Single-Pass Algorithm

A mathematical reformulation allows us to optimize the program and compute both the arithmetic mean and standard deviation in one pass through the array. We calculate the sums:

$$S_1 = \sum x_i \; ; \; S_2 = \sum x_i^2$$

The arithmetic mean follows directly:

$$\overline{x} = \frac{S_1}{N}$$

And the standard deviation is calculated as

$$\sigma = \sqrt{\frac{S_2}{N} - \left(\frac{S_1}{N}\right)^2}$$

The formula can be proven as follows. Expanding the expression for standard deviation:

$$\sigma = \sqrt{\frac{\sum (x_i - \overline{x})^2}{N}} = \sqrt{\frac{\sum (x_i^2 - 2x_i \overline{x} + \overline{x}^2)}{N}} = \sqrt{\frac{\sum x_i^2 - 2\overline{x} \sum x_i + N \overline{x}^2}{N}}$$

Given that $\overline{x} = \dfrac{S_1}{N}$ and $\sum x_i = S_1$, we get

$$\sigma = \sqrt{\frac{S_2 - 2\frac{S_1}{N} \cdot S_1 + N \cdot \frac{S_1^2}{N^2}}{N}} = \sqrt{\frac{S_2}{N} - 2\frac{S_1^2}{N^2} + \frac{S_1^2}{N^2}} = \sqrt{\frac{S_2}{N} - \left(\frac{S_1}{N}\right)^2}$$

We now implement this with our new formulas.

```
1   package com.nonpareilcoder.floatingpoint;
2
3   public class MeanDeviationSinglePass {
4     static public float[] compute(float[] input) {
5       int N = input.length;
```

```
 6
 7          float s1 = 0.0f, s2 = 0.0f;
 8
 9        for (float v : input) {
10           float v2 = v * v;
11
12            s1 += v;
13            s2 += v2;
14          }
15
16        float mean = (float) s1 / N;
17        float dev = (float) StrictMath.sqrt(s2 * N - s1 * s1) / N;
18
19        return new float[]{mean, dev};
20      }
21    }
22
```

- The single loop in lines 9–14 accumulates both sums as running totals.

- The sample's arithmetic mean is computed in line 16.

- The standard deviation is calculated in line 17.

Despite being mathematically correct and fast, the single-pass algorithm is numerically unstable because computing long sums introduces rounding errors. We can try to minimize the errors using Kahan's algorithm, as described in the previous chapter.

```
 1    package com.nonpareilcoder.floatingpoint;
 2
 3    public class MeanDeviationSingleCorrected {
 4      static public float[] compute(float[] input) {
 5        int N = input.length;
 6
 7        float s1 = 0.0f, s2 = 0.0f;
 8        float c1 = 0.0f, c2 = 0.0f;
 9
```

```
10      for (float v : input) {
11        float t1 = s1 + v;
12        c1 += (s1 - t1) + v;
13        s1 = t1;
14
15        float v2 = v * v;
16        float t2 = s2 + v2;
17        c2 += (s2 - t2) + v2;
18        s2 = t2;
19      }
20
21      s1 += c1;
22      s2 += c2;
23
24      float mean = (float) s1 / N;
25      float dev = (float) StrictMath.sqrt(s2 * N - s1 * s1) / N;
26
27      return new float[]{mean, dev};
28    }
29  }
30
```

- Lines 11–13 calculate the first sum and, separately, the accumulated rounding error.

- Lines 15–18 calculate the second sum and its accumulated rounding error.

- Lines 21–22 perform the sum corrections.

- The arithmetic mean is computed in line 24.

- The standard deviation is calculated in line 25.

Table 3-1. *Comparison of mean and standard deviation algorithms*

Algorithm	Mean	Error	Standard Deviation	Error
Double precision	0.50682557		0.28694576	
Two passes without correction	0.50682545	1.2E-07	0.28694564	1.2E-07
One pass without correction	0.5068264	8.3E-07	0.28694525	5.1E-07
One pass with correction	0.50682557	0	0.2869458	4E-08

As we can see from Table 3-1, the results with and without correction differ noticeably. Which one is more correct? We cannot answer that question without using specialized arbitrary-precision number libraries, but for comparison, we shall compute the same sums in two passes using double-precision numbers. We shall additionally correct the result using Kahan's algorithm and treat that as our reference.

```
1    package com.nonpareilcoder.floatingpoint;
2
3    public class MeanDeviationDoubleCorrected {
4      static public float[] compute(float[] input) {
5        int N = input.length;
6
7        double s1 = 0.0, s2 = 0.0;
8        double c1 = 0.0f, c2 = 0.0f;
9
10       for (float v : input) {
11         double t1 = s1 + v;
12         c1 += (s1 - t1) + v;
13         s1 = t1;
14
15         double v2 = v * v;
16         double t2 = s2 + v2;
17         c2 += (s2 - t2) + v2;
18         s2 = t2;
19       }
20
21       s1 += c1;
```

```
22        s2 += c2;
23
24        float mean = (float) s1 / N;
25        float dev = (float) StrictMath.sqrt(s2 * N - s1 * s1) / N;
26
27        return new float[]{mean, dev};
28      }
29    }
30
```

Vector Approach

We rewrite the loop implementation for computing sums in the single-pass algorithm using vector-length-agnostic instructions.

```
1     package com.nonpareilcoder.floatingpoint;
2
3     import jdk.incubator.vector.*;
4     import static jdk.incubator.vector.VectorOperators.*;
5
6     public class MeanDeviationReduced {
7       static final VectorSpecies<Float> SP =
8           FloatVector.SPECIES_PREFERRED;
9
10      static public float[] compute(float[] input) {
11        int N = input.length;
12
13        float s1 = 0.0f, s2 = 0.0f;
14
15        for (int i = 0; i < N; i += SP.length()) {
16          var _mask = SP.indexInRange(i, N);
17
18          FloatVector _v1 = FloatVector.fromArray(SP, input, i, _mask);
19          FloatVector _v2 = _v1.mul(_v1);
20
```

```
21              s1 += _v1.reduceLanes(ADD);
22              s2 += _v2.reduceLanes(ADD);
23          }
24
25      float mean = (float) s1 / N;
26      float dev = (float) StrictMath.sqrt(s2 * N - s1 * s1) / N;
27
28      return new float[]{mean, dev};
29      }
30  }
31
```

- Line 15 steps through the array with a stride equal to the vector register length.

- Line 16 creates a special mask that identifies the actually existing array elements in the current data chunk. This is necessary for correctly handling cases where the array size is not a multiple of the vector length.

- Line 18 loads available elements into the vector register according to the mask.

- Line 19 computes the squares of the vector elements. This operation executes in parallel for all vector elements.

- Line 21 sums all vector elements using the **reduceLanes** method. The result is added to the running total.

- Similarly, line 22 forms the sum of squared elements.

So far, we have encountered only element-wise operations on two vectors. We shall call such operations **vertical** (a term we adopt for this book). **reduceLanes** belongs to a different class of vector operations, which we will call **horizontal**. A horizontal operation performs actions on elements within a single vector, combining them to produce a single result or redistributing data between elements within the vector. Besides **reduceLanes**, examples of such operations include element permutations. To better understand the differences between types of vector operations, consider this analogy:

- Vertical (element-wise) operations are like driving on a multi-lane highway where each lane functions relatively independently from others.

- Horizontal operations resemble a stretch of motorway with frequent lane changes.

Horizontal operations are characterized by

- They require additional logic circuits for exchanging data between vector lanes.

- They consume more die area.

- They draw more power.

- They perform worse than vertical operations.

Though horizontal operations are sometimes unavoidable, you should follow these principles:

- Carefully analyze the necessity of each horizontal operation.

- Minimize the use of horizontal operations where possible.

- Use algorithms that minimize horizontal operations.

- Profile code to identify bottlenecks related to horizontal operations.

In our first vector implementation, the **reduceLanes** operation is called inside the loop on each iteration. This means the horizontal operation executes repeatedly, which substantially degrades performance. It is much more efficient to accumulate partial sums in vector registers using vertical operations, then perform the horizontal addition just once after the loop completes.

We now apply these principles to our problem.

```
1   package com.nonpareilcoder.floatingpoint;
2
3   import jdk.incubator.vector.*;
4   import static jdk.incubator.vector.VectorOperators.*;
5
6   public class MeanDeviationLanewise {
7     static final VectorSpecies<Float> SP =
```

```java
 8              FloatVector.SPECIES_PREFERRED;
 9
10     static public float[] compute(float[] input) {
11       int N = input.length;
12
13       FloatVector _s1 = FloatVector.zero(SP);
14       FloatVector _s2 = FloatVector.zero(SP);
15
16       for (int i = 0; i < N; i += SP.length()) {
17         var _mask = SP.indexInRange(i, N);
18
19         FloatVector _v1 = FloatVector.fromArray(SP, input, i, _mask);
20         FloatVector _v2 = _v1.mul(_v1);
21
22         _s1 = _s1.add(_v1);
23         _s2 = _s2.add(_v2);
24       }
25
26       float s1 = _s1.reduceLanes(ADD);
27       float s2 = _s2.reduceLanes(ADD);
28
29       float mean = (float) s1 / N;
30       float dev = (float) StrictMath.sqrt(s2 * N - s1 * s1) / N;
31
32       return new float[]{mean, dev};
33     }
34   }
35
36
```

- Line 22 inside the loop now performs element-wise addition. This way, we accumulate a vector of partial sums.

- Line 26, after the loop completes, horizontally adds the partial sums, forming the final sum.

- Similarly, lines 23 and 27 calculate the sum of squares.

Thus, the algorithm uses just two horizontal operations, which are moved outside the loop body.

We run our test problem on systems with different vector lengths and compare with the reference.

Table 3-2. *Accuracy comparison across different vector lengths*

Vector Length	Mean	Error	Standard Deviation	Error
Double precision (reference)	0.50682557		0.28694576	
128	0.50682527	3E-07	0.28694603	2.7E-07
256	0.50682557	0	0.28694573	3E-08
512	0.50682557	0	0.28694573	3E-08

Notably, the results in Table 3-2 vary with vector length, even though the processing algorithm remains unchanged and works correctly. This instability stems from the following mechanism:

- With different vector lengths, the problem splits into different numbers of partial sums.

- Each partial sum accumulates its own computation error.

- The pattern of error accumulation differs depending on the number of partial sums.

With a vector length of 128 bits, only four partial sums accumulate, and they become large enough for rounding errors to occur. With longer vectors, the partial sums are smaller, and rounding errors do not accumulate significantly. However, this should not create false confidence: the more data processed, the greater the likelihood of rounding errors appearing at any vector length.

Kahan's correction solves this problem because it tracks and compensates for rounding errors at each computation step. Regardless of how many partial sums accumulate (which depends on vector length), Kahan's algorithm corrects each of them, ensuring uniform accuracy in the final result. Thus, corrected sums produce a stable result independent of vector length.

```java
1    package com.nonpareilcoder.floatingpoint;
2
3    import jdk.incubator.vector.*;
4    import static jdk.incubator.vector.VectorOperators.*;
5
6    public class MeanDeviationLanewiseCorrected {
7      static final VectorSpecies<Float> SP =
8        FloatVector.SPECIES_512;
9
10     static public float[] compute(float[] input) {
11       int N = input.length;
12
13       FloatVector _s1 = FloatVector.zero(SP);
14       FloatVector _s2 = FloatVector.zero(SP);
15
16       FloatVector _c1 = FloatVector.zero(SP);
17       FloatVector _c2 = FloatVector.zero(SP);
18
19       for (int i = 0; i < N; i += SP.length()) {
20         var _mask = SP.indexInRange(i, N);
21
22         FloatVector _v1 = FloatVector.fromArray(SP, input, i, _mask);
23         FloatVector _v2 = _v1.mul(_v1);
24
25         FloatVector _t1 = _s1.add(_v1);
26         FloatVector _t2 = _s1.add(_v2);
27         _c1 = _s1.sub(_t1).add(_v1).add(_c1);
28         _c2 = _s2.sub(_t2).add(_v2).add(_c2);
29         _s1 = _t1;
30         _s2 = _t2;
31       }
32
33       float s1 = _s1.add(_c1).reduceLanes(ADD);
34       float s2 = _s2.add(_c2).reduceLanes(ADD);
35
```

```
36          float mean = (float) s1 / N;
37          float dev = (float) StrictMath.sqrt(s2 * N - s1 * s1) / N;
38
39          return new float[]{mean, dev};
40      }
41  }
42
```

Now our solution fully satisfies the definition of vector-length agnosticism: any vector length produces the same result. At least until accumulated errors exceed the correction mechanism's capacity.

In practice, I would not introduce Kahan's correction into vectorized code if the scalar version omits it. If the uncorrected scalar code is "accurate enough," the vectorized version should be equally acceptable. Indeed, spreading the rounding error across lanes often improves accuracy.

However, I often add corrections for a different reason: defending vectorized code against skeptical colleagues. Vector code necessarily uses a different order of operations than scalar code, producing different rounding errors. In my experience, team members less familiar with vectorization often blame the next bug on the "new, untested" vector implementation, pointing to the "different" arithmetic result as evidence. A prudent strategy is to prepare both corrected scalar and corrected vector implementations in advance, then demonstrate that both produce rounding errors, with the vector version typically faring better. This helps convince the team that result differences stem from operation ordering, not from bugs in the code.

Benchmarks

Table 3-3 and Table 3-5 show the raw execution timing, while Table 3-4 and Table 3-6 present the speedup relative to the scalar baseline.

Table 3-3. *Execution timing on x86 platforms (lower is better)*

Variant	GL	Z2	IL	SR	Z5	Units
doubleCorrected	589	177	190	143	117	ms/op
lanewise	357	41	25	27	31	ms/op
lanewiseX4	484	53	28	26	27	ms/op
lanewiseCorrected	2673	1222	34	89	59	ms/op
lanewiseCorrectedX4	2798	1331	33	29	33	ms/op
reduced	362	58	41	35	79	ms/op
single	327	186	244	141	90	ms/op
singleCorrected	340	151	171	106	98	ms/op
singlePass	152	93	120	59	45	ms/op

The X86 benchmark results demonstrate that vectorized statistics computation can achieve excellent speedups, but Kahan's correction introduces severe overhead on older hardware. Still, on modern CPUs, the corrected variant with 3× the operations is only 20% slower—the additional arithmetic can execute in parallel with memory fetches, hiding much of the computational overhead.

The singlePass variant provides consistent 2.01–2.40× speedups across all platforms by eliminating one array traversal. This confirms that our workload is memory-bound: the CPU spends most of its time waiting for data, leaving ample cycles for additional arithmetic. Indeed, a single addition per element is not enough to keep the execution units busy.

Z5 (AMD Turin) is the absolute leader in all scalar benchmarks. However, the unrolled vector code performs best on the SR (Intel Sapphire Rapids) core. This is an excellent example that vectorization can not only improve performance but also influence the choice of compute platform.

How much is gained by vectorization?

Table 3-4. *Single-core speedup on x86 platforms (higher is better)*

Variant	GL	Z2	IL	SR	Z5
doubleCorrected	0.56	1.05	1.28	0.99	0.77
lanewise	0.92	4.58	9.68	5.26	2.95
lanewiseX4	0.68	3.54	8.62	5.46	3.40
lanewiseCorrected	0.12	0.15	7.12	1.58	1.53
lanewiseCorrectedX4	0.12	0.14	7.32	4.88	2.73
reduced	0.90	3.20	5.94	3.98	1.15
single	1.00	1.00	1.00	1.00	1.00
singleCorrected	0.96	1.23	1.42	1.33	0.92
singlePass	2.15	2.01	2.03	2.40	2.02

IL (Intel Ice Lake) achieves peak performance with lanewise at 9.68× speedup, showcasing AVX-512's efficiency for floating-point accumulation with properly structured partial sums.

The variant with per-iteration horizontal reduction shows progressively worse scaling from IL (5.94×) to Z5 (1.15×), confirming that moving the reduction outside the loop is critical for performance.

The biggest disappointment is the GL (Intel Gemini Lake) chip. It appears that the compiler has failed to produce SSE vector code for all of our tests. Thus, GL has become an example of graceful degradation. All code runs without errors, but performance is significantly inferior to the scalar implementation. We will not repeat ourselves in subsequent chapters but will keep GL results as a reminder of our failure.

Table 3-5. *Execution timing on ARM platforms (lower is better)*

Variant	M4	06	CO	NV	G3	Units
doubleCorrected	69	242	183	73	159	ms/op
lanewise	44	26	24	14	17	ms/op
lanewiseX4	91	28	28	12	16	ms/op
lanewiseCorrected	450	1558	1144	933	1370	ms/op
lanewiseCorrectedX4	466	1555	1267	966	1504	ms/op
reduced	73	46	42	15	96	ms/op
single	103	166	115	95	130	ms/op
singleCorrected	67	183	148	73	130	ms/op
singlePass	58	95	63	52	77	ms/op

The ARM benchmark results reveal that Kahan's correction causes catastrophic performance degradation across all platforms, while uncorrected vectorization achieves excellent speedups. It appears that the compiler has failed to properly vectorize Kahan's algorithm.

The leaderboard changes with vectorization are even more dramatic in the ARM realm. The Apple M4 chip achieves scalar performance second only to NV. However, in vector benchmarks, M4 drops to last place.

The singlePass optimization delivers consistent 1.69–1.84× speedups across all ARM platforms, confirming that reducing memory passes is a universally beneficial strategy regardless of vector capabilities. The speedup does not reach the 2× mark, suggesting that we are still compute-bound.

Table 3-6. *Single-core speedup on ARM platforms (higher is better)*

Variant	M4	O6	CO	NV	G3
doubleCorrected	1.50	0.69	0.63	1.30	0.82
lanewise	2.31	6.48	4.69	6.84	7.65
lanewiseX4	1.13	5.86	4.14	7.71	8.24
lanewiseCorrected	0.23	0.11	0.10	0.10	0.09
lanewiseCorrectedX4	0.22	0.11	0.09	0.10	0.09
reduced	1.41	3.64	2.71	6.34	1.35
single	1.00	1.00	1.00	1.00	1.00
singleCorrected	1.54	0.91	0.77	1.31	1.00
singlePass	1.78	1.75	1.82	1.84	1.69

G3 (Amazon Graviton 3) achieves the best uncorrected vectorization performance with lanewiseX4 at 8.24× and lanewise at 7.65×, demonstrating that its 256-bit SVE vectors excel at floating-point accumulation. NV (Nvidia Grace) shows interesting behavior where lanewiseX4 (7.71×) outperforms lanewise (6.84×), unlike other 128-bit platforms, suggesting its quad-vector-instruction pipeline benefits from explicit unrolling.

From this point forward, our benchmark discussions will focus primarily on single-core speedup to isolate the algorithmic efficiency of vectorization. However, readers should bear in mind that optimizing for real-world production systems is a multidimensional challenge. A holistic performance strategy must consider a myriad of additional factors, including multi-core scaling and contention, cache hierarchy dynamics and coherency, NUMA (Non-uniform Memory Access) architectural implications, memory bandwidth saturation, storage I/O throughput, and network interconnect latencies.

What's Next

We now shift gears from pure numerical computation to our first Project Euler exploration. In the next chapter, we tackle the classic problem of summing multiples of 3 or 5: a simple-sounding challenge that reveals deep insights into JIT compilation. We will examine the assembly code generated by the C1 and C2 compilers, encounter Lemire's divisibility test, and learn how masked operations enable branch-free conditional logic.

CHAPTER 4

Multiples of Three or Five

Project Euler is a non-profit initiative that shows how mathematics and computer science combine to produce elegant, efficient code. In my view, if you add vectorization to the mix, the results become even more intriguing. Consider the project's first and simplest problem and see what additional lessons we can learn.

Problem Statement

Find the sum of all natural numbers less than 1000 that are multiples of 3 or 5.

In This Chapter

1. How JIT compilation transforms Java bytecode into optimized machine instructions

2. Lemire's divisibility test for efficient modulo-free divisibility checking

3. Masked operations and the blend operation for branch-free conditional logic

4. Reading and interpreting JIT-generated assembly code

Scalar Solution

The naive implementation is straightforward:

```
1    package com.nonpareilcoder.projecteuler;
2
3    public class MultiplesOf3Or5Naive {
```

```
4      public static int compute(int n) {
5        int sum = 0;
6        for (int i = 3; i < n; i++) {
7          if (i % 3 == 0 || i % 5 == 0) {
8            sum += i;
9          }
10       }
11       return sum;
12     }
13   }
14
```

We loop over natural numbers, find remainders when dividing by 3 and 5, and if at least one equals zero, we add the number to a running sum.

This is one of the smallest programs in this book—and that is precisely what makes it valuable. With so little logic to obscure the view, we can peer directly into the JVM's machinery: how the JIT compiler transforms our humble loop into optimized machine code and what that assembly reveals about the JVM's inner workings.

The initial execution of the program happens through bytecode interpretation. A Java program is first compiled to bytecode, which serves as an intermediate representation. This bytecode is executed by the Java Virtual Machine (JVM) using an interpreter. When a code fragment executes repeatedly, the JVM may determine that this section is resource-intensive and requires compilation. At this point, the first-level JIT compiler— C1—kicks in. It works quickly and performs simple optimizations. Here is what we get on our trusty Ice Lake processor:

```
1    ======================= C1-compiled nmethod =========================
2    --------------------------- Assembly -------------------------------
3
4    Compiled method (c1) 282   862         3
5    com.nonpareilcoder.projecteuler.MultiplesOf3Or5Naive::compute
6    (33 bytes)
7    total in heap  [0x000001766f2d3b88,0x000001766f2d3eb0] = 808
8    main code      [0x000001766f2d3c80,0x000001766f2d3e70] = 496
9    stub code      [0x000001766f2d3e70,0x000001766f2d3ea8] = 56
10   oops           [0x000001766f2d3ea8,0x000001766f2d3eb0] = 8
```

```
11   mutable data     [0x000001760a62fb50,0x000001760a62fb98] = 72
12   relocation       [0x000001760a62fb50,0x000001760a62fb90] = 64
13   metadata         [0x000001760a62fb90,0x000001760a62fb98] = 8
14   immutable data   [0x000001760a94c510,0x000001760a94c5d8] = 200
15   dependencies     [0x000001760a94c510,0x000001760a94c518] = 8
16   nul chk table    [0x000001760a94c518,0x000001760a94c530] = 24
17   scopes pcs       [0x000001760a94c530,0x000001760a94c5a0] = 112
18   scopes data      [0x000001760a94c5a0,0x000001760a94c5d8] = 56
19
20   [Disassembly]
21   -----------------------------------------------------------------
22   [Constant Pool (empty)]
23
24   -----------------------------------------------------------------
25
26   [Verified Entry Point]
27     # {method} {0x0000017606497e60} 'compute' '(I)I' in
28     # 'com/nonpareilcoder/projecteuler/MultiplesOf3Or5Naive'
29     # parm0:    rdx       = int
30     #             [sp+0x30]  (sp of caller)
31     0x000001766f2d3c80:   mov     %eax,-0x8000(%rsp)
32     0x000001766f2d3c87:   push    %rbp
33     0x000001766f2d3c88:   sub     $0x20,%rsp
34     0x000001766f2d3c8c:   cmpl    $0x0,0x20(%r15)
35     0x000001766f2d3c94:   je      0x000001766f2d3c9b
36     ; {runtime_call Stub::method_entry_barrier}
37     0x000001766f2d3c96:   call    Stub::method_entry_barrier
38     0x000001766f2d3c9b:   mov     %rdx,%rsi
39     ; {metadata(method data for {method} {0x0000017606497e60}
40     ;   'compute' '(I)I' in 'com/.../MultiplesOf3Or5Naive')}
41     0x000001766f2d3c9e:   movabs  $0x1760649c4c8,%rax
42     0x000001766f2d3ca8:   mov     0x90(%rax),%edx
43     0x000001766f2d3cae:   add     $0x2,%edx
44     0x000001766f2d3cb1:   mov     %edx,0x90(%rax)
45     0x000001766f2d3cb7:   and     $0x7fe,%edx
```

```
46        0x000001766f2d3cbd:    test    %edx,%edx
47        0x000001766f2d3cbf:    je      0x000001766f2d3dea
48        0x000001766f2d3cc5:    mov     $0x3,%edi
49        0x000001766f2d3cca:    mov     $0x0,%ebx
50        0x000001766f2d3ccf:    nop
51        0x000001766f2d3cd0:    cmp     %esi,%edi
52        ; {metadata(method data for {method} {0x0000017606497e60}
53        ;    'compute' '(I)I' in 'com/.../MultiplesOf3Or5Naive')}
54        0x000001766f2d3cd2:    movabs  $0x1760649c4c8,%rax
55        0x000001766f2d3cdc:    mov     $0xd8,%edx
56        0x000001766f2d3ce1:    jge     0x000001766f2d3ce8
57        0x000001766f2d3ce3:    mov     $0xe8,%edx
58        0x000001766f2d3ce8:    mov     (%rax,%rdx,1),%rcx
59        0x000001766f2d3cec:    lea     0x1(%rcx),%rcx
60        0x000001766f2d3cf0:    mov     %rcx,(%rax,%rdx,1)
61        0x000001766f2d3cf4:    jge     0x000001766f2d3dd7
62        0x000001766f2d3cfa:    mov     %rdi,%rax
63        0x000001766f2d3cfd:    mov     $0x3,%ecx
64        0x000001766f2d3d02:    cmp     $0x80000000,%eax
65        0x000001766f2d3d07:    jne     0x000001766f2d3d18
66        0x000001766f2d3d0d:    xor     %edx,%edx
67        0x000001766f2d3d0f:    cmp     $0xffffffff,%ecx
68        0x000001766f2d3d12:    je      0x000001766f2d3d1b
69        0x000001766f2d3d18:    cltd
70        ; implicit exception: dispatches to 0x000001766f2d3e0b
71        0x000001766f2d3d19:    idiv    %ecx
72        0x000001766f2d3d1b:    test    %edx,%edx
73        ; {metadata(method data for {method} {0x0000017606497e60}
74        ;    'compute' '(I)I' in 'com/.../MultiplesOf3Or5Naive')}
75        0x000001766f2d3d1d:    movabs  $0x1760649c4c8,%rax
76        0x000001766f2d3d27:    mov     $0xf8,%edx
77        0x000001766f2d3d2c:    je      0x000001766f2d3d33
78        0x000001766f2d3d2e:    mov     $0x108,%edx
79        0x000001766f2d3d33:    mov     (%rax,%rdx,1),%rcx
80        0x000001766f2d3d37:    lea     0x1(%rcx),%rcx
```

```
 81   0x000001766f2d3d3b:   mov    %rcx,(%rax,%rdx,1)
 82   0x000001766f2d3d3f:   je     0x000001766f2d3d90
 83   0x000001766f2d3d45:   mov    %rdi,%rax
 84   0x000001766f2d3d48:   mov    $0x5,%ecx
 85   0x000001766f2d3d4d:   cmp    $0x80000000,%eax
 86   0x000001766f2d3d52:   jne    0x000001766f2d3d63
 87   0x000001766f2d3d58:   xor    %edx,%edx
 88   0x000001766f2d3d5a:   cmp    $0xffffffff,%ecx
 89   0x000001766f2d3d5d:   je     0x000001766f2d3d66
 90   0x000001766f2d3d63:   cltd
 91   ; implicit exception: dispatches to 0x000001766f2d3e10
 92   0x000001766f2d3d64:   idiv   %ecx
 93   0x000001766f2d3d66:   test   %edx,%edx
 94   ; {metadata(method data for {method} {0x0000017606497e60}
 95   ;    'compute' '(I)I' in 'com/.../MultiplesOf3Or5Naive')}
 96   0x000001766f2d3d68:   movabs $0x1760649c4c8,%rax
 97   0x000001766f2d3d72:   mov    $0x118,%edx
 98   0x000001766f2d3d77:   jne    0x000001766f2d3d7e
 99   0x000001766f2d3d79:   mov    $0x128,%edx
100   0x000001766f2d3d7e:   mov    (%rax,%rdx,1),%rcx
101   0x000001766f2d3d82:   lea    0x1(%rcx),%rcx
102   0x000001766f2d3d86:   mov    %rcx,(%rax,%rdx,1)
103   0x000001766f2d3d8a:   jne    0x000001766f2d3d92
104   0x000001766f2d3d90:   add    %edi,%ebx
105   0x000001766f2d3d92:   inc    %edi
106   ; {metadata(method data for {method} {0x0000017606497e60}
107   ;    'compute' '(I)I' in 'com/.../MultiplesOf3Or5Naive')}
108   0x000001766f2d3d94:   movabs $0x1760649c4c8,%rax
109   0x000001766f2d3d9e:   mov    0x94(%rax),%edx
110   0x000001766f2d3da4:   add    $0x2,%edx
111   0x000001766f2d3da7:   mov    %edx,0x94(%rax)
112   0x000001766f2d3dad:   and    $0x3ffe,%edx
113   0x000001766f2d3db3:   test   %edx,%edx
114   0x000001766f2d3db5:   je     0x000001766f2d3e15
115   ; ImmutableOopMap {}
```

```
116    ; *goto {reexecute=1 rethrow=0 return_oop=0}
117    ; - (reexecute) com/.../MultiplesOf3Or5Naive::compute@28 (line 6)
118    0x000001766f2d3dbb:   mov     0x30(%r15),%r10
119    ; {poll}
120    0x000001766f2d3dbf:   test    %eax,(%r10)
121    ; {metadata(method data for {method} {0x0000017606497e60}
122    ;    'compute' '(I)I' in 'com/.../MultiplesOf3Or5Naive')}
123    0x000001766f2d3dc2:   movabs  $0x1760649c4c8,%rax
124    0x000001766f2d3dcc:   incl    0x138(%rax)
125    0x000001766f2d3dd2:   jmp     0x000001766f2d3cd0
126    0x000001766f2d3dd7:   mov     %rbx,%rax
127    0x000001766f2d3dda:   add     $0x20,%rsp
128    0x000001766f2d3dde:   pop     %rbp
129    ; {poll_return}
130    0x000001766f2d3ddf:   cmp     0x28(%r15),%rsp
131    0x000001766f2d3de3:   ja      0x000001766f2d3e33
132    0x000001766f2d3de9:   ret
133    ; {metadata({method} {0x0000017606497e60}
134    ;    'compute' '(I)I' in 'com/.../MultiplesOf3Or5Naive')}
135    0x000001766f2d3dea:   movabs  $0x17606497e58,%r10
136    0x000001766f2d3df4:   mov     %r10,0x8(%rsp)
137    0x000001766f2d3df9:   movq    $0xffffffffffffffff,(%rsp)
138    ; ImmutableOopMap {}
139    ; *synchronization entry
140    ; - com/.../MultiplesOf3Or5Naive::compute@-1 (line 5)
141    ; {runtime_call C1 Runtime counter_overflow_blob}
142    0x000001766f2d3e01:   call    0x000001767682a360
143    0x000001766f2d3e06:   jmp     0x000001766f2d3cc5
144    ; ImmutableOopMap {}
145    ; *irem {reexecute=0 rethrow=0 return_oop=0}
146    ; - com/.../MultiplesOf3Or5Naive::compute@11 (line 7)
147    ; {runtime_call C1 Runtime throw_div0_exception_blob}
148    0x000001766f2d3e0b:   call    0x0000017676823ee0
149    ; ImmutableOopMap {}
150    ; *irem {reexecute=0 rethrow=0 return_oop=0}
```

```
151    ; - com/.../MultiplesOf3Or5Naive::compute@17 (line 7)
152    ; {runtime_call C1 Runtime throw_div0_exception_blob}
153    0x000001766f2d3e10:    call    0x0000017676823ee0
154    ; {metadata({method} {0x0000017606497e60}
155    ;   'compute' '(I)I' in 'com/.../MultiplesOf3Or5Naive')}
156    0x000001766f2d3e15:    movabs $0x17606497e58,%r10
157    0x000001766f2d3e1f:    mov     %r10,0x8(%rsp)
158    0x000001766f2d3e24:    movq    $0x1c,(%rsp)
159    ; ImmutableOopMap {}
160    ; *goto {reexecute=1 rethrow=0 return_oop=0}
161    ; - (reexecute) com/.../MultiplesOf3Or5Naive::compute@28 (line 6)
162    ; {runtime_call C1 Runtime counter_overflow_blob}
163    0x000001766f2d3e2c:    call    0x000001767682a360
164    0x000001766f2d3e31:    jmp     0x000001766f2d3dbb
165    ; {internal_word}
166    0x000001766f2d3e33:    movabs $0x1766f2d3ddf,%r10
167    0x000001766f2d3e3d:    mov     %r10,0x4e0(%r15)
168    ; {runtime_call SafepointBlob}
169    0x000001766f2d3e44:    jmp     0x0000017676752260
170    0x000001766f2d3e49:    mov     0x588(%r15),%rax
171    0x000001766f2d3e50:    movq    $0x0,0x588(%r15)
172    0x000001766f2d3e5b:    movq    $0x0,0x590(%r15)
173    0x000001766f2d3e66:    add     $0x20,%rsp
174    0x000001766f2d3e6a:    pop     %rbp
175    ; {runtime_call C1 Runtime unwind_exception_blob}
176    0x000001766f2d3e6b:    jmp     0x00000176768232e0
177 [Exception Handler]
178    ; {runtime_call C1 Runtime handle_exception_from_callee_blob}
179    0x000001766f2d3e70:    call    0x00000176768263e0
180    ; {external_word}
181    0x000001766f2d3e75:    movabs $0x7ffac9720838,%rcx
182    0x000001766f2d3e7f:    and     $0xfffffffffffffff0,%rsp
183    ; {runtime_call}
184    0x000001766f2d3e83:    movabs $0x7ffac9358c50,%rax
185    0x000001766f2d3e8d:    call    *%rax
```

```
186      0x000001766f2d3e8f:    hlt
187    [Deopt Handler Code]
188      ; {section_word}
189      0x000001766f2d3e90:    movabs $0x1766f2d3e90,%r10
190      0x000001766f2d3e9a:    push   %r10
191      ; {runtime_call DeoptimizationBlob}
192      0x000001766f2d3e9c:    jmp    0x00000176767509e0
193      0x000001766f2d3ea1:    hlt
194      0x000001766f2d3ea2:    hlt
195      0x000001766f2d3ea3:    hlt
196      0x000001766f2d3ea4:    hlt
197      0x000001766f2d3ea5:    hlt
198      0x000001766f2d3ea6:    hlt
199      0x000001766f2d3ea7:    hlt
200    ----------------------------------------------------------------------
201    [/Disassembly]
202
```

Let us walk through this assembly listing in detail:

- **Method Header and Statistics** (lines 1–19). The output begins with metadata about the compiled method: its name (compute), signature ((I)I—takes an int, returns an int), and memory layout. The "main code" occupies 496 bytes, which is substantial for such a simple loop.

- **Stack Frame Setup** (lines 31–37). The method entry establishes a stack frame.

- Line 31 performs a stack banging check by writing to an address 32KB below the stack pointer, ensuring sufficient stack space is available.

- Lines 32–33 save the frame pointer and allocate 32 bytes of local space.

- Lines 34–37 check a thread-local flag to see if a memory barrier is needed (for garbage collector safepoints). If the flag is set, a runtime stub is called.

- **Profiling and Invocation Counter** (lines 38–50). C1 generates code that collects execution statistics.

- Line 41 loads the address of the method's profiling data structure (MethodData).

- Lines 42–46 increment an invocation counter. When this counter reaches a threshold, the method becomes a candidate for C2 recompilation.

- Line 47 checks if the counter has overflowed; if so, it jumps to line 170 to trigger recompilation.

- Lines 48–49 initialize the loop variable i = 3 (in edi) and the accumulator sum = 0 (in ebx).

- **Loop Condition Check** (lines 51–61). The loop header compares i against the limit n.

- Line 51 compares edi (loop counter) with esi (the parameter n).

- Lines 52–60 update branch profiling counters—the JVM tracks how often each branch is taken to guide future optimizations.

- Line 61 exits the loop if i >= n.

- **Division by 3** (lines 62–82). This is the first modulo operation.

- Lines 62–68 handle a special case: when the dividend equals Integer.MIN_VALUE and the divisor is −1, the result would overflow. The JVM must guard against this.

- Line 69 (cltd) sign-extends eax into edx:eax, preparing for signed division.

- Line 71 (idiv %ecx) performs the actual division. The quotient goes to eax, the remainder to edx. This single instruction is one of the slowest in the x86 repertoire—it can take 20–80 cycles depending on the processor.

- Lines 72–82 check if the remainder is zero and update branch profiling data.

- **Division by 5** (lines 83–103). The pattern repeats for the second divisibility test.

- Line 84 loads the divisor 5 into ecx.

- Line 92 performs idiv again—another expensive operation.

- Lines 93–103 check the remainder and update profiling counters.

- **Conditional Addition and Loop Increment** (lines 104–125).

- Line 104 adds i to sum if divisible by 3 or 5.

- Line 105 increments the loop counter.

- Lines 106–114 update the backedge counter (tracking loop iterations) for compilation decisions.

- Lines 118–120 perform a safepoint poll—checking if the JVM needs to pause this thread for garbage collection or other VM operations.

- Line 125 jumps back to the loop header.

- **Method Exit** (lines 126–132).

- Line 126 moves the result from ebx to eax (the return register).

- Lines 127–128 restore the stack frame.

- Lines 130–131 perform a final safepoint check before returning.

- **Exception Handlers** (lines 133–176). The remaining code handles edge cases:

- Lines 148 and 153 call runtime stubs to throw ArithmeticException if division by zero occurs.

- Lines 177–186 handle exceptions that propagate from callees.

- Lines 187–199 contain the deoptimization handler—if an assumption made during compilation proves wrong, execution transfers back to the interpreter.

In summary, this C1-generated code is correct but unoptimized. The two idiv instructions dominate execution time, and the extensive profiling overhead adds further cost.

If, after C1 compilation, the code continues to consume significant execution time, the JVM may invoke the C2 compiler. This is a more sophisticated and resource-intensive compiler that performs deep code optimization.

Once upon a time, when JIT technology was just being developed, the C1 compiler was created for client applications, while C2 was for the server version of Java. Over time, they merged into a unified system where both compilers are used as needed, depending on the application type, system load, nature of operations, and available resources.

```
1   ======================= C2-compiled nmethod =======================
2   --------------------------- Assembly ---------------------------
3
4   Compiled method (c2) 289   864          4
5    com.nonpareilcoder.projecteuler.MultiplesOf3Or5Naive::compute
6    (33 bytes)
7    total in heap    [0x0000017676cb8d88,0x0000017676cb9028] = 672
8    main code        [0x0000017676cb8e80,0x0000017676cb9008] = 392
9    stub code        [0x0000017676cb9008,0x0000017676cb9020] = 24
10   oops             [0x0000017676cb9020,0x0000017676cb9028] = 8
11   mutable data     [0x000001760a96d4f0,0x000001760a96d510] = 32
12   relocation       [0x000001760a96d4f0,0x000001760a96d508] = 24
13   metadata         [0x000001760a96d508,0x000001760a96d510] = 8
14   immutable data   [0x000001760a62f2e0,0x000001760a62f328] = 72
15   dependencies     [0x000001760a62f2e0,0x000001760a62f2e8] = 8
16   scopes pcs       [0x000001760a62f2e8,0x000001760a62f318] = 48
17   scopes data      [0x000001760a62f318,0x000001760a62f328] = 16
18
19   [Disassembly]
20   ------------------------------------------------------------------
21   [Constant Pool (empty)]
22
23   ------------------------------------------------------------------
24
25   [Verified Entry Point]
26     # {method} {0x0000017606497e60} 'compute' '(I)I' in
27     # 'com/nonpareilcoder/projecteuler/MultiplesOf3Or5Naive'
28     # parm0:   rdx        = int
```

```
29      #               [sp+0x20]  (sp of caller)
30      0x0000017676cb8e80:    sub     $0x18,%rsp
31      0x0000017676cb8e87:    mov     %rbp,0x10(%rsp)
32      0x0000017676cb8e8c:    cmpl    $0x0,0x20(%r15)
33      0x0000017676cb8e94:    jne     0x0000017676cb8ffa
34      0x0000017676cb8e9a:    xor     %r10d,%r10d
35      0x0000017676cb8e9d:    cmp     $0x3,%edx
36      0x0000017676cb8ea0:    jle     0x0000017676cb8fe0
37      0x0000017676cb8ea6:    movslq  %edx,%r11
38      0x0000017676cb8ea9:    dec     %r11
39      0x0000017676cb8eac:    mov     $0x4,%r8d
40      0x0000017676cb8eb2:    mov     $0x3,%eax
41      0x0000017676cb8eb7:    mov     $0xffffffff80000000,%r9
42      0x0000017676cb8ebe:    cmp     $0xffffffff80000000,%r11
43      0x0000017676cb8ec5:    cmovl   %r9,%r11
44      0x0000017676cb8ec9:    mov     %r11d,%r11d
45      0x0000017676cb8ecc:    cmp     $0x4,%r11d
46      0x0000017676cb8ed0:    jle     0x0000017676cb8f8f
47      0x0000017676cb8ed6:    mov     $0x7d0,%ecx
48      0x0000017676cb8edb:    jmp     0x0000017676cb8f6f
49      0x0000017676cb8ee0:    add     %eax,%r13d
50      0x0000017676cb8ee3:    mov     %r13d,%eax
51      0x0000017676cb8ee6:    data16 nopw 0x0(%rax,%rax,1)
52      0x0000017676cb8ef0:    add     $0x2,%r8d
53      0x0000017676cb8ef4:    cmp     %r9d,%r8d
54      0x0000017676cb8ef7:    jge     0x0000017676cb8f63
55      0x0000017676cb8ef9:    movslq  %r8d,%rbx
56      0x0000017676cb8efc:    imul    $0x55555556,%rbx,%rsi
57      0x0000017676cb8f03:    imul    $0x66666667,%rbx,%rbp
58      0x0000017676cb8f0a:    mov     %rsi,%rbx
59      0x0000017676cb8f0d:    sar     $0x20,%rbx
60      0x0000017676cb8f11:    mov     %ebx,%edi
61      0x0000017676cb8f13:    lea     (%rdi,%rdi,2),%edi
62      0x0000017676cb8f16:    cmp     %edi,%r8d
63      0x0000017676cb8f19:    je      0x0000017676cb8f2c
```

```
64    0x0000017676cb8f1b:    mov     %rbp,%rbx
65    0x0000017676cb8f1e:    sar     $0x21,%rbx
66    0x0000017676cb8f22:    mov     %ebx,%ebx
67    0x0000017676cb8f24:    lea     (%rbx,%rbx,4),%ebx
68    0x0000017676cb8f27:    cmp     %ebx,%r8d
69    0x0000017676cb8f2a:    jne     0x0000017676cb8f2f
70    0x0000017676cb8f2c:    add     %r8d,%eax
71    0x0000017676cb8f2f:    lea     0x1(%r8),%r13d
72    0x0000017676cb8f33:    add     $0x55555556,%rsi
73    0x0000017676cb8f3a:    sar     $0x20,%rsi
74    0x0000017676cb8f3e:    mov     %esi,%ebx
75    0x0000017676cb8f40:    lea     (%rbx,%rbx,2),%ebx
76    0x0000017676cb8f43:    cmp     %ebx,%r13d
77    0x0000017676cb8f46:    je      0x0000017676cb8ee0
78    0x0000017676cb8f48:    add     $0x66666667,%rbp
79    0x0000017676cb8f4f:    sar     $0x21,%rbp
80    0x0000017676cb8f53:    mov     %ebp,%ebx
81    0x0000017676cb8f55:    lea     (%rbx,%rbx,4),%edi
82    0x0000017676cb8f58:    cmp     %edi,%r13d
83    0x0000017676cb8f5b:    je      0x0000017676cb8ee0
84    0x0000017676cb8f61:    jmp     0x0000017676cb8ef0
85    ; ImmutableOopMap {}
86    ; *goto {reexecute=1 rethrow=0 return_oop=0}
87    ; - (reexecute) com/.../MultiplesOf3Or5Naive::compute@28 (line 6)
88    0x0000017676cb8f63:    mov     0x30(%r15),%r9
89    ; {poll}
90    0x0000017676cb8f67:    test    %eax,(%r9)
91    0x0000017676cb8f6a:    cmp     %r11d,%r8d
92    0x0000017676cb8f6d:    jge     0x0000017676cb8f8f
93    0x0000017676cb8f6f:    mov     %r11d,%r9d
94    0x0000017676cb8f72:    sub     %r8d,%r9d
95    0x0000017676cb8f75:    cmp     %r8d,%r11d
96    0x0000017676cb8f78:    cmovl   %r10d,%r9d
97    0x0000017676cb8f7c:    cmp     $0x7d0,%r9d
98    0x0000017676cb8f83:    cmova   %ecx,%r9d
```

```
 99      0x0000017676cb8f87:    add     %r8d,%r9d
100      0x0000017676cb8f8a:    jmp     0x0000017676cb8ef9
101      0x0000017676cb8f8f:    cmp     %edx,%r8d
102      0x0000017676cb8f92:    jge     0x0000017676cb8fd0
103      0x0000017676cb8f94:    movslq  %r8d,%r10
104      0x0000017676cb8f97:    imul    $0x55555556,%r10,%r11
105      0x0000017676cb8f9e:    sar     $0x20,%r11
106      0x0000017676cb8fa2:    mov     %r11d,%r9d
107      0x0000017676cb8fa5:    lea     (%r9,%r9,2),%r11d
108      0x0000017676cb8fa9:    cmp     %r11d,%r8d
109      0x0000017676cb8fac:    je      0x0000017676cb8fc5
110      0x0000017676cb8fae:    imul    $0x66666667,%r10,%r10
111      0x0000017676cb8fb5:    sar     $0x21,%r10
112      0x0000017676cb8fb9:    mov     %r10d,%r10d
113      0x0000017676cb8fbc:    lea     (%r10,%r10,4),%r11d
114      0x0000017676cb8fc0:    cmp     %r11d,%r8d
115      0x0000017676cb8fc3:    jne     0x0000017676cb8fc8
116      0x0000017676cb8fc5:    add     %r8d,%eax
117      0x0000017676cb8fc8:    inc     %r8d
118      0x0000017676cb8fcb:    cmp     %edx,%r8d
119      0x0000017676cb8fce:    jl      0x0000017676cb8f94
120      0x0000017676cb8fd0:    add     $0x10,%rsp
121      0x0000017676cb8fd4:    pop     %rbp
122      ; {poll_return}
123      0x0000017676cb8fd5:    cmp     0x28(%r15),%rsp
124      0x0000017676cb8fd9:    ja      0x0000017676cb8fe4
125      0x0000017676cb8fdf:    ret
126      0x0000017676cb8fe0:    xor     %eax,%eax
127      0x0000017676cb8fe2:    jmp     0x0000017676cb8fd0
128      ; {internal_word}
129      0x0000017676cb8fe4:    movabs  $0x17676cb8fd5,%r10
130      0x0000017676cb8fee:    mov     %r10,0x4e0(%r15)
131      ; {runtime_call SafepointBlob}
132      0x0000017676cb8ff5:    jmp     0x0000017676752260
133      ; {runtime_call Stub::method_entry_barrier}
```

```
134     0x0000017676cb8ffa:    call    Stub::method_entry_barrier
135     0x0000017676cb8fff:    jmp     0x0000017676cb8e9a
136     0x0000017676cb9004:    hlt
137     0x0000017676cb9005:    hlt
138     0x0000017676cb9006:    hlt
139     0x0000017676cb9007:    hlt
140  [Exception Handler]
141     ; {runtime_call ExceptionBlob}
142     0x0000017676cb9008:    jmp     0x000001767682bc60
143  [Deopt Handler Code]
144     0x0000017676cb900d:    call    0x0000017676cb9012
145     0x0000017676cb9012:    subq    $0x5,(%rsp)
146     ; {runtime_call DeoptimizationBlob}
147     0x0000017676cb9017:    jmp     0x00000176767509e0
148     0x0000017676cb901c:    hlt
149     0x0000017676cb901d:    hlt
150     0x0000017676cb901e:    hlt
151     0x0000017676cb901f:    hlt
152  ----------------------------------------------------------------
153  [/Disassembly]
154
```

The C2 output is dramatically different from C1. Let us examine it in detail:

- **Method Header and Statistics** (lines 1–18). The first thing to notice is the reduced code size: "main code" is now 392 bytes compared to C1's 496 bytes. More importantly, "scopes data" shrunk from 56 to 16 bytes—C2 strips out most profiling instrumentation since the method has already been deemed hot.

- **Stack Frame Setup** (lines 30–34). The entry sequence is leaner.

- Line 30 allocates only 24 bytes of stack space (C1 used 32).

- Line 31 saves the frame pointer.

- Lines 32–33 check the barrier flag, jumping to the slow path at line 134 only if needed.

- Line 34 initializes the accumulator r10d to zero.

- **Early Exit and Loop Preparation** (lines 35–48).

- Lines 35–36 handle the edge case: if n <= 3, jump directly to return zero.

- Lines 37–44 compute the loop bound, handling potential overflow with a conditional move.

- Lines 45–46 check if the loop has enough iterations for the unrolled version; if not, jump to the loop epilogue at line 143.

- Line 47 loads the constant 0x7d0 (2000 decimal) into ecx—this limits inner loop iterations to prevent excessive time between safepoint checks.

The most striking feature of the C2 implementation is the absence of division instruction. It has been replaced by multiplication. Daniel Lemire (Lemire, Kaser, & Kurz, 2019) describes this technique in his article on fast divisibility testing. Here is a variant for 32-bit numbers:

If we know the divisor d in advance, we can compute a magic constant at compile time:

```
static const uint32_t c = 0xFFFFFFFF / d + 1;
```

Then the quotient and remainder when dividing an arbitrary 32-bit number n by d can be computed using multiplication:

```
void div_rem(uint32_t n, uint32_t c, uint32_t d, uint32_t& div,
uint32_t &rem) {
  uint64_t prod = (uint64_t)c * n;
  div = (uint32_t)(prod >> 32);
  rem = (uint32_t)(((uint64_t)(uint32_t)prod * d) >> 32);
}
```

The quotient is computed with one multiplication and shift. Another multiplication and shift yield the remainder. C2 compiler uses this technique to replace a 20–80 cycle idiv with a 3–4 cycle imul plus a 1-cycle shift.

- **The Unrolled Main Loop** (lines 49–84). C2 has unrolled the loop to process two iterations simultaneously.

- *First iteration (processing index in r8d)*

- Line 56 multiplies r8d by the magic constant 0x55555556. This constant equals $\lceil 2^{33}/3 \rceil$, enabling division by 3 through multiplication.

- Line 57 similarly multiplies by 0x66666667 $= \lceil 2^{34}/5 \rceil$ for division by 5.

- Lines 59-62 extract the quotient: shift right by 32 bits, then compute quotient * 3 using `lea (%rdi,%rdi,2),%edi` (which calculates $rdi + rdi \times 2 = rdi \times 3$).

- Line 63 compares the original number with $\lfloor n/3 \rfloor \times 3$. If equal, n is divisible by 3.

- Lines 64-69 repeat this pattern for divisibility by 5, using `lea (%rbx,%rbx,4),%ebx` to compute quotient * 5.

- Line 70 adds r8d to the sum if either divisibility test passed.

- *Second iteration (processing index r8d + 1 in r13d)*

- Line 71 computes `r13d = r8d + 1`.

- Lines 72-77 test divisibility by 3 for the next number, reusing the previous multiplication result by simply adding the magic constant. This is an interesting trick on top of the trick replacing 3-4 cycle `imul` with a 1-cycle addition.

- Lines 78-83 test divisibility by 5 similarly.

- Lines 49-50 (at the top of the loop) add the second number to the sum if divisible.

- **Safepoint Polling** (lines 88-92). Unlike C1's per-iteration polling, C2 places safepoints only at loop backedges and limits iterations between checks to 2000 (line 97). This dramatically reduces overhead while still allowing the JVM to pause threads for garbage collection.

- **Loop Epilogue** (lines 101-119). When the remaining iteration count is too small for the unrolled loop, execution falls through to this simpler version that processes one element at a time. The same multiplication-based divisibility tests are used.

- **Method Exit** (lines 120-127)

- Lines 120–121 restore the stack and frame pointer.

- Lines 123–125 perform a final safepoint check before returning.

- Lines 126–127 handle the early-exit case where n <= 3.

- **Exception and Deoptimization Handlers** (lines 140–151). These are much smaller than C1's handlers because C2 has proven that division by zero cannot occur (the divisors are compile-time constants 3 and 5), eliminating the need for runtime checks.

In summary, C2 applies three major optimizations: (1) replacing division with multiplication, (2) loop unrolling to amortize overhead, and (3) removing unnecessary profiling and exception checks. The result is code that runs significantly faster than C1's output.

Vector Loop

The core optimization by C2 is calculating the remainder with two multiplications instead of a lengthy division instruction.

But Lemire went further and derived an efficient divisibility test for d:

```
bool is_divisible(uint32_t c, uint32_t n) {
  return n * c < c;
}
```

Why does this work? A number n is divisible by d if and only if $n \bmod d = 0$. But $n \bmod d = n - d \cdot \lfloor n/d \rfloor$. Using the fact that $c \approx 2^{32}/d$, we get $n \cdot c \approx n \cdot 2^{32}/d$. When dividing evenly by d, the low bits of the product $n \cdot c$ will be small (less than c). If there is a remainder, the low bits will be large. Thus, the condition $n \cdot c < c$ is equivalent to n being divisible by d.

With Lemire's test, we can check divisibility of n by d with just one multiplication. Armed with this knowledge, we can outperform the compiler's optimization:

```
1    package com.nonpareilcoder.projecteuler;

2

3    import jdk.incubator.vector.*;

4
```

```
 5   import static jdk.incubator.vector.VectorOperators.*;
 6
 7   public class MultiplesOf3Or5Vectorized {
 8     static final VectorSpecies<Integer> SP =
 9       IntVector.SPECIES_PREFERRED;
10
11     static final int c3 = 0x55555556;
12     static final int c5 = 0x33333334;
13
14     public static int compute(int n) {
15       var _idx = VectorShuffle.iota(SP, 0, 1, false)
16         .toVector().reinterpretAsInts();
17
18       IntVector _sum = IntVector.zero(SP);
19
20       for (int i = 0; i < n; i += SP.length()) {
21         var _mask = SP.indexInRange(i, n);
22
23         var _mask3 = _idx.mul(c3).compare(ULT, c3, _mask);
24         var _mask5 = _idx.mul(c5).compare(ULT, c5, _mask);
25
26         _sum = _sum.add(_idx, _mask3.or(_mask5));
27
28         _idx = _idx.add(SP.length());
29       }
30
31       int sum = _sum.reduceLanes(ADD);
32
33       return sum;
34     }
35   }
36
```

- The standard vector loop header is presented in lines 20–21.

- Since the algorithm is formulated for unsigned integers, lines 23–24 use unsigned number comparison. This is a perfect example of how vector operations let us bring unsigned arithmetic into Java, even though unsignet ty was not included in the base language.

- Line 31 performs the reduction of partial sums into the final result. We managed to pull the horizontal operation out of the loop body, which improved vector code performance.

In this algorithm, we encounter **masked operations** for the first time. This is an important concept in vector programming.

A mask is a vector of Boolean values that determines which vector elements should have an operation performed on them or, from the hardware perspective, what vector lanes should be activated. In our case, the masks `divisibleBy3` and `divisibleBy5` indicate which numbers are divisible by 3 or 5, respectively. The `blend` operation uses the mask for selective merging of two vectors: it takes elements from the first vector where the mask is true and from the second where the mask is false.

Masked operations eliminate the need for branching in vector code. Instead of checking a condition for each element separately (which would destroy parallelism), we compute the mask for all vector elements at once, then apply it to vector operations. This is a key technique that enables efficient vectorization of algorithms with conditional logic.

The generated machine code shows

```
1    ========================= C2-compiled nmethod =========================
2    --------------------------------- Assembly ---------------------------------
3
4    Compiled method (c2) 925 1376        4
5    com.nonpareilcoder.projecteuler.MultiplesOf3Or5Vectorized::compute
6    (128 bytes)
7    total in heap  [0x00000229eab60b88,0x00000229eab61110] = 1416
8    constants      [0x00000229eab60c80,0x00000229eab60ca0] = 32
9    main code      [0x00000229eab60ca0,0x00000229eab610e0] = 1088
10   stub code      [0x00000229eab610e0,0x00000229eab610f8] = 24
11   oops           [0x00000229eab610f8,0x00000229eab61110] = 24
12   mutable data   [0x00000229fdadf600,0x00000229fdadf988] = 904
```

```
13   relocation      [0x00000229fdadf600,0x00000229fdadf630] = 48
14   metadata        [0x00000229fdadf630,0x00000229fdadf988] = 856
15   immutable data  [0x00000229fdad3ea0,0x00000229fdad40b0] = 528
16   dependencies    [0x00000229fdad3ea0,0x00000229fdad3f98] = 248
17   scopes pcs      [0x00000229fdad3f98,0x00000229fdad3fe8] = 80
18   scopes data     [0x00000229fdad3fe8,0x00000229fdad40b0] = 200
19
20   [Disassembly]
21   -----------------------------------------------------------------
22
23   [Constant Pool]
24             Address             hex4                      hex8
25     0x00000229eab60c80:    0x00000010        0x5555555600000010
26     0x00000229eab60c84:    0x55555556
27     0x00000229eab60c88:    0x33333334        0xf4f4f4f433333334
28     0x00000229eab60c8c:    0xf4f4f4f4
29     0x00000229eab60c90:    0xf4f4f4f4        0xf4f4f4f4f4f4f4f4
30     0x00000229eab60c94:    0xf4f4f4f4
31     0x00000229eab60c98:    0xf4f4f4f4        0xf4f4f4f4f4f4f4f4
32     0x00000229eab60c9c:    0xf4f4f4f4
33
34   -----------------------------------------------------------------
35
36   [Verified Entry Point]
37     # {method} {0x00000229f949c738} 'compute' '(I)I' in
38     # 'com/nonpareilcoder/projecteuler/MultiplesOf3Or5Vectorized'
39     # parm0:     rdx        = int
40     #            [sp+0xe0]  (sp of caller)
41     ; {other}
42     0x00000229eab60ca0:    mov      %eax,-0x8000(%rsp)
43     0x00000229eab60ca7:    push     %rbp
44     0x00000229eab60ca8:    sub      $0xd0,%rsp
45     0x00000229eab60caf:    nop
46     0x00000229eab60cb0:    cmpl     $0x0,0x20(%r15)
47     0x00000229eab60cb8:    jne      0x00000229eab610d6
```

```
48       0x00000229eab60cbe:    vpxor   %xmm7,%xmm7,%xmm7
49       0x00000229eab60cc2:    xor     %r10d,%r10d
50       0x00000229eab60cc5:    test    %edx,%edx
51       0x00000229eab60cc7:    jle     0x00000229eab60fcf
52       ; {oop([I{0x0000000705e54ed8})}
53       0x00000229eab60ccd:    movabs  $0x705e54ed8,%r11
54       0x00000229eab60cd7:    vmovdqu32 0x10(%r11),%zmm5
55       0x00000229eab60ce1:    cmp     $0x7ffffff0,%edx
56       0x00000229eab60ce7:    jg      0x00000229eab6104c
57       0x00000229eab60ced:    movslq  %edx,%rbx
58       0x00000229eab60cf0:    mov     $0xffffffff,%r8d
59       0x00000229eab60cf6:    kmovd   %r8d,%k3
60       0x00000229eab60cfb:    kshiftrd $0x10,%k3,%k3
61       0x00000229eab60d01:    cmp     $0x10,%edx
62       0x00000229eab60d04:    jl      0x00000229eab61011
63       0x00000229eab60d0a:    kmovq   %k3,%k7
64       0x00000229eab60d0f:    lea     -0x30(%rbx),%r11
65       0x00000229eab60d13:    mov     $0xffffffff80000000,%r8
66       0x00000229eab60d1a:    cmp     $0xffffffff80000000,%r11
67       0x00000229eab60d21:    cmovl   %r8,%r11
68       0x00000229eab60d25:    mov     %r11d,%edi
69       ; {section_word}
70       0x00000229eab60d28:    vpbroadcastd -0xaa(%rip),%zmm0
71       0x00000229eab60d32:    vpmulld %zmm0,%zmm5,%zmm1
72       0x00000229eab60d38:    vpcmpltud %zmm0,%zmm1,%k6{%k7}
73       ; {section_word}
74       0x00000229eab60d3f:    vpbroadcastd -0xc9(%rip),%zmm1
75       0x00000229eab60d49:    vpaddd %zmm5,%zmm1,%zmm2
76       ; {section_word}
77       0x00000229eab60d4f:    vpbroadcastd -0xd5(%rip),%zmm3
78       0x00000229eab60d59:    vpmulld %zmm3,%zmm5,%zmm4
79       0x00000229eab60d5f:    vpcmpltud %zmm3,%zmm4,%k7{%k7}
80       0x00000229eab60d66:    mov     $0x10,%r11d
81       0x00000229eab60d6c:    korw    %k7,%k6,%k7
82       0x00000229eab60d70:    vpaddd %zmm5,%zmm7,%zmm7{%k7}
```

```
 83   0x00000229eab60d76:   cmp        $0x10,%edi
 84   0x00000229eab60d79:   jle        0x00000229eab61074
 85   0x00000229eab60d7f:   mov        $0xfa00,%eax
 86   0x00000229eab60d84:   jmp        0x00000229eab60f53
 87   0x00000229eab60d89:   nopl       0x0(%rax)
 88   0x00000229eab60d90:   kmovq      %k3,(%rsp)
 89   0x00000229eab60d96:   lea        -0x20(%r9),%ecx
 90   0x00000229eab60d9a:   cmp        $0x10,%ecx
 91   0x00000229eab60d9d:   jl         0x00000229eab60ee5
 92   0x00000229eab60da3:   kmovq      (%rsp),%k5
 93   0x00000229eab60da9:   add        $0xffffffd0,%r9d
 94   0x00000229eab60dad:   cmp        $0x10,%r9d
 95   0x00000229eab60db1:   jl         0x00000229eab60f18
 96   0x00000229eab60db7:   kmovq      (%rsp),%k6
 97   0x00000229eab60dbd:   vpmulld    %zmm2,%zmm3,%zmm4
 98   0x00000229eab60dc3:   vpcmpltud  %zmm3,%zmm4,%k4{%k7}
 99   0x00000229eab60dca:   kmovq      %k4,0x8(%rsp)
100   0x00000229eab60dd1:   vpmulld    %zmm2,%zmm0,%zmm4
101   0x00000229eab60dd7:   vpcmpltud  %zmm0,%zmm4,%k7{%k7}
102   0x00000229eab60dde:   kmovq      %k7,0x10(%rsp)
103   0x00000229eab60de5:   vpaddd     %zmm2,%zmm1,%zmm4
104   0x00000229eab60deb:   vpaddd     %zmm4,%zmm1,%zmm5
105   0x00000229eab60df1:   vpmulld    %zmm4,%zmm3,%zmm6
106   0x00000229eab60df7:   vpcmpltud  %zmm3,%zmm6,%k4{%k3}
107   0x00000229eab60dfe:   vpmulld    %zmm5,%zmm3,%zmm6
108   0x00000229eab60e04:   vpmulld    %zmm5,%zmm0,%zmm8
109   0x00000229eab60e0a:   vpmulld    %zmm4,%zmm0,%zmm9
110   0x00000229eab60e10:   vpaddd     %zmm5,%zmm1,%zmm10
111   0x00000229eab60e16:   vpaddd     %zmm10,%zmm1,%zmm11
112   0x00000229eab60e1c:   vpmulld    %zmm10,%zmm0,%zmm12
113   0x00000229eab60e22:   vpmulld    %zmm10,%zmm3,%zmm13
114   0x00000229eab60e28:   vpcmpltud  %zmm3,%zmm6,%k2{%k5}
115   0x00000229eab60e2f:   vpcmpltud  %zmm3,%zmm13,%k7{%k6}
116   0x00000229eab60e36:   vpcmpltud  %zmm0,%zmm12,%k6{%k6}
117   0x00000229eab60e3d:   vpcmpltud  %zmm0,%zmm9,%k3{%k3}
```

```
118   0x00000229eab60e44:   vpcmpltud %zmm0,%zmm8,%k1{%k5}
119   ; {other}
120   0x00000229eab60e4b:   korw     %k6,%k7,%k5
121   0x00000229eab60e4f:   korw     %k2,%k1,%k7
122   0x00000229eab60e53:   kmovq    0x10(%rsp),%k2
123   0x00000229eab60e5a:   kmovq    0x8(%rsp),%k1
124   0x00000229eab60e61:   korw     %k1,%k2,%k6
125   0x00000229eab60e65:   vpaddd   %zmm2,%zmm7,%zmm7{%k6}
126   0x00000229eab60e6b:   korw     %k4,%k3,%k6
127   0x00000229eab60e6f:   vpaddd   %zmm4,%zmm7,%zmm7{%k6}
128   0x00000229eab60e75:   vpaddd   %zmm5,%zmm7,%zmm7{%k7}
129   0x00000229eab60e7b:   vpaddd   %zmm10,%zmm7,%zmm7{%k5}
130   0x00000229eab60e81:   add      $0x40,%r11d
131   0x00000229eab60e85:   cmp      %esi,%r11d
132   0x00000229eab60e88:   jge      0x00000229eab60f3b
133   0x00000229eab60e8e:   vmovdqu64 %zmm11,%zmm2
134   0x00000229eab60e94:   kmovq    (%rsp),%k3
135   0x00000229eab60e9a:   mov      %edx,%r9d
136   0x00000229eab60e9d:   sub      %r11d,%r9d
137   0x00000229eab60ea0:   movslq   %r11d,%rbp
138   0x00000229eab60ea3:   mov      %rbx,%r13
139   0x00000229eab60ea6:   sub      %rbp,%r13
140   0x00000229eab60ea9:   cmp      $0x10,%r9d
141   0x00000229eab60ead:   jl       0x00000229eab60f02
142   0x00000229eab60eaf:   kmovq    %k3,%k7
143   0x00000229eab60eb4:   lea      -0x10(%r9),%r8d
144   0x00000229eab60eb8:   cmp      $0x10,%r8d
145   0x00000229eab60ebc:   jge      0x00000229eab60d90
146   0x00000229eab60ec2:   kmovq    %k3,(%rsp)
147   0x00000229eab60ec8:   lea      -0x10(%r13),%r8
148   0x00000229eab60ecc:   movabs   $0xffffffffffffffff,%rcx
149   0x00000229eab60ed6:   bzhi     %r8,%rcx,%rcx
150   0x00000229eab60edb:   kmovq    %rcx,%k3
151   0x00000229eab60ee0:   jmp      0x00000229eab60d96
152   0x00000229eab60ee5:   add      $0xffffffffffffffe0,%r13
```

```
153    0x00000229eab60ee9:    movabs  $0xffffffffffffffff,%r8
154    0x00000229eab60ef3:    bzhi    %r13,%r8,%r8
155    0x00000229eab60ef8:    kmovq   %r8,%k5
156    0x00000229eab60efd:    jmp     0x00000229eab60da9
157    0x00000229eab60f02:    movabs  $0xffffffffffffffff,%r8
158    0x00000229eab60f0c:    bzhi    %r13,%r8,%r8
159    0x00000229eab60f11:    kmovq   %r8,%k7
160    0x00000229eab60f16:    jmp     0x00000229eab60eb4
161    0x00000229eab60f18:    add     $0x30,%rbp
162    0x00000229eab60f1c:    mov     %rbx,%r8
163    0x00000229eab60f1f:    sub     %rbp,%r8
164    0x00000229eab60f22:    movabs  $0xffffffffffffffff,%r9
165    0x00000229eab60f2c:    bzhi    %r8,%r9,%r9
166    0x00000229eab60f31:    kmovq   %r9,%k6
167    0x00000229eab60f36:    jmp     0x00000229eab60dbd
168    ; ImmutableOopMap {}
169    ; *goto {reexecute=1 rethrow=0 return_oop=0}
170    ; - (reexecute) com/.../MultiplesOf3Or5Vectorized::compute@115
171    ;     (line 16)
172    0x00000229eab60f3b:    mov     0x30(%r15),%r8
173    ; {poll}
174    0x00000229eab60f3f:    test    %eax,(%r8)
175    0x00000229eab60f42:    cmp     %edi,%r11d
176    0x00000229eab60f45:    jge     0x00000229eab60f70
177    0x00000229eab60f47:    vmovdqu64 %zmm11,%zmm2
178    0x00000229eab60f4d:    kmovq   (%rsp),%k3
179    0x00000229eab60f53:    mov     %edi,%esi
180    0x00000229eab60f55:    sub     %r11d,%esi
181    0x00000229eab60f58:    cmp     %r11d,%edi
182    0x00000229eab60f5b:    cmovl   %r10d,%esi
183    0x00000229eab60f5f:    cmp     $0xfa00,%esi
184    0x00000229eab60f65:    cmova   %eax,%esi
185    0x00000229eab60f68:    add     %r11d,%esi
186    0x00000229eab60f6b:    jmp     0x00000229eab60e9a
187    0x00000229eab60f70:    kmovq   (%rsp),%k3
```

```
188        0x00000229eab60f76:    cmp       %edx,%r11d
189        0x00000229eab60f79:    jge       0x00000229eab60fcf
190        0x00000229eab60f7b:    nop
191        0x00000229eab60f7c:    cmp       %edx,%r11d
192        0x00000229eab60f7f:    jge       0x00000229eab6107f
193        0x00000229eab60f85:    mov       %edx,%r9d
194        0x00000229eab60f88:    sub       %r11d,%r9d
195        0x00000229eab60f8b:    cmp       $0x10,%r9d
196        0x00000229eab60f8f:    jl        0x00000229eab6102a
197        0x00000229eab60f95:    kmovq     %k3,%k7
198        0x00000229eab60f9a:    vpmulld %zmm11,%zmm3,%zmm2
199        0x00000229eab60fa0:    vpcmpltud %zmm3,%zmm2,%k6{%k7}
200        0x00000229eab60fa7:    vpmulld %zmm11,%zmm0,%zmm2
201        0x00000229eab60fad:    vpcmpltud %zmm0,%zmm2,%k7{%k7}
202        0x00000229eab60fb4:    korw      %k6,%k7,%k7
203        0x00000229eab60fb8:    vpaddd %zmm11,%zmm7,%zmm7{%k7}
204        0x00000229eab60fbe:    add       $0x10,%r11d
205        0x00000229eab60fc2:    cmp       %edx,%r11d
206        0x00000229eab60fc5:    jge       0x00000229eab60fcf
207        0x00000229eab60fc7:    vpaddd %zmm11,%zmm1,%zmm11
208        0x00000229eab60fcd:    jmp       0x00000229eab60f7c
209        0x00000229eab60fcf:    vextracti64x4 $0x1,%zmm7,%ymm1
210        0x00000229eab60fd6:    vpaddd %ymm7,%ymm1,%ymm1
211        0x00000229eab60fda:    vphaddd %ymm1,%ymm1,%ymm0
212        0x00000229eab60fdf:    vextracti128 $0x1,%ymm0,%xmm1
213        0x00000229eab60fe5:    vpaddd %xmm1,%xmm0,%xmm0
214        0x00000229eab60fe9:    vphaddd %xmm0,%xmm0,%xmm0
215        0x00000229eab60fee:    vmovd     %r10d,%xmm1
216        0x00000229eab60ff3:    vpaddd %xmm1,%xmm0,%xmm0
217        0x00000229eab60ff7:    vmovd     %xmm0,%eax
218        0x00000229eab60ffb:    vzeroupper
219        0x00000229eab60ffe:    add       $0xd0,%rsp
220        0x00000229eab61005:    pop       %rbp
221        ; {poll_return}
222        0x00000229eab61006:    cmp       0x28(%r15),%rsp
```

```
223    0x00000229eab6100a:    ja      0x00000229eab610c0
224    0x00000229eab61010:    ret
225    0x00000229eab61011:    movabs $0xffffffffffffffff,%r11
226    0x00000229eab6101b:    bzhi    %rbx,%r11,%r11
227    0x00000229eab61020:    kmovq   %r11,%k7
228    0x00000229eab61025:    jmp     0x00000229eab60d0f
229    0x00000229eab6102a:    movslq %r11d,%r8
230    0x00000229eab6102d:    mov     %rbx,%r9
231    0x00000229eab61030:    sub     %r8,%r9
232    0x00000229eab61033:    movabs $0xffffffffffffffff,%r8
233    0x00000229eab6103d:    bzhi    %r9,%r8,%r8
234    0x00000229eab61042:    kmovq   %r8,%k7
235    0x00000229eab61047:    jmp     0x00000229eab60f9a
236    0x00000229eab6104c:    mov     %edx,(%rsp)
237    0x00000229eab6104f:    vmovdqu64 %zmm7,0x40(%rsp)
238    0x00000229eab61057:    vmovdqu64 %zmm5,0x80(%rsp)
239    0x00000229eab6105f:    mov     $0xffffff66,%edx
240    0x00000229eab61064:    vzeroupper
241    ; ImmutableOopMap {}
242    ; *if_icmpge {reexecute=1 rethrow=0 return_oop=0}
243    ; - (reexecute) com/.../MultiplesOf3Or5Vectorized::compute@27
244    ;   (line 16)
245    ; {runtime_call UncommonTrapBlob}
246    0x00000229eab61067:    call    0x00000229ea6ab960
247    ; {post_call_nop}
248    0x00000229eab6106c:    nopl    0x10004e4(%rax,%rax,1)
249    0x00000229eab61074:    vmovdqu64 %zmm2,%zmm11
250    0x00000229eab6107a:    jmp     0x00000229eab60f76
251    0x00000229eab6107f:    vpmovm2b %k3,%xmm0
252    0x00000229eab61085:    vpabsb %xmm0,%xmm0
253    0x00000229eab6108a:    mov     %r11d,0x4(%rsp)
254    0x00000229eab6108f:    mov     %edx,0x8(%rsp)
255    0x00000229eab61093:    vmovdqu64 %zmm7,0x40(%rsp)
256    0x00000229eab6109b:    vmovdqu64 %zmm11,0x80(%rsp)
257    0x00000229eab610a3:    vmovdqu %xmm0,0x10(%rsp)
```

```
258     0x00000229eab610a9:    mov     $0xffffff45,%edx
259     0x00000229eab610ae:    xchg    %ax,%ax
260     0x00000229eab610b0:    vzeroupper
261     ; ImmutableOopMap {}
262     ; *if_icmplt {reexecute=1 rethrow=0 return_oop=0}
263     ; - (reexecute) jdk/.../AbstractMask::indexInRange@17 (line 216)
264     ; - jdk/.../AbstractSpecies::indexInRange@7 (line 225)
265     ; - com/.../MultiplesOf3Or5Vectorized::compute@35 (line 17)
266     ; {runtime_call UncommonTrapBlob}
267     0x00000229eab610b3:    call    0x00000229ea6ab960
268     ; {post_call_nop}
269     0x00000229eab610b8:    nopl    0x2000530(%rax,%rax,1)
270     ; {internal_word}
271     0x00000229eab610c0:    movabs  $0x229eab61006,%r10
272     0x00000229eab610ca:    mov     %r10,0x4e0(%r15)
273     ; {runtime_call SafepointBlob}
274     0x00000229eab610d1:    jmp     0x00000229ea5d2260
275     ; {runtime_call Stub::method_entry_barrier}
276     0x00000229eab610d6:    call    Stub::method_entry_barrier
277     0x00000229eab610db:    jmp     0x00000229eab60cbe
278 [Exception Handler]
279     ; {runtime_call ExceptionBlob}
280     0x00000229eab610e0:    jmp     0x00000229ea6abc60
281 [Deopt Handler Code]
282     0x00000229eab610e5:    call    0x00000229eab610ea
283     0x00000229eab610ea:    subq    $0x5,(%rsp)
284     ; {runtime_call DeoptimizationBlob}
285     0x00000229eab610ef:    jmp     0x00000229ea5d09e0
286     0x00000229eab610f4:    hlt
287     0x00000229eab610f5:    hlt
288     0x00000229eab610f6:    hlt
289     0x00000229eab610f7:    hlt
290 --------------------------------------------------------------------------
291 [/Disassembly]
292
```

This listing showcases AVX-512 vector code—the most advanced SIMD instruction set available on modern x86 processors. Let us examine how the JVM translates our Java Vector API code into these powerful instructions.

- **Method Header and Statistics** (lines 1–18). The "main code" occupies 1088 bytes—larger than the scalar C2 version (392 bytes). This increase reflects the complexity of vector instructions and the extensive loop unrolling. However, this larger code processes data far more efficiently.

- **Constant Pool** (lines 23–32). The compiler embeds several constants directly in the code section:

- 0x55555556: The magic multiplier for Lemire's divisibility test by 3, equal to $\lfloor 2^{32}/3 \rfloor + 1$.

- 0x33333334: The magic multiplier for divisibility test by 5, equal to $\lfloor 2^{32}/5 \rfloor + 1$.

- 0x00000010 (decimal 16): The vector increment, since each ZMM register holds 16 32-bit integers.

- **Stack Frame Setup** (lines 42–51). The stack frame is set up as follows:

- Line 42 performs the stack banging check.

- Line 44 allocates 208 bytes (0xd0)—much larger than scalar code because vector registers may need to be spilled to memory.

- Line 48 (vpxor %xmm7,%xmm7,%xmm7) initializes the accumulator register zmm7 to zero. This idiom uses XMM (128-bit) operands but implicitly zeros the entire 512-bit ZMM register.

- Lines 50–51 handle the early exit case when n <= 0.

- **Vector Initialization** (lines 53–62). The vector initialization code is as follows:

- Lines 53–54 load the initial index vector from a pre-computed array: zmm5 = [0, 1, 2, 3, ..., 15]. This vector represents the first 16 values to test.

- Lines 55–56 check for potential overflow: if n > 0x7FFFFFF0, execution jumps to a slow path.

- Lines 58–60 initialize the mask register k3. The `kmovd` and `kshiftrd` instructions create a 16-bit mask with all ones, indicating all 16 lanes are active.

- Lines 61–62 check if we have at least 16 elements; if not, jump to the masked epilogue.

- **First Vector Iteration** (lines 70–82). This section implements Lemire's divisibility test for the first 16 numbers.

- Line 70 (`vpbroadcastd`) loads the constant 0x55555556 and broadcasts it to all 16 lanes of zmm0.

- Line 71 (`vpmulld %zmm0,%zmm5,%zmm1`) multiplies each index by the magic constant—this is the core of Lemire's test.

- Line 72 (`vpcmpltud %zmm0,%zmm1,%k6{k7}`) performs an *unsigned* comparison: if `product < constant`, the number is divisible by 3. The result is stored in mask register k6. The {k7} suffix means the comparison is only performed for lanes where k7 is set (write masking).

- Lines 74–75 add an increment vector to prepare for the next iteration.

- Lines 77–79 repeat the pattern for divisibility by 5, using the constant 0x33333334.

- Line 81 (`korw %k7,%k6,%k7`) combines the two masks with a bitwise OR—a lane is set if the number is divisible by 3 *or* 5.

- Line 82 (`vpaddd %zmm5,%zmm7,%zmm7{k7}`) performs a **masked addition:** only lanes where k7 is set add their values to the accumulator zmm7. This single instruction replaces 16 conditional branches in scalar code.

- **The Unrolled Main Loop** (lines 87–167). The compiler has aggressively unrolled the loop to process 64 elements (four 16-element vectors) per iteration:

- Lines 97–102 compute divisibility tests for the second vector of 16 elements.

- Lines 103–118 process the third and fourth vectors, computing all multiplications and comparisons.

- Lines 120–129 combine the masks and perform four masked additions to the accumulator.

- Line 130 increments the loop counter by 64 (0x40).

- This aggressive unrolling amortizes loop overhead and enables instruction-level parallelism—modern CPUs can execute multiple vector operations simultaneously.

- **Dynamic Masking with \texttt{bzhi}** (lines 147–167). When the remaining element count is not a multiple of 16, the code uses the bzhi (bit zero high) instruction to create a partial mask:

- bzhi extracts the low n bits from a source register, zeroing the rest.

- For example, if 7 elements remain, bzhi creates the mask 0x007F (binary 0000000001111111).

- This mask ensures that only valid elements participate in the computation, preventing out-of-bounds access or incorrect results.

- **Safepoint Polling** (lines 172–174). The safepoint check appears only at the outer loop backedge, not inside the unrolled body. Combined with the iteration limit (line 85 shows 0xfa00 = 64000), this ensures the JVM can pause the thread for garbage collection within a reasonable time.

- **Scalar Epilogue** (lines 188–208). When fewer than 16 elements remain after the main loop, this section processes them with a simpler (non-unrolled) vector loop. The same Lemire divisibility tests are used, but only one vector per iteration.

- **Horizontal Reduction** (lines 209–217). After the loop completes, the partial sums in zmm7 must be combined into a single scalar result. This requires a series of "horizontal" operations:

- Line 209 (vextracti64x4 \\$0x1,%zmm7,%ymm1) extracts the upper 256 bits of zmm7 into ymm1.

- Line 210 (vpaddd %ymm7,%ymm1,%ymm1) adds the upper and lower 256-bit halves, reducing from 16 to 8 elements.

- Lines 211–214 continue the reduction: vphaddd performs horizontal pairwise addition within the vector, and vextracti128 extracts the upper 128 bits.

- Lines 215–217 add any remaining scalar accumulator value and move the final result to eax.

- **AVX-SSE Transition** (line 218). The vzeroupper instruction clears the upper 256 bits of all YMM registers. This is critical for performance: if legacy SSE code runs after AVX-512 code without this instruction, the processor incurs a severe penalty (potentially hundreds of cycles) due to internal state transitions.

- **Method Exit** (lines 219–224). Standard cleanup: restore the stack, check the safepoint flag, and return.

- **Uncommon Traps** (lines 236–269). These sections handle rare conditions that the compiler didn't optimize for.

- Line 246 handles the case where n exceeds 0x7FFFFFF0.

- Lines 262–267 handle mask-related edge cases in the Vector API's indexInRange method.

- When triggered, these "uncommon traps" transfer control to the interpreter and may trigger recompilation with different assumptions.

This vector code demonstrates several key techniques: Lemire's divisibility test implemented with unsigned comparisons, aggressive loop unrolling, dynamic masking with bzhi, masked vector operations for conditional logic, and horizontal reduction for final summation. The result processes 16 (or 64 with unrolling) numbers simultaneously, achieving substantial speedup over scalar code.

Arithmetic Progression

Adding some mathematics can improve this result. Numbers that are multiples of 3, 5, or 15 form an arithmetic progression. The number of progression terms up to n (exclusive) equals

$$K = \frac{n-1}{3}; L = \frac{n-1}{5}; M = \frac{n-1}{15}$$

The sum of the first K terms of an arithmetic progression with first term a_1 and common difference d is $S = \frac{K(a_1 + a_K)}{2} = \frac{K(2a_1 + d(K-1))}{2}$. For numbers divisible by 3, we have $a_1 = 3$, $d = 3$, $a_K = 3K$, giving us $S_3 = \frac{K(3+3K)}{2} = \frac{3K(K+1)}{2}$. Similarly for numbers divisible by 5 and 15.

Using the arithmetic progression sum formula, we derive a formula for solving the problem:

$$S = \frac{3K(K+1)}{2} + \frac{5L(L+1)}{2} - \frac{15M(M+1)}{2}$$

The third term—or rather, subtrahend—is needed so that numbers divisible by both 3 and 5 (meaning divisible by 15) are not counted twice. This applies the inclusion-exclusion principle: $|A \cup B| = |A| + |B| - |A \cap B|$, where A is the set of numbers divisible by 3, B is the set divisible by 5, and $A \cap B$ is numbers divisible by both (i.e., divisible by LCM(3,5) = 15). Now we can solve the problem without using a loop:

```
1    package com.nonpareilcoder.projecteuler;
2
3    public class MultiplesOf3Or5Smart {
4      public static int compute(int n) {
5        int k = (n - 1) / 3;
6        int l = (n - 1) / 5;
7        int m = (n - 1) / 15;
8
9        int sum =
10          3 * k * (k + 1) / 2 +
```

```
11                5 * l * (l + 1) / 2 -
12                15 * m * (m + 1) / 2;
13
14          return sum;
15      }
16  }
17
```

This is the optimal solution Project Euler expects. But we will go further. Since the three sum components are computed using the same operations, we can vectorize the fast solution.

The key idea: instead of sequentially computing the three sums S_3, S_5, and S_{15}, we can pack the values K, L, M into one vector, the corresponding multipliers 3, 5, 15 into another vector, and then apply element-wise vector multiplication and addition operations. All three computations execute in parallel with one vector instruction. The final reduction gives us the needed sum, accounting for signs (the third term is subtracted).

```java
1   package com.nonpareilcoder.projecteuler;
2
3   import jdk.incubator.vector.IntVector;
4   import jdk.incubator.vector.VectorSpecies;
5
6   import static jdk.incubator.vector.VectorOperators.*;
7
8   public class MultiplesOf3Or5Fast {
9     static final VectorSpecies<Integer> SP =
10      IntVector.SPECIES_128;
11
12     static final IntVector _c = IntVector
13       .fromArray(SP, new int[]{0x5556, 0x3334, 0x1112, 0}, 0);
14     static final IntVector _d = IntVector
15       .fromArray(SP, new int[]{3, 5, -15, 0}, 0);
16
17     public static int compute(int n) {
18       var _klm = _c.mul(n - 1).lanewise(LSHR, 16);
```

```
19
20      var _sum = _klm.add(1).mul(_klm).lanewise(LSHR, 1).mul(_d);
21
22      int sum = _sum.reduceLanes(ADD);
23
24      return sum;
25    }
26  }
27
```

Practice in writing vector code helps you find vectorization opportunities in algorithms that might seem unsuitable for it.

Benchmarks

Table 4-1 and Table 4-2 compare the algorithmic optimization approaches.

Table 4-1. *Single-core speedup on x86 platforms (higher is better)*

Variant	GL	Z2	IL	SR	Z5
fast	2555.70	2060.53	2545.70	2495.58	2307.40
naïve	1.00	1.00	1.00	1.00	1.00
smart	2560.16	2060.53	2536.13	2504.72	2307.40
vectorized	0.11	1563.98	2565.06	1330.33	2161.36

It is possible to read the X86 benchmark results in two ways. On the one hand, it is a dramatic illustration of the power of algorithmic optimization over brute-force computation, with speedups exceeding 2000× for the mathematical solutions. On the other hand, the brute force augmented with vectorization delivers practically identical results compared to mathematical trickery.

Table 4-2. *Single-core speedup on ARM platforms (higher is better)*

Variant	M4	O6	CO	NV	G3
fast	1753.72	2552.00	2016.84	1832.80	2329.95
naive	1.00	1.00	1.00	1.00	1.00
smart	1719.11	2428.60	1901.32	1825.53	2387.28
vectorized	1736.25	2753.48	1857.00	1840.13	2387.28

The ARM benchmark results demonstrate remarkably consistent performance across all optimized variants, with speedups in the same range of 2000× over the naive implementation. Apple M4 emerges as a relative outlier with the lowest speedups (1700×), likely due to its NEON-only implementation. The vectorized, smart, and fast variants achieve nearly identical performance on each platform, with differences under 5%, indicating that all three approaches are equally viable on ARM architectures. The uniform performance across variants confirms that for this problem, the choice between a mathematical solution and a vectorized loop is largely a matter of code clarity rather than performance on ARM.

What's Next

We now turn from mathematical puzzles to a classic algorithmic challenge. The next chapter tackles removing duplicates from a sorted array—a common interview problem that introduces the powerful **compress** operation. This operation selectively writes vector elements based on a mask, enabling efficient data filtering that would otherwise require costly branching.

CHAPTER 5

Removing Duplicates

Consider an integer array sorted in non-descending order. We need to remove duplicate elements in place, leaving only unique elements. The original order of elements must be preserved. Return the number of unique elements in the array.

In This Chapter

1. The **compress** operation for selectively packing vector elements based on a mask

2. The **slice** operation for efficient data access across vector boundaries

3. How to vectorize the classic two-pointer method

4. Trade-offs between extra memory loads and slice-based approaches

Two-Pointer Method

The standard scalar solution uses the two-pointer method.

```
1    package com.nonpareilcoder.realleetcode;
2
3    public class RemoveDuplicatesScalar {
4      public static int compress(int[] array) {
5        int arraySize = array.length;
6
7        int writeIndex = 1;
8
```


© Roman Snytsar 2026
R. Snytsar, *Mastering SIMD with Java Vector API*, https://doi.org/10.1007/979-8-8688-2676-4_5

```
 9          if (arraySize > 0) {
10            for (int ri = 1; ri < arraySize; ri++) {
11              if (array[ri] != array[ri - 1])
12                array[writeIndex++] = array[ri];
13            }
14          }
15
16          return writeIndex;
17        }
18      }
```

The algorithm is simple and frequently appears in programming interviews. However, it appears to resist parallelization.

- The decision whether to write the next element to the output array depends on the program execution history.

- The write position likewise depends on history.

We can circumvent this dependency by splitting the task into two stages. First, for each vector, determine in parallel which elements need to be kept (a local decision independent of other vectors). Then compress the selected elements and write them to the output array, updating the global write pointer. This approach allows vectorizing the main computational part of the algorithm.

Vector Compression

Modern vector instruction sets include the **compress** operation, illustrated in Figure 5-1. It selects vector elements by mask and packs the selected elements at the beginning of the vector.

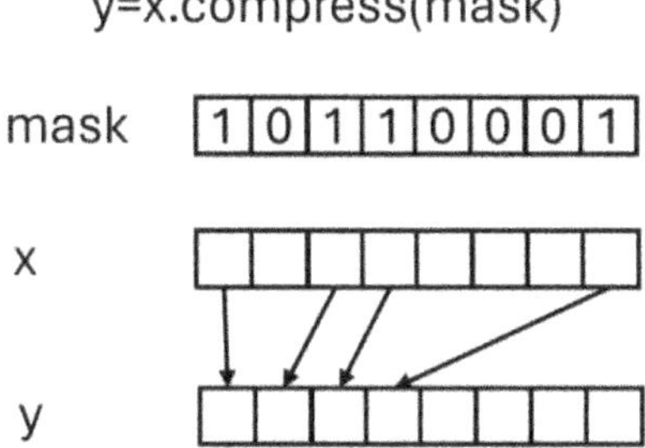

Figure 5-1. *The compress operation*

More precisely, the operation

```
vector = input.compress(mask);
```

means

```
for(int i = 0, j = 0; i < SP.length(); i++) {
  if(mask[i]) {
    vector[j++] = input[i];
  }
}
```

Observe that the decision to write an element to the output array can be made by examining only the current and previous elements. If they are identical, the current element should be skipped.

One subtlety: for the first element of each vector, the previous element is the last element of the previous vector. Access to it is provided by the **slice** operation (see Figure 5-2), which concatenates two vectors sequentially and then extracts a new vector from the concatenation, starting at a specified position.

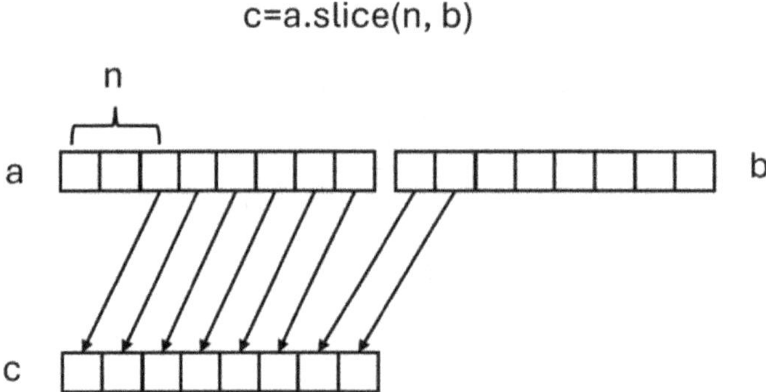

Figure 5-2. *The slice operation*

A special case is the very first element of the array. It has no previous element for comparison, so it must always be written to the output array. This can be implemented either by handling the first element separately before the loop or by using a special initial value for the "previous" element that is guaranteed to differ from any array element. Any number less than the first element or greater than the last element of the array works as such a sentinel element.

The vector implementation follows:

```
1    package com.nonpareilcoder.realleetcode;
2
3    import jdk.incubator.vector.*;
4
5    import static jdk.incubator.vector.VectorOperators.*;
6
7    public class RemoveDuplicatesShuffle {
8      static final VectorSpecies<Integer> SP =
9        IntVector.SPECIES_PREFERRED;
10     static final int vl = SP.length();
11
12     public static int compress(int[] array) {
13       int arraySize = array.length;
14
15       int writeIndex = 1;
16
17       if (arraySize > 0) {
```

```
18        int[] a = array;
19        IntVector _prev = IntVector.broadcast(SP, a[0]);
20
21        for (int i = 1; i < arraySize; i += vl) {
22          var _mask = SP.indexInRange(i, arraySize);
23          var _current = IntVector.fromArray(SP, a, i, _mask);
24          var _shifted = _prev.slice(vl - 1, _current);
25          _prev = _current;
26
27          var _neq = _current.compare(NE, _shifted).and(_mask);
28
29          var _write = _neq.compress();
30
31          _current.compress(_neq).intoArray(a, writeIndex, _write);
32
33          writeIndex += _neq.trueCount();
34        }
35      }
36
37    return writeIndex;
38    }
39 }
```

- Line 22 creates a mask that identifies the actually existing array elements in the current data chunk.

- Line 23 loads the next batch of data according to the mask.

- Line 24 forms the shifted vector.

- Line 27 computes the mask of elements for compression.

- We also need to form a mask for writing the selected elements to the array. Strictly speaking, this is not necessary—writing extra elements would not affect correctness, but explicit masking improves clarity. The write mask is derived from the selection mask using the same compression operation: if the selection mask contains, for example, the set [true, false, true, false], with k true elements, then after compression we obtain the write mask [true, true, false, false], where the first k positions are true.

- Line 31 compresses the data and writes it back to the array. This is where both masks from lines 27 and 29 are used.

- Line 33 counts how many elements were compressed and written and advances the write pointer by that count.

Extra Memory Access

The **slice** operation may be unavailable or slow on some architectures. An alternative approach is to load the previous vector shifted by one element (i.e., starting from position $i - 1$ instead of i). This creates an additional memory access but eliminates the need for **slice**. The choice between these approaches depends on the specific hardware platform: on systems with fast memory and slow **slice**, the second variant may be preferable.

Important   When loading from position $i - 1$, special care must be taken for the first iteration where $i = 0$. Accessing memory before the array start risks a segmentation fault if the array begins at a page boundary. The implementation must either handle the first element separately (scalar peeling) or ensure the array is padded with a valid sentinel value before its start.

```
1    package com.nonpareilcoder.realleetcode;
2
3    import jdk.incubator.vector.*;
4
5    import static jdk.incubator.vector.VectorOperators.*;
6
7    public class RemoveDuplicatesLoad {
8      static final VectorSpecies<Integer> SP =
9        IntVector.SPECIES_PREFERRED;
10     static final int vl = SP.length();
```

```
11
12    public static int compress(int[] array) {
13      int arraySize = array.length;
14
15      int writeIndex = 1;
16
17      if (arraySize > 0) {
18        for (int i = 1; i < arraySize; i += vl) {
19          var _mask = SP.indexInRange(i, arraySize);
20          var _shifted = IntVector.fromArray(SP, array, i - 1, _mask);
21          var _current = IntVector.fromArray(SP, array, i, _mask);
22
23          var _neq = _current.compare(NE, _shifted).and(_mask);
24
25          var _write = _neq.compress();
26
27          _current.compress(_neq).intoArray(array, writeIndex, _write);
28
29          writeIndex += _neq.trueCount();
30        }
31      }
32
33      return writeIndex;
34    }
35  }
```

- The main difference from the previous version lies in how the comparison vector is obtained. In line 20, instead of the **slice** operation, an additional memory load is used with a one-element backward shift.

- This approach eliminates potential data dependencies that could arise when using **slice** and may be more efficient on architectures with high memory bandwidth.

- The rest of the algorithm logic in lines 23–29, namely, mask formation, compression, and writing, remains identical to the first variant.

Benchmarks

Table 5-1 and Table 5-2 compare the compress-based duplicate removal approaches.

Table 5-1. *Single-core speedup on x86 platforms (higher is better)*

Variant	GL	Z2	IL	SR	Z5
baseline	1.00	1.00	1.00	1.00	1.00
load	0.04	0.16	1.09	0.63	0.42
shuffle	0.03	0.23	2.47	1.77	2.28
shuffleX4	0.03	0.24	2.67	1.93	2.27

The X86 benchmark results demonstrate a stark divide between processors with and without AVX-512 compress instruction support. Z2 (AMD Rome) with AVX2 struggles severely (0.16–0.24x), revealing that efficient compress support is essential for this algorithm. IL (Intel Ice Lake) emerges as the standout performer with 2.67× speedup for unrolled shuffleX4, benefiting from native AVX-512 compress instructions that pack selected elements in a few cycles. The load variant using extra memory access instead of slice operations performs poorly, confirming that the slice operation is more efficient when properly supported. The shuffle variants consistently outperform the load variant by 10–15× on AVX-512 platforms, validating the design choice to use slice for obtaining the comparison vector.

Table 5-2. *Single-core speedup on ARM platforms (higher is better)*

Variant	M4	O6	CO	NV	G3
baseline	1.00	1.00	1.00	1.00	1.00
load	0.26	1.14	0.79	0.92	1.27
shuffle	0.32	2.99	2.15	3.48	2.39
shuffleX4	0.30	3.45	2.44	3.99	2.69

The ARM benchmark results present a striking contrast between NEON and SVE implementations for the duplicate removal algorithm. Apple M4 stands out as a severe outlier with slowdowns across all variants (0.26–0.32×), indicating that NEON lacks efficient support for the compress operation required by this algorithm. NV (Nvidia Grace) achieves exceptional performance with shuffleX4 reaching 4× speedup, demonstrating that its advanced pipeline can execute the compress and slice operations efficiently despite having only 128-bit SVE vectors. The O6 (CIX CD8180) also performs remarkably well at 3.45× for shuffleX4, suggesting that power-efficient ARM designs with SVE can still excel at this workload. The load variant shows mixed results, confirming that slice-based comparison is generally superior on SVE platforms. Overall, the shuffle variants deliver excellent speedups of 2.15–3.99× across SVE-capable ARM processors, making this algorithm highly amenable to vectorization on modern ARM server chips.

What's Next

Having seen how the compress operation enables efficient data filtering, we now examine the prefix sum: one of the most fundamental operations in parallel computing. The next chapter reveals why this seemingly simple operation resists efficient vectorization and how understanding its limitations prepares us for more sophisticated algorithms.

CHAPTER 6

Prefix Sum

Consider a sequence of numbers:

$$\left[x_0 ; x_1 ; x_2 ; \ldots ; x_k ; \ldots ; x_n \right]$$

We seek to compute the **prefix sum**—a sequence

$$\left[p_0 ; p_1 ; p_2 ; \ldots ; p_k ; \ldots ; p_n \right]$$

defined by the recurrence relation

$$p_0 = x_0 ,$$

$$p_k = p_{k-1} + x_k .$$

Analogously, the **suffix sum**

$$\left[s_0 ; s_1 ; s_2 ; \ldots ; s_k ; \ldots ; s_n \right]$$

is defined by the recurrence relation

$$s_n = x_n ,$$

$$s_k = s_{k+1} + x_k$$

The term **cumulative sum** encompasses both prefix and suffix sums. Prefix sums arise frequently in practice: converting time intervals to absolute timestamps, computing cumulative distributions, building range query data structures, and implementing parallel algorithms for sorting and searching.

© Roman Snytsar 2026
R. Snytsar, *Mastering SIMD with Java Vector API*, https://doi.org/10.1007/979-8-8688-2676-4_6

In This Chapter

1. Vector scan algorithms for computing prefix and suffix sums

2. The fundamental tension between sequential dependencies and parallelism

3. Why prefix sum resists efficient vectorization despite its importance

4. How vector scan serves as a building block for more complex algorithms

Scalar Solution

```
1    package com.nonpareilcoder.realleetcode;
2
3    public class AdditiveScanScalar {
4      public static void prefixAdd(int[] input, int[] output) {
5        int acc = 0;
6        for (int i = 0; i < input.length; i++) {
7          acc += input[i];
8          output[i] = acc;
9        }
10     }
11
12     public static void suffixAdd(int[] input, int[] output) {
13       int acc = 0;
14       for (int i = input.length; i-- > 0; ) {
15         acc += input[i];
16         output[i] = acc;
17       }
18     }
19
20   }
21
```

The code above computes **inclusive** prefix and suffix sums. Consider the difference between **inclusive** and **exclusive** sums. An inclusive prefix sum includes the current element: $p_k = x_0 + x_1 + \dots + x_k$. An exclusive prefix sum excludes the current element: $p_k = x_0 + x_1 + \dots + x_{k-1}$. For example, for the sequence $[1, 2, 3, 4]$, the inclusive prefix sum yields $[1, 3, 6, 10]$, while the exclusive version yields $[0, 1, 3, 6]$. **Note:** Swapping lines 7 and 8 (or 15 and 16) produces the exclusive variant.

Vector Solution

The parallel approach relies on the associativity property of addition

$$(a+b)+c = a+(b+c)$$

We take the initial vector

$$\left[x_0 ; x_1 ; x_2 ; x_3 ; x_4 ; x_5 ; x_6 ; x_7 ; \dots \right]$$

shift it one element to the right, and add it to the original (see Figure 6-1).

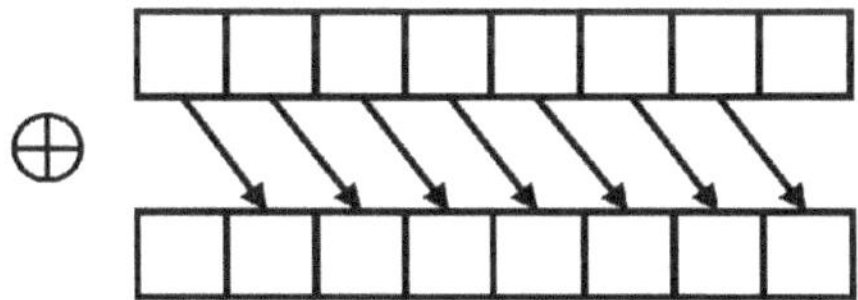

Figure 6-1. *Vector scan step 1*

This operation yields

$$\left[x_0 ; x_0 + x_1 ; x_1 + x_2 ; x_2 + x_3 ; x_3 + x_4 ; x_4 + x_5 ; x_5 + x_6 ; x_6 + x_7 ; \dots \right]$$

We shift the intermediate result by two positions and add the shifted version to the unshifted version (Figure 6-2).

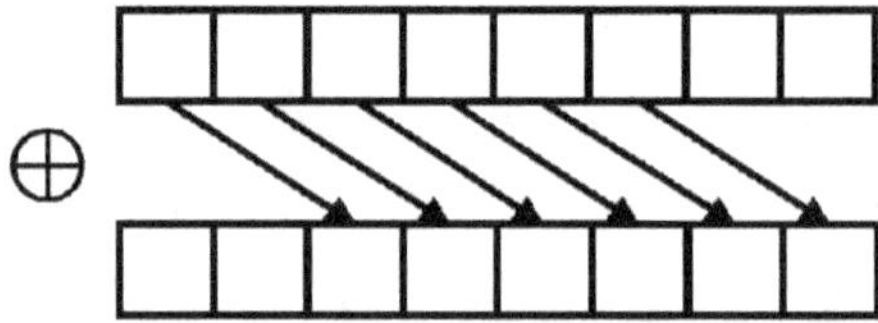

Figure 6-2. *Vector scan step 2*

This yields

$$[x_0; x_0 + x_1; x_0 + x_1 + x_2; x_0 + x_1 + x_2 + x_3;$$

$$x_1 + x_2 + x_3 + x_4; x_2 + x_3 + x_4 + x_5; x_3 + x_4 + x_5 + x_6; x_4 + x_5 + x_6 + x_7; \ldots]$$

Because partial sums combine pairwise, the operation must be associative for the result to be correct.

Now we repeat the procedure once more, but this time shifting by four elements—the next power of two (Figure 6-3).

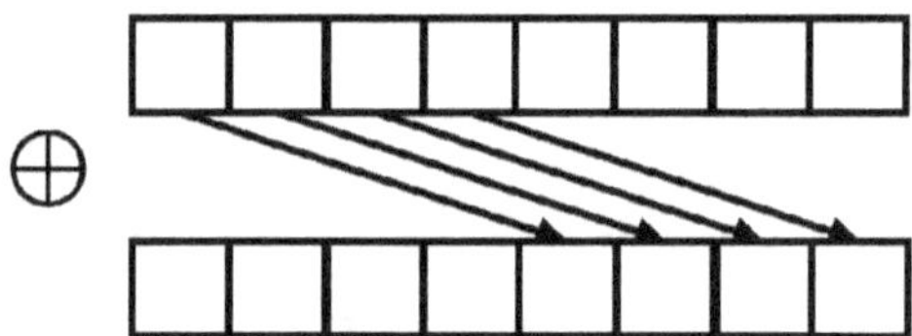

Figure 6-3. *Vector scan step 3*

$$[x_0; x_0 + x_1; x_0 + x_1 + x_2; x_0 + x_1 + x_2 + x_3; x_0 + x_1 + x_2 + x_3 + x_4;$$

$$x_0 + x_1 + x_2 + x_3 + x_4 + x_5; x_0 + x_1 + x_2 + x_3 + x_4 + x_5 + x_6;$$

$$x_0 + x_1 + x_2 + x_3 + x_4 + x_5 + x_6 + x_7; \ldots]$$

Thus, after $log_2 W$ shift-add operations, a vector of length W contains the cumulative sum of the original vector. We will call the described algorithm **vector scan**.

Observe that the last element of the result contains the sum of all elements in the original vector, meaning we have simultaneously obtained a **vector reduction** algorithm in the same $log_2 W$ steps.

The algorithms' optimality and complexity can be justified as follows. Any parallel prefix sum algorithm requires at least $log_2 W$ steps, since information about the first element must propagate to the last, and information can propagate between at most two elements per step (because each operation can combine only two values at a time). Thus, our algorithms demonstrate optimal execution time in terms of vector steps. However, the main drawback of vector reduction is extremely high computational complexity. The sum of W elements can be computed with $W - 1$ additions. Our vector algorithm executes $log_2 W$ vector addition instructions—optimal in terms of instruction count. However, each vector instruction performs W element-wise additions in parallel, so the total number of element operations is $W \cdot log_2 W$, compared to just $W - 1$ for the scalar algorithm. This incurs roughly $log_2 W$ times as many element operations as necessary—a significant computational and energy cost.

Vector scan is less wasteful, but still performs unnecessary work. On the first step (shift by 1), the rightmost element has no pair for addition, leaving one unused element. On the second step (shift by 2), two right elements go out of bounds, adding two more unused elements. On the third step (shift by 4), we add four more unused elements. In general, at step i, 2^{i-1} elements remain unused. Summing across all $log_2 W$ steps:

$$1 + 2 + 4 + \ldots + \frac{W}{2} = 2^0 + 2^1 + \ldots + 2^{log_2 W - 1} = W - 1$$ elements are unused throughout the

algorithm. Nearly a full vector's worth of computation is wasted. Worse still, vector scan prevents out-of-order instruction execution: each operation requires the result of the previous one.

We might call vector scan a "super-horizontal" operation: clumsy and sluggish, yet indispensable for vectorizing a broad class of problems.

The implementation follows:

```java
1    package com.nonpareilcoder.realleetcode;
2
3    import jdk.incubator.vector.*;
4
5    public class AdditiveScanHorizontal {
6      static final VectorSpecies<Integer> SP =
7        IntVector.SPECIES_PREFERRED;
8      static final int vl = SP.length();
9
10     public static void prefixAdd(int[] input, int[] output) {
```

```
11        int arraySize = input.length;
12        if (arraySize == 0)
13          return;
14
15        final IntVector _zero = IntVector.broadcast(SP, 0);
16
17        int nIterations = arraySize / vl;
18        int nRemainder = arraySize % vl;
19
20        int acc = 0;
21
22        int pos = 0;
23        for (int i = 0; i < nIterations; i++) {
24          var _current = IntVector.fromArray(SP, input, pos);
25
26          for (int step = 1; step < vl; step <<= 1) {
27            var _shifted = _zero.slice(vl - step, _current);
28            _current = _current.add(_shifted);
29          }
30
31          _current = _current.add(acc);
32
33          acc = _current.lane(vl - 1);
34
35          _current.intoArray(output, pos);
36
37          pos += vl;
38        }
39
40      while (nRemainder-- > 0) {
41        acc += input[pos];
42        output[pos++] = acc;
43      }
44    }
45
46    public static void suffixAdd(int[] input, int[] output) {
```

```java
47        int arraySize = input.length;
48        if (arraySize == 0)
49          return;
50
51        final IntVector _zero = IntVector.broadcast(SP, 0);
52
53        int nIterations = arraySize / vl;
54        int nRemainder = arraySize % vl;
55
56        int acc = 0;
57
58        int pos = input.length;
59        while (nRemainder-- > 0) {
60          acc += input[--pos];
61          output[pos] = acc;
62        }
63
64        for (int i = 0; i < nIterations; i++) {
65          pos -= vl;
66
67          var _current = IntVector.fromArray(SP, input, pos);
68
69          for (int step = 1; step < vl; step <<= 1) {
70            var _shifted = _current.slice(step, _zero);
71            _current = _current.add(_shifted);
72          }
73
74          _current = _current.add(acc);
75
76          acc = _current.lane(0);
77
78          _current.intoArray(output, pos);
79        }
80      }
81    }
82
```

The prefix and suffix algorithms are symmetric, but the suffix sum proves slightly more elegant in vector form. We examine it in detail below.

- The array is processed from end to beginning.

- Lines 58–62 compute the array's "tail" that is shorter than the vector length, using the ordinary scalar algorithm.

- Then lines 64–79 execute the vector loop.

- Line 67 loads the next batch of values from the input array.

- Lines 69–72 run the inner loop—the vector scan.

- Line 74 adds the running total to each result element, propagating accumulated sums across the entire array.

- Line 76 records the new sum.

- Line 78 stores the result into the output array.

The correctness of the sum propagation can be clarified as follows. After the vector scan, the last element of the vector contains the sum of all elements in the current vector. This value is saved as the preceding sum. When processing the next (left for suffix sum) vector, the vector scan computes local cumulative sums within that vector. To obtain global cumulative sums, we need to add the sum of all elements to the right (i.e., the preceding sum) to each element. This ensures continuity of the suffix sum calculation at vector boundaries.

Vector scan generalizes to any associative operation, as subsequent chapters demonstrate.

Benchmarks

Table 6-1 and Table 6-2 demonstrate the challenges of vectorizing prefix sum.

Table 6-1. *Single-core speedup on x86 platforms (higher is better)*

Variant	GL	Z2	IL	SR	Z5
horizontalPrefix	0.07	0.52	0.62	0.98	0.82
horizontalPrefixX4	0.06	0.66	0.90	1.15	0.89
horizontalSuffix	0.08	0.54	0.73	1.03	0.94
horizontalSuffixX4	0.06	0.76	0.99	1.12	1.13
scalarPrefix	1.00	1.00	1.00	1.00	1.00
scalarSuffix	1.00	1.00	1.00	1.00	1.00

The benchmark results reveal several important trends that apply broadly across processor architectures.

- Vector scan underperforms scalar code. Most speedup values fall below 1.0, indicating that the vectorized prefix sum runs slower than the straightforward scalar loop. This outcome aligns with the theoretical analysis: vector scan performs $Wlog_2W$ additions compared to $W-1$ for scalar code, and the sequential dependency chain prevents out-of-order execution from hiding latency.

- Loop unrolling provides consistent improvement. The X4 variants, which unroll the outer loop by a factor of four, outperform their non-unrolled counterparts across all platforms. Unrolling reduces loop overhead and enables the processor to better schedule independent operations between iterations.

- Suffix sum slightly outperforms prefix sum. This modest advantage likely stems from memory access patterns. The suffix algorithm processes arrays from end to beginning, which may interact more favorably with hardware prefetching in certain scenarios.

- Newer microarchitectures narrow the gap. More recent processor generations show speedup values closer to 1.0, and some achieve parity or slight gains with the unrolled variants. Improvements in branch prediction, larger reorder buffers, and faster shuffle operations all contribute to reducing the overhead of vector scan.

Table 6-2. *Single-core speedup on ARM platforms (higher is better)*

Variant	M4	06	CO	NV	G3
horizontalPrefix	0.26	0.39	0.43	0.51	0.60
horizontalPrefixX4	0.30	0.50	0.54	0.54	0.61
horizontalSuffix	0.29	0.46	0.46	0.50	0.66
horizontalSuffixX4	0.34	0.62	0.63	0.52	0.94
scalarPrefix	1.00	1.00	1.00	1.00	1.00
scalarSuffix	1.00	1.00	1.00	1.00	1.00

- ARM platforms show more consistent behavior. The ARM results cluster more tightly than x86, reflecting the more uniform microarchitectural characteristics across ARM implementations compared to the diverse x86 landscape spanning multiple generations and vendors.

The central lesson is sobering: prefix sum resists efficient vectorization. The inherent sequential dependency—each output element requires the previous one—fundamentally limits parallelism. Vector scan remains valuable not for its absolute performance, but for enabling vectorization of algorithms that embed prefix sum as a component. When the surrounding computation offers sufficient parallelism, the overhead of vector scan becomes acceptable.

What's Next

We now turn to a trio of classic problems that showcase how naturally bitwise operations lend themselves to SIMD vectorization. The next chapter explores finding unique elements using XOR reduction and trit arithmetic—techniques that demonstrate both the elegance and the limitations of vectorized bit manipulation.

CHAPTER 7

Finding the Unique Element

This chapter covers three classic problems that illustrate how naturally bitwise operations lend themselves to SIMD vectorization. All three problems involve finding a unique element in an array where every other element appears a fixed number of times.

Problem Statement

Given an array of integers where each element appears **an even number of times**, except for one element that appears **exactly once**. Find that single element.

Examples:

```
Input:  [4, 1, 2, 1, 2]
Answer: 4

Input:  [2, 2, 1]
Answer: 1
```

In This Chapter

1. XOR reduction for finding unique elements in pairs

2. Trit arithmetic and modulo-3 counting for the triples variant

3. How branch misprediction affects performance decisions

4. Vectorized bit manipulation techniques

© Roman Snytsar 2026

R. Snytsar, *Mastering SIMD with Java Vector API*, https://doi.org/10.1007/979-8-8688-2676-4_7

Scalar Solution

The scalar solution is elegantly simple and relies on the properties of XOR (exclusive OR):

1. **Commutativity:** $a \oplus b = b \oplus a$ (order does not matter)

2. **Associativity:** $(a \oplus b) \oplus c = a \oplus (b \oplus c)$ (grouping does not matter)

3. **Identity element:** $a \oplus 0 = a$ (XOR with 0 yields the number itself)

4. **Self-inverse:** $a \oplus a = 0$ (XOR with itself yields 0)

To find the unique element, we fold the array using XOR reduction. All paired elements cancel each other out, leaving only the unpaired element we seek.

$$[a,b,a,c,b] \rightarrow a \oplus b \oplus a \oplus c \oplus b$$

$$= (a \oplus a) \oplus (b \oplus b) \oplus c$$

$$= 0 \oplus 0 \oplus c$$

$$= c$$

```
1    package com.nonpareilcoder.realleetcode;
2
3    public class SingleNumberPairsScalar {
4      public static int find(int[] input) {
5        int result = 0;
6
7        for (int num : input) {
8          result ^= num;
9        }
10
11        return result;
12      }
13    }
14
```

Vector Solution

The solution mirrors computing a sum, except XOR replaces addition.

```java
1   package com.nonpareilcoder.realleetcode;
2
3   import jdk.incubator.vector.*;
4
5   import static jdk.incubator.vector.VectorOperators.*;
6
7   public class SingleNumberPairsVectorized {
8     static final VectorSpecies<Integer> SP =
9       IntVector.SPECIES_PREFERRED;
10
11    public static int find(int[] input) {
12      IntVector _ones = IntVector.zero(SP);
13
14      for (int i = 0; i < input.length; i += SP.length()) {
15        var _mask = SP.indexInRange(i, input.length);
16
17        IntVector _num = IntVector.fromArray(SP, input, i, _mask);
18
19        _ones = _ones.lanewise(XOR, _num);
20      }
21
22      int result = _ones.reduceLanes(XOR);
23
24      return result;
25    }
26  }
27
```

- XOR does not have a dedicated method. Line 19 therefore uses the
  universal **lanewise** operator.

Two Unique Elements

Consider a slight modification of the problem: given an array of integers where each element appears **an even number of times**, except for **two** unique elements, each appearing **exactly once**. Find both unique elements.

The problem is similar to the previous one; we will try to reduce it to the solution we already know.

```java
1   package com.nonpareilcoder.realleetcode;
2
3   import java.util.*;
4
5   public class SingleNumberPairs2Scalar {
6     public static int[] find(int[] input) {
7       int result = 0;
8       for (int num : input) {
9         result ^= num;
10      }
11
12      int set = result & (-result);
13
14      int[] uniques = new int[2];
15
16      for (int num : input) {
17        if ((num & set) == set)
18          uniques[0] ^= num;
19        else
20          uniques[1] ^= num;
21      }
22
23      Arrays.sort(uniques);
24
25      return uniques;
26    }
27  }
28
```

- Lines 7–10 repeat the previous solution. The resulting sum (for lack of a better term, we call the XOR result a sum) equals the sum of **two** unique elements. We need to split this sum into its components.

- Since the problem guarantees distinct, unique elements, they differ in at least one bit. The XOR result has a 1 in positions where the elements differ. Line 12 isolates the rightmost set bit of the sum—a bit that differs between the two components.

- The original array can now be partitioned into two groups: elements where the isolated bit is zero and elements where it is one. Each group contains repeated elements and exactly **one** unique element. Finding that unique element requires applying the previous algorithm to the group. Applying the algorithm a third time to the other group yields the second unique element. The passes over both groups are fused into the loop in lines 16–21.

Vector Solution

The vector solution follows the same pattern as the previous one. The interesting aspect lies in vectorizing the conditional operator.

```
1    package com.nonpareilcoder.realleetcode;
2
3    import jdk.incubator.vector.*;
4    import static jdk.incubator.vector.VectorOperators.*;
5
6    import java.util.Arrays;
7
8    public class SingleNumberPairs2Vectorized {
9      static final VectorSpecies<Integer> SP =
10         IntVector.SPECIES_PREFERRED;
11
12     public static int[] find(int[] input) {
13       IntVector _ones = IntVector.zero(SP);
14
```

```java
15      for (int i = 0; i < input.length; i += SP.length()) {
16        var _mask = SP.indexInRange(i, input.length);
17
18        IntVector _num = IntVector.fromArray(SP, input, i, _mask);
19
20        _ones = _ones.lanewise(XOR, _num);
21      }
22
23    int result = _ones.reduceLanes(XOR);
24
25    int set = result & (-result);
26
27    _ones = IntVector.zero(SP);
28    IntVector _zeroes = IntVector.zero(SP);
29
30      for (int i = 0; i < input.length; i += SP.length()) {
31        var _mask = SP.indexInRange(i, input.length);
32
33        IntVector _num = IntVector.fromArray(SP, input, i, _mask);
34
35        VectorMask<Integer> _set = _num.and(set).eq(set);
36
37        _ones = _ones.lanewise(XOR, _num, _set);
38        var _notSet = _set.not();
39        _zeroes = _zeroes.lanewise(XOR, _num, _notSet);
40      }
41
42    int[] uniques = new int[2];
43
44    uniques[0] = _zeroes.reduceLanes(XOR);
45    uniques[1] = _ones.reduceLanes(XOR);
46
47    Arrays.sort(uniques);
48
49    return uniques;
```

```
50      }
51    }
52
```

- Lines 15–21 repeat the loop from the previous solution.

- Lines 30–40 perform the second pass over the array. Mask operations replace the conditional operator.

Replacing conditionals with mask-based computation has both drawbacks and benefits. On one hand, each array element participates in computation twice, which is suboptimal. On the other hand, the danger of branch misprediction disappears.

The processor attempts to exploit instruction-level parallelism by executing instructions ahead of time, speculatively advancing through the program. When a conditional branch instruction appears in the instruction stream, the processor predicts which path execution will take and fills the pipeline with instructions from the predicted branch. If the prediction proves wrong, the processor rolls back all speculatively executed instructions, flushes the pipeline, and refills it with instructions from the correct branch. Each misprediction costs dozens of stall cycles. Prediction is based on execution history. If a conditional branch controls loop exit, for instance, prediction succeeds until the loop terminates. In the case of selection based on a particular bit, prediction accuracy drops to just 50%. Mask-based instructions avoid conditional branches entirely, eliminating branch misprediction altogether.

Finding Among Triples

Now we vary a different aspect of the problem: given an array of integers where each element appears **three times or a multiple of three times**, except for one element that appears **exactly once**. Find that single element.

The XOR approach fails for triples, but the underlying principle guides us toward a general solution.

XOR can be interpreted as the addition of bits independently at each position modulo 2. Similarly, solving the modified problem requires adding bits at each position modulo 3. Then bits from triplets of identical numbers cancel out, and the remaining bits form the sought number.

We represent each ternary digit (trit) with two bits. The first bit is set when the trit value is 1. The second bit is set when the trit value is 2. Setting both bits simultaneously represents an invalid state. The addition rules are shown in Table 7-1.

Table 7-1. *Addition table for a trit plus a bit modulo 3*

Input			Output	
Ones	Twos	Bit	Ones	Twos
0	0	0	0	0
0	0	1	1	0
1	0	0	1	0
1	0	1	0	1
0	1	0	0	1
0	1	1	0	0
1	1	0	-	-
1	1	1	-	-

The bottom two rows correspond to the invalid state.

State transitions are easily described with standard logic functions. Working with bits brings me joy—not only because of the intrinsic parallelism but also because it sits right on the boundary between software and hardware, where abstraction gives way to physical reality. Though I abandoned my hardware engineering ambitions long ago, working on low-level optimizations keeps me close to that world.

```
1    package com.nonpareilcoder.realleetcode;
2
3    public class SingleNumberTriplesScalar {
4      public static int find(int[] input) {
5        int ones = 0;
6        int twos = 0;
7
8        for (int num : input) {
9          twos |= ones & num;
10
11          ones ^= num;
```

```
12
13            int threes = ones & twos;
14
15          ones &= ~threes;
16          twos &= ~threes;
17        }
18
19      return ones;
20    }
21  }
22
```

- Line 9 updates the twos counter.

- Line 11 updates the ones counter.

- Lines 13–16 reset both counters when the invalid state would occur.

Vector Solution

All logic operations vectorize naturally because each bitwise operation works in parallel. The challenge lies in the final reduction: we must define trit addition modulo 3.

- If the second operand is zero, nothing needs to be done.

- If the second operand is one, we already know how to add one using the table above.

- If the second operand is two, we reduce to the previous case and add one twice.

The implementation:

```
1  package com.nonpareilcoder.realleetcode;
2
3  import jdk.incubator.vector.*;
4
5  import static jdk.incubator.vector.VectorOperators.*;
6
```

```
 7    public class SingleNumberTriplesVectorized {
 8      static final VectorSpecies<Integer> SP =
 9        IntVector.SPECIES_PREFERRED;
10
11      public static int find(int[] input) {
12        IntVector _zero = IntVector.zero(SP);
13        IntVector _ones = IntVector.zero(SP);
14        IntVector _twos = IntVector.zero(SP);
15        IntVector _threes;
16
17        for (int i = 0; i < input.length; i += SP.length()) {
18          var _mask = SP.indexInRange(i, input.length);
19
20          IntVector _num = IntVector.fromArray(SP, input, i, _mask);
21
22          _twos = _ones.and(_num).or(_twos);
23          _ones = _ones.lanewise(XOR, _num);
24          _threes = _ones.and(_twos);
25          _ones = _ones.lanewise(AND_NOT, _threes);
26          _twos = _twos.lanewise(AND_NOT, _threes);
27        }
28
29        for (int step = 1; step < SP.length(); step <<= 1) {
30          IntVector _os = _ones.slice(step, _zero);
31          IntVector _ts = _twos.slice(step, _zero);
32
33          _os = _os.or(_ts);
34
35          _twos = _ones.and(_os).or(_twos);
36          _ones = _ones.lanewise(XOR, _os);
37          _threes = _ones.and(_twos);
38          _ones = _ones.lanewise(AND_NOT, _threes);
39          _twos = _twos.lanewise(AND_NOT, _threes);
40
41          _twos = _ones.and(_ts).or(_twos);
```

```
42          _ones = _ones.lanewise(XOR, _ts);
43          _threes = _ones.and(_twos);
44          _ones = _ones.lanewise(AND_NOT, _threes);
45          _twos = _twos.lanewise(AND_NOT, _threes);
46        }
47
48        int result = _ones.lane(0);
49
50        return result;
51      }
52    }
53
```

- Lines 17–27 contain the trivially parallel part of the algorithm.

- Lines 29–46 perform the final reduction outside the main loop.

- The optimization in line 33 exploits the fact that the twos counter and ones counter cannot be set simultaneously. The addition rule can therefore be reformulated as follows: if either counter is set, add one. Also, if the twos counter is set, add another one.

Practical Applications

Despite their simplicity, these educational problems demonstrate bit manipulation techniques that frequently appear in real industrial systems:

- **Error detection and correction**: Parity bits, checksums, Reed-Solomon codes

- **RAID systems**: XOR parity for data redundancy

- **Data deduplication**:Finding unique elements in streams

- **Cryptography**: Stream ciphers, one-time pads

- **Network protocols**: Checksum computation (parallelized with SIMD)

- **Digital signal processing**: Removal of periodic noise

- **Hardware testing**: Triple modular redundancy

Benchmarks

Table 7-2 and Table 7-3 compare the XOR-based and trit-based algorithms.

Table 7-2. *Single-core speedup on x86 platforms (higher is better)*

Variant	GL	Z2	IL	SR	Z5
pairsScalar	1.00	1.00	1.00	1.00	1.00
pairsVectorized	0.39	1.21	1.61	1.70	1.16
triplesScalar	1.00	1.00	1.00	1.00	1.00
triplesVectorized	1.11	3.56	7.95	4.38	3.40

The X86 benchmark results reveal a striking difference between the pairs and triples problems despite their apparent similarity. The triplesVectorized variant achieves substantially higher speedups (3.40–7.95×) compared to pairsVectorized (1.16–1.70×), because the triples algorithm's more complex trit arithmetic translates into more computational work that benefits from parallelization.

Table 7-3. *Single-core speedup on ARM platforms (higher is better)*

Variant	M4	O6	CO	NV	G3
pairsScalar	1.00	1.00	1.00	1.00	1.00
pairsVectorized	0.43	1.88	1.63	1.92	2.66
triplesScalar	1.00	1.00	1.00	1.00	1.00
triplesVectorized	0.93	2.02	1.96	2.00	3.83

The ARM benchmark results show consistent speedups across SVE-capable platforms. Apple M4 stands out as a clear outlier with slowdowns for pairsVectorized (0.43×) and near-parity for triplesVectorized (0.93×), indicating that NEON's 128-bit vectors and the horizontal reduction overhead negate vectorization benefits on this platform. G3 (Amazon Graviton 3) achieves the highest speedups at 2.66× for pairs and 3.83× for triples, demonstrating that its 256-bit SVE width provides meaningful parallelism for these bitwise reduction operations. The SVE platforms with 128-bit vectors—O6 (CIX CD8180), CO (Microsoft Cobalt), and NV (Nvidia Grace)—show consistent performance around 1.88–2.02×, suggesting that the algorithms scale predictably with available vector width. The triplesVectorized variant again outperforms pairsVectorized on all platforms, reinforcing the observation that more complex per-element computation provides better vectorization efficiency. NV shows identical results for both problems (1.92× and 2.00×), indicating that its advanced pipeline provides uniform benefits regardless of operation complexity.

What's Next

We return to Project Euler with a mathematically elegant problem involving Fibonacci numbers. The next chapter introduces matrix exponentiation as a vectorization strategy and explores the crucial distinction between Array of Structures and Structure of Arrays data layouts—a choice that profoundly affects vectorization efficiency.

CHAPTER 8

Even Fibonacci Numbers

Project Euler. Problem 2.

Each new term in the Fibonacci sequence is formed by adding the two previous terms. Starting with 1 and 2, the first ten terms are

$$1,2,3,5,8,13,21,34,55,89....$$

Find the sum of all even-valued terms in the Fibonacci sequence that do not exceed four million.

In This Chapter

1. Matrix exponentiation as a strategy for parallelizing recurrence relations

2. The distinction between Array of Structures and Structure of Arrays layouts

3. How prefix products enable parallel computation of dependent sequences

4. When algorithmic optimization outperforms vectorization

Scalar Algorithm

The scalar program works according to the recursive formula for Fibonacci numbers:

$$f_n = f_{n-1} + f_{n-2}$$

© Roman Snytsar 2026
R. Snytsar, *Mastering SIMD with Java Vector API*, https://doi.org/10.1007/979-8-8688-2676-4_8

```
1    package com.nonpareilcoder.projecteuler;
2
3    public class EvenFibonacciNumbersScalar {
4      public static int compute(int limit) {
5        int fib1 = 1, fib2 = 2, sum = fib2;
6
7        while (true) {
8          int fib3 = fib1 + fib2;
9          fib1 = fib2;
10         fib2 = fib3;
11
12         if (fib2 > limit)
13           break;
14
15         if (fib2 % 2 == 0)
16           sum += fib2;
17       }
18
19       return sum;
20     }
21   }
22
```

- Lines 8–10 compute the next term of the sequence.

- Lines 12–13 check the loop exit condition.

- Lines 15–16 update the running sum.

The program does not offer much parallelism; each new term depends on two(!) previous ones, creating a chain dependency. Is it possible to apply a prefix sum algorithm in such a situation?

Vector Algorithm

We can represent the two previous sequence terms as a two-component vector. This leads naturally to the following recursive representation of the Fibonacci sequence:

$$\begin{bmatrix} f_{n+1} \\ f_n \end{bmatrix} = \begin{bmatrix} 1 & 1 \\ 1 & 0 \end{bmatrix} \begin{bmatrix} f_n \\ f_{n-1} \end{bmatrix}$$

Performing the multiplication yields

$$\begin{bmatrix} 1 & 1 \\ 1 & 0 \end{bmatrix} \begin{bmatrix} f_n \\ f_{n-1} \end{bmatrix} = \begin{bmatrix} f_n + f_{n-1} \\ f_n \end{bmatrix} = \begin{bmatrix} f_{n+1} \\ f_n \end{bmatrix}$$

Indeed, the first component of the result equals $f_n + f_{n-1} = f_{n+1}$ by the Fibonacci definition, while the second component contains f_n. Denoting this matrix as F, we see that multiplying by F advances the sequence by one step.

Then the Fibonacci sequence can be represented as a sequence of first elements from vectors obtained by multiplying the suffix product of matrices

$$...; F^n; ...; F^3; F^2; F$$

by an initial vector. Since matrix multiplication has the associative property, we can compute the suffix product using a parallel algorithm. Moreover, using the fact that all matrices in the product are identical, we can pull the suffix sum computation out of the loop, minimizing the number of horizontal operations.

The parallelization scheme is based on the following idea: instead of sequentially computing $F \cdot f$, then $F \cdot (F \cdot f)$, and so on, we can simultaneously compute several powers of matrix F: $F^W, ..., F^3, F^2, F$, where W is the vector length. These powers are computed in $logW$ steps using a vector scan (similar to a prefix sum, but using matrix multiplication instead of addition). Then we multiply each power by the initial vector, generating W consecutive Fibonacci numbers in parallel.

```
1    package com.nonpareilcoder.projecteuler;
2
3    import jdk.incubator.vector.*;
4
5    import static jdk.incubator.vector.VectorOperators.*;
```

```
 6
 7   public class EvenFibonacciNumbersVectorized {
 8     static final VectorSpecies<Integer> SP =
 9       IntVector.SPECIES_PREFERRED;
10
11     public static int compute(int limit) {
12       final IntVector _zero = IntVector.zero(SP);
13       final IntVector _one = IntVector.broadcast(SP, 1);
14
15       IntVector _a00 = _one, _a01 = _one, _a10 = _one;
16       IntVector _a11 = _zero;
17
18       for (int step = 1; step < SP.length(); step <<= 1) {
19         IntVector _b00 = _a00.slice(step, _one);
20         IntVector _b01 = _a01.slice(step, _zero);
21         IntVector _b10 = _a10.slice(step, _zero);
22         IntVector _b11 = _a11.slice(step, _one);
23
24         IntVector _c00 = _a00.mul(_b00).add(_a01.mul(_b10));
25         IntVector _c01 = _a00.mul(_b01).add(_a01.mul(_b11));
26         IntVector _c10 = _a10.mul(_b00).add(_a11.mul(_b10));
27         IntVector _c11 = _a10.mul(_b01).add(_a11.mul(_b11));
28
29         _a00 = _c00;
30         _a01 = _c01;
31         _a10 = _c10;
32         _a11 = _c11;
33       }
34
35       IntVector _sum = _zero;
36
37       int f0 = 2, f1 = 1;
38
39       while (true) {
40         IntVector _c0 = _a00.mul(f0).add(_a01.mul(f1));
41         IntVector _c1 = _a10.mul(f0).add(_a11.mul(f1));
```

```
42
43          var _mask = _c0.compare(LE, limit);
44
45          var _even = _c0.and(0x01).compare(EQ, _zero, _mask);
46          _sum = _sum.add(_c0, _even);
47
48          if (!_mask.allTrue())
49            break;
50
51          f0 = _c0.lane(0);
52          f1 = _c1.lane(0);
53        }
54
55        int sum = 2 + _sum.reduceLanes(ADD);
56
57        return sum;
58      }
59    }
60
```

- Lines 18–33 compute the suffix product of *F* matrices.

- Lines 40–41 multiply the matrices by the initial vector.

- Line 46 updates the running sum.

- Lines 48–49 check the loop exit condition.

- Lines 51–52 update the initial vector for the next loop iteration.

Interestingly, inside the loop, we use element-wise scalar multiplication operations to implement vector multiplication.

Within the object-oriented paradigm typical of Java, it would be logical to create some data structure to describe the matrix, then pack these structures into some container, say, an array. This approach is called **Array of Structures** in the literature. Being low-level programmers, we do not concern ourselves with more sophisticated containers. Array of Structures is poorly suited for vectorization: elements of one component are scattered through memory with a stride equal to the structure size, requiring expensive gather/ scatter operations or multiple loads and permutations to access them.

We store matrices element-wise in different vectors. This data organization method is called **Structure of Arrays**. It is much better suited for vector programs. Elements with the same name from all matrices (e.g., all a_{11} elements) are already laid out sequentially in memory and can be loaded with a single vector instruction. Even if you do not use vector programming directly, element-wise data storage significantly facilitates automatic code vectorization by the compiler. The transition to element-wise storage is akin to database normalization, whose advantages are extensively discussed in the literature.

Scalar Hopping

Adding some mathematics helps here. We will reason by induction.

1. Note that f_1 is odd, while f_2 is even.

2. Suppose that for some k, f_{k-1} is odd and f_k is even.

3. Then f_{k+1} is the sum of odd and even, hence odd. f_{k+2} is the sum of even and odd, meaning odd. f_{k+3} is the sum of odd and odd and therefore even.

Consequently, starting from f_2, only every third term in the sequence is even. Applying this conclusion optimizes the program: instead of computing all Fibonacci numbers and checking each for evenness, we can jump three positions in the sequence each time, computing only even-valued terms. This reduces the number of loop iterations by a factor of three and completely eliminates the evenness check.

```
1    package com.nonpareilcoder.projecteuler;
2
3    public class EvenFibonacciNumbersLeapScalar {
4      public static int compute(int limit) {
5        int fib1 = 1, fib2 = 2, sum = fib2;
6
7        while (true) {
8          int fib3 = fib1 + fib2;
9          fib1 = fib2 + fib3;
10         fib2 = fib3 + fib1;
11
```

```
12        if (fib2 > limit)
13          break;
14
15        sum += fib2;
16      }
17
18    return sum;
19    }
20  }
21
```

- Lines 8–10 jump the sequence forward by three positions at once.

- Line 15 now computes the running sum unconditionally.

Vector Hopping

The improved vector program differs from program 6.3 in that the prefix product involves not F matrices but F^3 matrices. The choice of the third power is directly connected to the property we proved earlier: only every third Fibonacci term is even. Multiplying by matrix F^3 advances the sequence by three positions at once, allowing us to generate only even-valued terms without intermediate computations of odd-valued terms.

$$H = F^3 = \begin{bmatrix} 1 & 1 \\ 1 & 0 \end{bmatrix} \times \begin{bmatrix} 1 & 1 \\ 1 & 0 \end{bmatrix} \times \begin{bmatrix} 1 & 1 \\ 1 & 0 \end{bmatrix} = \begin{bmatrix} 3 & 2 \\ 2 & 1 \end{bmatrix}$$

```
1   package com.nonpareilcoder.projecteuler;
2
3   import jdk.incubator.vector.*;
4
5   import static jdk.incubator.vector.VectorOperators.*;
6
7   public class EvenFibonacciNumbersLeapVectorized {
8     static final VectorSpecies<Integer> SP =
9       IntVector.SPECIES_PREFERRED;
```

```
10
11      public static int compute(int limit) {
12        final IntVector _zero = IntVector.zero(SP);
13        final IntVector _one = IntVector.broadcast(SP, 1);
14
15        IntVector _a00 = IntVector.broadcast(SP, 3);
16        IntVector _a01 = IntVector.broadcast(SP, 2);
17        IntVector _a10 = _a01;
18        IntVector _a11 = _one;
19
20        for (int step = 1; step < SP.length(); step <<= 1) {
21          IntVector _b00 = _a00.slice(step, _one);
22          IntVector _b01 = _a01.slice(step, _zero);
23          IntVector _b10 = _a10.slice(step, _zero);
24          IntVector _b11 = _a11.slice(step, _one);
25
26          IntVector _c00 = _a00.mul(_b00).add(_a01.mul(_b10));
27          IntVector _c01 = _a00.mul(_b01).add(_a01.mul(_b11));
28          IntVector _c10 = _a10.mul(_b00).add(_a11.mul(_b10));
29          IntVector _c11 = _a10.mul(_b01).add(_a11.mul(_b11));
30
31          _a00 = _c00;
32          _a01 = _c01;
33          _a10 = _c10;
34          _a11 = _c11;
35        }
36
37        IntVector _sum = _zero;
38
39        int f0 = 2, f1 = 1;
40
41        while (true) {
42          IntVector _c0 = _a00.mul(f0).add(_a01.mul(f1));
43          IntVector _c1 = _a10.mul(f0).add(_a11.mul(f1));
44
```

```
45            var _mask = _c0.compare(ULE, limit);
46
47            _sum = _sum.add(_c0, _mask);
48
49            if (!_mask.allTrue())
50              break;
51
52            f0 = _c0.lane(0);
53            f1 = _c1.lane(0);
54          }
55
56          int sum = 2 + _sum.reduceLanes(ADD);
57
58          return sum;
59        }
60      }
61
```

Since vectors _c0 and _c1 now contain only every third sequence term, values grow much faster and, with a 512-bit vector length, exceed the Integer type range but fit within Unsigned Integer. With a 512-bit vector and 32-bit element size, 16 elements fit in the vector. One loop iteration generates 16 consecutive even Fibonacci numbers, corresponding to 48 positions in the full sequence. Already by the second or third iteration, values exceed $2^{31} - 1$ but remain below $2^{32} - 1$. That is why line 45 computes the mask using unsigned comparison. This allowed us to stay within the IntVector type, but we are walking a fine line. If vector length increases further in the future (say, to 1024 bits), the number of simultaneously generated numbers will double, and values will exceed unsigned integer limits already in the first or second iteration. In that case, we would need to switch to wider vector elements (LongVector) or reconsider how we divide the problem into chunks.

Benchmarks

Table 8-1 and Table 8-2 compare the Fibonacci computation approaches.

Table 8-1. *Single-core speedup on x86 platforms (higher is better)*

Variant	GL	Z2	IL	SR	Z5
baseline	1.00	1.00	1.00	1.00	1.00
leapScalar	4.02	2.98	4.04	3.97	4.40
leapVectorized	0.13	1.02	1.24	0.88	1.78
vectorized	0.06	0.69	1.08	0.81	1.48

The X86 benchmark results reveal that for Fibonacci computation, the scalar leap optimization consistently outperforms vectorization across all platforms. The vectorized variant without the leap optimization performs worst (0.06–1.48×), confirming that the overhead of matrix prefix products exceeds the benefits of parallelism for this problem's small iteration count. These results demonstrate that algorithmic improvements (skipping two-thirds of iterations) can outweigh vectorization benefits when the computation is inherently small.

Table 8-2. *Single-core speedup on ARM platforms (higher is better)*

Variant	M4	06	CO	NV	G3
baseline	1.00	1.00	1.00	1.00	1.00
vectorized	0.77	0.79	0.63	0.56	0.85
leapScalar	4.07	4.34	4.02	3.92	4.10
leapVectorized	1.61	1.85	1.50	2.01	1.21

The ARM benchmark results strongly favor the scalar leap optimization over any vectorized approach for Fibonacci computation. The clear lesson from ARM results is that for problems with sequential data dependencies like Fibonacci recurrences, algorithmic optimization can sometimes beat vectorization. The vectorization techniques are still important to practice and keep in one's toolkit.

What's Next

Vector computations excel when processing large volumes of data. The next chapter addresses a fundamental question: How do we generate test data quickly? We explore vectorizing the Linear Congruential Generator behind java.util.Random, applying prefix sums and products to leap ahead in the pseudorandom sequence.

CHAPTER 9

Random Number Generator

Vector computations excel when processing large volumes of data. Often, the simplest way to obtain a suitable dataset for testing, debugging, or profiling is to generate it randomly.

Many tests in our project use a method that fills an array with random values.

```java
public static float[] generateRandomArray() {
  Random rand = new Random(arraySeed);
  float[] array = new float[arraySize];

  for (int i = 0; i < arraySize; i++) {
    array[i] = rand.nextFloat(arrayMax);
  }

  return array;
}
```

Since every test begins with such a method, we end up waiting for the loop to finish before reaching the interesting part: our own code. I confess to growing impatient watching random numbers trickle out one by one. Worse, benchmark runs repeat this data generation over thousands of iterations, adding hours to total execution time.

Can we speed up random number generation using vector computations?

In This Chapter

1. The mathematics behind java.util.Random and Linear Congruential Generators

2. How to vectorize seemingly sequential algorithms using prefix sums and products

3. The nature of the modular bias

4. The compress operation for handling rejection sampling without branches

java.util.Random

Consider the algorithm behind `java.util.Random`. It is a classic Linear Congruential Generator (LCG) (Knuth, 1997). The sequence is completely determined by the initial value X_0 (*seed*). Each subsequent value is computed by the formula

$$X_{n+1} = (a \cdot X_n + c) \bmod m$$

where

- X_n: Current state

- a: Multiplier

- c: Increment

- m: Modulus

For `java.util.Random`, the parameters are

$$a = 25214903917$$

$$c = 11$$

$$m = 2^{48}$$

The parameter m, being a power of two, saves us from division and remainder operations (though we already know how to compute remainders efficiently using Lemire's method). The remainder is obtained very quickly by applying a bitmask. The parameter m also determines the period of the pseudorandom sequence, approximately 2^{48}.

The Hull–Dobell theorem (Hull & Dobell, 1962) states the necessary and sufficient conditions for achieving maximum period in an LCG:

1. c and m are coprime: $gcd(c, m) = 1$.

2. $a - 1$ is divisible by all prime factors of m.

3. If m is divisible by 4, then $a - 1$ is also divisible by 4.

For $m = 2^{48}$, the only prime factor is 2, so the conditions simplify:

- c must be odd. The value $c = 11$ satisfies this requirement.

- $a - 1$ must be divisible by 4. Indeed,
  $a - 1 = 25214903916 = 4 \cdot 6303725979$.

Satisfying the Hull–Dobell conditions only guarantees maximum period, however. The quality of random numbers depends on the spectral characteristics of the generator. The spectral test measures the uniformity of point distribution $(X_n, X_{n+1}, ..., X_{n+k})$ in k-dimensional space. A poor choice of a causes points to fall on a small number of hyperplanes, forming noticeable regular structures. The value $a = 25214903917$ was selected to minimize this effect and ensure good spectral test results for dimensions 2 through 6.

Interestingly, the k-dimensional space of the spectral test is mathematically related to the hyperparameter space in machine learning. In both cases, we explore a multidimensional space searching for optimal values. When tuning neural network hyperparameters (learning rate, batch size, number of layers and neurons), we move through the space seeking a point with minimum error. Similarly, when choosing parameter a for an LCG, we search for a value where points $(X_n, X_{n+1}, dots, X_{n+k})$ are distributed as uniformly as possible. Both cases employ optimization methods in multidimensional spaces, and the quality criterion is expressed through geometric properties of point distribution.

Even with optimal parameter selection, not all LCG bits are equally random. Examine the least significant bit more closely. Suppose for some number X_n this bit equals zero, meaning the number is even. Then $a \cdot X_n$ is even, $a \cdot X_n + c$ is odd, $(a \cdot X_n + c) \bmod m$ is odd, meaning X_{n+1} is odd. Similarly, if X_n is odd, then $a \cdot X_n$ is odd, $a \cdot X_n + c$ is even, $(a \cdot X_n + c) \bmod m$ is even, meaning X_{n+1} is even. The least significant bit therefore changes according to a completely non-random pattern with period 2. Following the same logic, one can show that bit number i has period 2^{i+1}. Consequently, the higher bits of an LCG have better statistical properties than the lower bits. The Java developers compensated for this effect.

The `nextFloat` method converts the 48-bit integer LCG value into a floating-point number. The number is shifted right by 24 bits, then the remaining 24 bits are converted to floating-point format and divided by 2^{24}. Recall that the mantissa in IEEE 754 format occupies 23 bits plus one hidden bit. Using more than 24 bits is therefore pointless—they would be truncated by rounding anyway. Since the higher LCG bits have better statistical properties, the higher bits are retained.

The nextInt method returns a value in the range $[0...n)$ following a uniform distribution, meaning all numbers should have equal probability of occurring. Reducing numbers from range $[0...m)$ to range $[0...n)$ is simple: divide by n and take the remainder. However, another statistical trap awaits us: modular bias, a systematic error in the distribution of generated random numbers.

Consider a simple LCG with $m = 4$. It outputs values from 0 to 4 exclusive with equal probability. We reduce these values to range $[0...3)$ by computing the remainder when divided by 3 (Table 9-1).

Table 9-1. *Remainder distribution*

Dividend	Remainder
0	0
1	1
2	2
3	0

Computing the probabilities of each value is straightforward (Table 9-2).

Table 9-2. *Remainder probabilities*

Value	Probability
0	$\dfrac{1}{2}$
1	$\dfrac{1}{4}$
2	$\dfrac{1}{4}$

The distribution differs from uniform. This probability non-uniformity manifests not only in our toy generator example but whenever m is not evenly divisible by n. Mathematicians have invented numerous ways to avoid modular bias, and Java uses the most common: rejection sampling. If the next LCG value $X_k < (m - m \% n)$, it is used to compute $(X_k \% n)$. Otherwise, it is discarded, and we proceed to the next LCG value.

We reproduce the standard random number generator.

```
 1   package com.nonpareilcoder.floatingpoint;
 2
 3   public class RandomGeneratorScalar {
 4     static final long a = 25_214_903_917L;
 5     static final long b = 11L;
 6     static final long mask = (1L << 48) - 1;
 7
 8     static float scale = ((float) (1 << 24));
 9
10     static public float[] generateFloatArray(
11       long seed, float arrayMax, int arraySize) {
12       float[] result = new float[arraySize];
13
14       long val = (seed ^ a) & mask;
15
16       for (int i = 0; i < arraySize; i++) {
17         val = (val * a + b) & mask;
18
19         int bits = (int) (val >>> 24);
20         result[i] = bits / scale * arrayMax;
21       }
22
23     return result;
24     }
25
26     static public int[] generateIntArray(
27       long seed, int arrayMax, int arraySize) {
28       int[] result = new int[arraySize];
29
30       long val = (seed ^ a) & mask;
31
32       for (int i = 0; i < arraySize; i++) {
33         int bits, rem;
34         do {
```

```
35                val = (val * a + b) & mask;
36                bits = (int) (val >>> 17);
37                rem = bits % arrayMax;
38            } while (bits - rem + (arrayMax - 1) < 0);
39
40            result[i] = rem;
41          }
42
43        return result;
44      }
45    }
46
```

- Lines 34–38 hide a vectorizer's nightmare: a non-deterministic loop that rejects unsuitable values. If our random number generator were truly random, the loop could even be infinite. The finite period of LCG ensures the loop terminates.

- In lines 19 and 36, the long-to-int conversion includes a right shift to preserve the more random higher bits.

- We have exactly reproduced the java.util.Random algorithm except for special cases, such as when n is a power of two. In the general case, our code produces bit-identical results to the library generator.

Vector Acceleration

The sequential nature of LCG appears to be an obstacle to vectorization: each subsequent value depends on the previous one. However, knowing the mathematical structure of the generator, we can compute several values ahead at once. Moreover, the formulas for these values are expressed through prefix sums and products—operations that we already know how to vectorize efficiently.

The vectorization approach is straightforward: given value X_n, find formulas for directly computing $X_{n+1}, X_{n+2}, ..., X_{n+w}$, where w is the vector size. The formula for X_{n+1} is already known (all operations below are implicitly performed modulo m):

$$X_{n+1} = a \cdot X_n + c$$

Then, for X_{n+2}

$$X_{n+2} = a \cdot (a \cdot X_n + c) + c = a^2 \cdot X_n + (1 + a) \cdot c$$

Similarly

$$X_{n+3} = a^3 \cdot X_n + (1 + a + a^2) \cdot c$$

In general

$$X_{n+k} = a^k \cdot X_n + c \cdot \sum_{i=0}^{k-1} a^i$$

The vector algorithm thus decomposes into a sequence of steps we already know:

- Compute A_k as a prefix product:

$$A_0 = 1; A_k = \prod_{i=1}^{k} a$$

- Compute B_k as a prefix sum:

$$B_k = \sum_{i=0}^{k-1} A_i$$

- Compute in parallel:

$$X_{n+k} = A_k \cdot X_n + B_k \cdot c$$

Time to code.

```
1    package com.nonpareilcoder.floatingpoint;
2
3    import jdk.incubator.vector.*;
4
5    import static jdk.incubator.vector.VectorOperators.*;
6
7    public class RandomGeneratorVectorized {
8      static final VectorSpecies<Long> SL =
```

```
9          LongVector.SPECIES_PREFERRED;
10      static final VectorSpecies<Float> SF =
11        FloatVector.SPECIES_PREFERRED;
12      static final VectorSpecies<Integer> SI =
13        IntVector.SPECIES_PREFERRED;
14      static final int vl = SL.length();
15
16      static final long a = RandomGeneratorScalar.a;
17      static final long b = RandomGeneratorScalar.b;
18      static final long mask = RandomGeneratorScalar.mask;
19
20      private static final long[] multiplier0;
21      private static final long[] multiplier1;
22      private static final long[] addend0;
23      private static final long[] addend1;
24
25      static {
26        multiplier0 = new long[vl];
27        multiplier1 = new long[vl];
28        addend0 = new long[vl];
29        addend1 = new long[vl];
30
31        final var _zero = LongVector.zero(SL);
32        final var _one = LongVector.broadcast(SL, 1L);
33
34        var _multiplier1 = LongVector.broadcast(SL, a);
35
36        _multiplier1 = _multiplier1.mul(_multiplier1).and(mask);
37
38        for (int step = 1; step < vl; step <<= 1) {
39          var _shifted = _one.slice(vl - step, _multiplier1);
40          _multiplier1 = _multiplier1.mul(_shifted).and(mask);
41        }
42
43        var _multiplier0 = _one.slice(vl - 1, _multiplier1);
```

```
44      _multiplier0 = _multiplier0.mul(a).and(mask);
45
46      _multiplier0.intoArray(multiplier0, 0);
47      _multiplier1.intoArray(multiplier1, 0);
48
49    var _addend0 = _multiplier0;
50    var _addend1 = _multiplier1;
51
52    for (int step = 1; step < vl; step <<= 1) {
53      var _shifted0 = _zero.slice(vl - step, _addend0);
54      var _shifted1 = _zero.slice(vl - step, _addend1);
55      _addend0 = _addend0.add(_shifted0).and(mask);
56      _addend1 = _addend1.add(_shifted1).and(mask);
57    }
58
59    var _t = _addend0.add(_addend1).and(mask);
60    _addend1 = _zero.slice(vl - 1, _addend1).add(_addend0).and(mask);
61    _addend0 = _zero.slice(vl - 1, _t).and(mask);
62
63    _addend0 = _addend0.add(1).mul(b).and(mask);
64    _addend1 = _addend1.add(1).mul(b).and(mask);
65
66    _addend0.intoArray(addend0, 0);
67    _addend1.intoArray(addend1, 0);
68  }
69
70  static float scale = RandomGeneratorScalar.scale;
71
72  static public float[] generateFloatArray(
73    long seed, float arrayMax, int arraySize) {
74    float[] result = new float[arraySize];
75
76    long val = (seed ^ a) & mask;
77
```

```
78        final var _multiplier0 = LongVector.fromArray(SL,
          multiplier0, 0);
79        final var _multiplier1 = LongVector.fromArray(SL,
          multiplier1, 0);
80        final var _addend0 = LongVector.fromArray(SL, addend0, 0);
81        final var _addend1 = LongVector.fromArray(SL, addend1, 0);
82
83        for (int i = 0; i < arraySize; i += vl * 2) {
84          var _part0 = _multiplier0.mul(val).and(mask)
85            .add(_addend0).and(mask);
86          var _part1 = _multiplier1.mul(val).and(mask)
87            .add(_addend1).and(mask);
88
89          val = _part1.lane(vl - 1);
90
91          _part0 = _part0.lanewise(LSHR, 24);
92          _part1 = _part1.lanewise(LSHR, 24);
93
94          _part1 = _part1.lanewise(LSHL, 32);
95          _part0 = _part1.or(_part0);
96
97          var _ival = _part0.reinterpretAsInts();
98
99          var _fval = (FloatVector) _ival.convert(I2F, 0);
100
101          _fval = _fval.div(scale).mul(arrayMax);
102
103          var _store = SF.indexInRange(i, arraySize);
104
105          _fval.intoArray(result, i, _store);
106        }
107
108      return result;
109    }
110
```

```
111    static public int[] generateIntArray(
112      long seed, int arrayMax, int arraySize) {
113      int[] result = new int[arraySize];
114
115      final long c = Long.divideUnsigned(-1L, arrayMax) + 1;
116
117      long val = (seed ^ a) & mask;
118
119      final var _multiplier0 = LongVector.fromArray(SL,
             multiplier0, 0);
120      final var _multiplier1 = LongVector.fromArray(SL,
             multiplier1, 0);
121      final var _addend0 = LongVector.fromArray(SL, addend0, 0);
122      final var _addend1 = LongVector.fromArray(SL, addend1, 0);
123
124      for (int i = 0; i < arraySize; ) {
125        var _part0 = _multiplier0.mul(val).and(mask)
126          .add(_addend0).and(mask);
127        var _part1 = _multiplier1.mul(val).and(mask)
128          .add(_addend1).and(mask);
129
130        val = _part1.lane(vl - 1);
131
132        _part0 = _part0.lanewise(LSHR, 17);
133        _part1 = _part1.lanewise(LSHR, 17);
134
135        var _low0 = _part0.mul(c);
136        var _low1 = _part1.mul(c);
137
138        var _lo0 = _low0.and(0xFFFFFFFFL);
139        var _lo1 = _low1.and(0xFFFFFFFFL);
140        var _hi0 = _low0.lanewise(LSHR, 32);
141        var _hi1 = _low1.lanewise(LSHR, 32);
142        _lo0 = _lo0.mul(arrayMax).lanewise(LSHR, 32);
143        _lo1 = _lo1.mul(arrayMax).lanewise(LSHR, 32);
```

```
144          _hi0 = _hi0.mul(arrayMax);
145          _hi1 = _hi1.mul(arrayMax);
146
147       var _rem0 = _hi0.add(_lo0).lanewise(LSHR, 32);
148       var _rem1 = _hi1.add(_lo1).lanewise(LSHR, 32);
149
150       _part1 = _part1.lanewise(LSHL, 32);
151       _part0 = _part1.or(_part0);
152
153       _rem1 = _rem1.lanewise(LSHL, 32);
154       _rem0 = _rem1.or(_rem0);
155
156       var _ival = _part0.reinterpretAsInts();
157       var _irem = _rem0.reinterpretAsInts();
158
159       var _keep = _ival.sub(_irem)
160          .add(arrayMax)
161          .compare(GE, 1);
162
163       var _store = SI
164          .indexInRange(i, arraySize).and(_keep);
165
166       _irem.compress(_keep).intoArray(result, i, _store);
167
168       i += _store.trueCount();
169     }
170
171    return result;
172   }
173  }
174
```

- Lines 34–41 compute values A_k for even k.

- Lines 43–44 form a second vector with A_k for odd k.

- Lines 49-67 compute values $B_k \cdot c$.

- Lines 84–85 compute a vector of 48-bit values X_{n+k} for even k.

- Similarly, lines 86–87 fill a LongVector with values X_{n+k} for odd k.

- Lines 91–97 truncate values to 24 bits and combine them, forming a single IntVector.

- Lines 99–101 create a vector of floating-point values in the specified range.

- Lines 135–148 implement the full Lemire remainder algorithm.

- Lines 159–166 eliminate the non-deterministic loop using the **compress** operation, previously used in the duplicate removal problem.

Practical Applications

Fast random number generation is in demand across many domains:

- **Testing and benchmarking**: Filling large arrays with test data before measuring performance.

- **Monte Carlo simulations**: Statistical modeling of systems with elements of chaos, from financial markets to nuclear reactors.

- **Computer graphics**: Procedural generation of textures, Perlin noise, and particle effects.

- **Machine learning**: Neural network weight initialization, stochastic gradient descent, and data augmentation.

- **Cryptography**: Key and initialization vector generation. Remember to use algorithms more resistant to attacks than LCG. For example, **java.security.SecureRandom**.

The vectorized generator is especially effective when a large buffer needs to be filled with random values in the minimum time.

Benchmarks

Table 9-3 and Table 9-4 compare the random number generator implementations.

Table 9-3. *Single-core speedup on x86 platforms (higher is better)*

Variant	GL	Z2	IL	SR	Z5
floatBaseline	1.00	1.00	1.00	1.00	1.00
floatScalar	2.01	3.55	6.17	6.91	4.11
floatVectorized	0.58	4.69	15.61	12.32	10.92
intBaseline	1.00	1.00	1.00	1.00	1.00
intScalar	1.36	0.76	4.45	5.30	3.28
intVectorized	0.39	2.20	10.69	7.15	11.10

The X86 benchmark results demonstrate that vectorized random number generation can achieve impressive speedups on AVX-512 platforms, but struggles on older hardware. IL (Intel Ice Lake) achieves the peak floatVectorized performance at 15.61× speedup, benefiting from efficient 512-bit multiplication and the ability to generate 16 random numbers per iteration. Z2 (AMD Rome) shows an unexpected slowdown for intScalar (0.76×) while achieving 2.20× for intVectorized, suggesting that the baseline java.util.Random is highly optimized for this platform's scalar pipeline. Z5 (AMD Turin) achieves the best intVectorized speedup at 11.10×, outperforming even IL for integer generation. The floatScalar variant provides consistent 2–7× improvements over java.util. Random across all platforms, indicating that eliminating the function call overhead in the baseline provides immediate benefits. This is the reason why all code in this book is written in a "poor" style that minimizes the number of function calls.

Table 9-4. *Single-core speedup on ARM platforms (higher is better)*

Variant	M4	O6	CO	NV	G3
floatBaseline	1.00	1.00	1.00	1.00	1.00
floatScalar	42.89	9.01	5.42	5.85	5.54
floatVectorized	23.50	8.03	4.92	5.55	7.51
intBaseline	1.00	1.00	1.00	1.00	1.00
intScalar	42.65	3.52	2.13	2.49	2.17
intVectorized	9.03	4.77	2.82	5.04	5.05

The ARM benchmark results reveal dramatically different performance characteristics across platforms, with Apple M4 emerging as a striking outlier. The M4 achieves extraordinary scalar speedups of 42.65–42.89× over the baseline, indicating that java.util.Random suffers severe performance penalties on this platform, likely due to the function call overhead interacting poorly with M4's architecture. The floatVectorized variant on M4 (23.50×) actually underperforms the floatScalar (42.89×), demonstrating that vectorization overhead exceeds its benefits when the baseline is already problematic. On SVE-capable platforms—O6 (CIX CD8180), CO (Microsoft Cobalt), NV (Nvidia Grace), and G3 (Amazon Graviton 3)—results are more modest but consistent, with floatVectorized achieving 4.92–8.03× speedups. G3 shows the best vectorized-over-scalar improvement ratio, where floatVectorized (7.51×) exceeds floatScalar (5.54×) by 35%, confirming that its 256-bit SVE effectively accelerates the LCG computation. The intVectorized variant generally outperforms intScalar on SVE platforms but not on M4, suggesting that the compress operation for rejection sampling works efficiently with SVE but struggles with NEON.

What's Next

Having mastered prefix sums with addition and prefix products with multiplication, we now extend these techniques to prefix maximum. The next chapter tackles the classic interview problem of trapping rainwater, introducing Guy Blelloch's work-optimal scan algorithm and the powerful technique of vector transposition.

CHAPTER 10

Trapping Rainwater

Given an array of n non-negative integers representing bar heights in an elevation map (each bar has unit width), compute the total volume of water trapped between bars after rain.

For example, the input array:

$$2,0,1,2,1,3,0,1$$

The answer is 5, as illustrated in Figure 10-1.

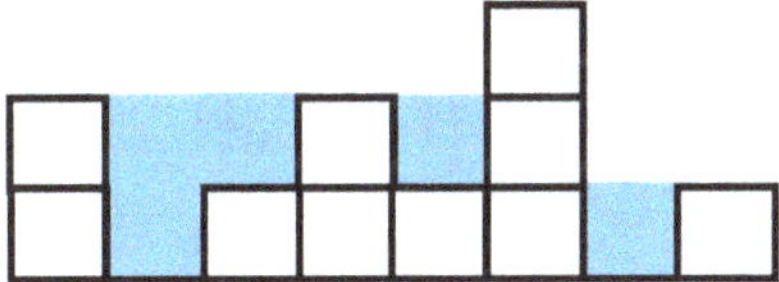

Figure 10-1. *Visualization of trapped rainwater between elevation bars*

In This Chapter

1. Blelloch's work-optimal parallel scan algorithm with upsweep and downsweep phases

2. Vector transposition using zip and unzip operations

3. The memoization technique for avoiding redundant vector pivots

4. How loop unrolling enables instruction-level parallelism within vector scans

Interview Solution

First, we need to compute the prefix maximum and suffix maximum of the input data. That is, cumulative maxima rather than cumulative sums.

The amount of water at each position x is determined by the height of "walls" to the left and right of it. The prefix maximum $prefix\_max\,[x]$ contains the maximum height to the left of the position (including it), and the suffix maximum $suffix\_max[x]$ contains the maximum height to the right. Water at position x can rise to at most the height of the shorter of the two walls: $min(prefix\_max\,[x], suffix\_max[x])$. Thus, the amount of water at the position equals the difference between the water level and the ground height: $min(prefix\_max[x], suffix\_max[x]) - input[x]$.

After computing cumulative sums, the amount of water in puddles is calculated by the formula

$$w = \sum_{0}^{n-1} min\left(prefix\_max[x], suffix\_max[x]\right) - input[x]$$

```java
1    package com.nonpareilcoder.realleetcode;
2
3    public class TrappingRainWaterScalar {
4      public static int trap(int[] input) {
5        int[] prefixMax = new int[input.length];
6        int[] suffixMax = new int[input.length];
7
8        computePrefixMax(input, prefixMax);
9        computeSuffixMax(input, suffixMax);
10
11        return reduceHeights(input, prefixMax, suffixMax);
12      }
13
14      static void computePrefixMax(int[] input, int[] prefixMax) {
15        for (int acc = 0, i = 0; i < input.length; i++) {
16          acc = Math.max(acc, input[i]);
17          prefixMax[i] = acc;
18        }
19      }
```

```
20
21    static void computeSuffixMax(int[] input, int[] suffixMax) {
22      for (int acc = 0, i = input.length; i-- > 0; ) {
23        acc = Math.max(acc, input[i]);
24        suffixMax[i] = acc;
25      }
26    }
27
28    static int reduceHeights(
29      int[] input, int[] prefixMax, int[] suffixMax) {
30      int trapped = 0;
31
32      for (int i = 0; i < prefixMax.length; i++) {
33        int minMax = Math.min(prefixMax[i], suffixMax[i]);
34        trapped += minMax - input[i];
35      }
36
37      return trapped;
38    }
39  }
40
```

- Lines 15–18 compute the prefix maximum.

- Lines 22–25 compute the suffix maximum.

- The loop in lines 32–35 forms the final sum.

- The program solves the problem in linear time, specifically, in three
  passes over the array. Moreover, the pass directions alternate, making
  our algorithm cache-oblivious.

Vector Scan

```
1   package com.nonpareilcoder.realleetcode;
2
3   import jdk.incubator.vector.*;
```

```
 4
 5    import static jdk.incubator.vector.VectorOperators.*;
 6
 7    public class TrappingRainWaterHorizontal {
 8      public static int trap(int[] input) {
 9        int[] prefixMax = new int[input.length];
10        int[] suffixMax = new int[input.length];
11
12        computePrefixMax(input, prefixMax);
13        computeSuffixMax(input, suffixMax);
14
15        return reduceHeights(input, prefixMax, suffixMax);
16      }
17
18      static final VectorSpecies<Integer> SP =
19        IntVector.SPECIES_PREFERRED;
20      static final int vl = SP.length();
21
22      static void computePrefixMax(int[] input, int[] prefixMax) {
23        final var _zero = IntVector.zero(SP);
24
25        int acc = 0, pos = 0;
26        for (int i = 0; i < input.length; i += vl) {
27          var _mask = SP.indexInRange(i, input.length);
28
29          var _current = IntVector.fromArray(SP, input, pos, _mask);
30
31          for (int step = 1; step < vl; step <<= 1) {
32            var _shifted = _zero.slice(vl - step, _current);
33            _current = _current.max(_shifted);
34          }
35
36          _current = _current.max(IntVector.broadcast(SP, acc));
37
38          acc = _current.lane(vl - 1);
39
142
```

```
40        _current.intoArray(prefixMax, pos, _mask);
41
42      pos += vl;
43    }
44  }
45
46  static void computeSuffixMax(int[] input, int[] suffixMax) {
47    final var _zero = IntVector.zero(SP);
48
49    int iterations = input.length / vl;
50    int remainder = input.length % vl;
51
52    int acc = 0, pos = input.length;
53    while (remainder-- > 0) {
54      acc = Math.max(acc, input[--pos]);
55      suffixMax[pos] = acc;
56    }
57
58    for (int i = 0; i < iterations; i++) {
59      pos -= vl;
60
61      var _current = IntVector.fromArray(SP, input, pos);
62
63      for (int step = 1; step < vl; step <<= 1) {
64        var _shifted = _current.slice(step, _zero);
65        _current = _current.max(_shifted);
66      }
67
68      _current = _current.max(
69        IntVector.broadcast(SP, acc));
70
71      acc = _current.lane(0);
72
73      _current.intoArray(suffixMax, pos);
74    }
```

```
75      }
76
77      static int reduceHeights(
78        int[] input, int[] prefixMax, int[] suffixMax) {
79        var _trapped = IntVector.zero(SP);
80
81        for (int i = 0; i < input.length; i += vl) {
82          var _mask = SP.indexInRange(i, input.length);
83          var _height = IntVector.fromArray(SP, input, i, _mask);
84          var _left = IntVector.fromArray(SP, prefixMax, i, _mask);
85          var _right = IntVector.fromArray(SP, suffixMax, i, _mask);
86
87          _trapped = _trapped.add(_left.min(_right).sub(_height));
88        }
89
90        return _trapped.reduceLanes(ADD);
91      }
92    }
93
```

- Lines 22–44 compute the prefix maximum. Code nearly identical to Chapter 5, with **add** replaced by **max**.

- Lines 46–75 compute the suffix maximum.

- Lines 77–91 form the final sum using vector reduction, very similar to code from Chapter 2.

- The main drawbacks, as discussed above, are data dependencies during cumulative sum calculation and the inability to execute instructions in parallel.

Unrolled Vector Scan

Next, we unroll the outer loop of the vector scan by four.

```
package com.nonpareilcoder.realleetcode;

import jdk.incubator.vector.*;

public class TrappingRainWaterHorizontalX4 {
  public static int trap(int[] input) {
    int[] prefixMax = new int[input.length];
    int[] suffixMax = new int[input.length];

    computePrefixMax(input, prefixMax);
    computeSuffixMax(input, suffixMax);

    return TrappingRainWaterHorizontal
      .reduceHeights(input, prefixMax, suffixMax);
  }

  static final VectorSpecies<Integer> SP =
    IntVector.SPECIES_PREFERRED;
  static final int vl = SP.length();

  static void computePrefixMax(int[] input, int[] prefixMax) {
    final IntVector _zero = IntVector.zero(SP);

    int iterations = input.length / (4 * vl);
    int remainder = input.length % (4 * vl);

    int acc = 0, pos = 0;
    for (int i = 0; i < iterations; i++) {
      var _part0 = IntVector.fromArray(SP, input, pos + 0 * vl);
      var _part1 = IntVector.fromArray(SP, input, pos + 1 * vl);
      var _part2 = IntVector.fromArray(SP, input, pos + 2 * vl);
      var _part3 = IntVector.fromArray(SP, input, pos + 3 * vl);

      for (int step = 1; step < vl; step <<= 1) {
        var _shifted0 = _zero.slice(vl - step, _part0);
```

```
36        var _shifted1 = _zero.slice(vl - step, _part1);
37        var _shifted2 = _zero.slice(vl - step, _part2);
38        var _shifted3 = _zero.slice(vl - step, _part3);
39        _part0 = _part0.max(_shifted0);
40        _part1 = _part1.max(_shifted1);
41        _part2 = _part2.max(_shifted2);
42        _part3 = _part3.max(_shifted3);
43      }
44
45      var _accV = IntVector.broadcast(SP, acc);
46      _part0 = _part0.max(_accV);
47      _accV = IntVector.broadcast(SP, _part0.lane(vl - 1));
48      _part1 = _part1.max(_accV);
49      _accV = IntVector.broadcast(SP, _part1.lane(vl - 1));
50      _part2 = _part2.max(_accV);
51      _accV = IntVector.broadcast(SP, _part2.lane(vl - 1));
52      _part3 = _part3.max(_accV);
53
54      acc = _part3.lane(vl - 1);
55
56      _part0.intoArray(prefixMax, pos + 0 * vl);
57      _part1.intoArray(prefixMax, pos + 1 * vl);
58      _part2.intoArray(prefixMax, pos + 2 * vl);
59      _part3.intoArray(prefixMax, pos + 3 * vl);
60
61      pos += 4 * vl;
62    }
63
64    while (remainder-- > 0) {
65      acc = Math.max(acc, input[pos]);
66      prefixMax[pos++] = acc;
67    }
68  }
69
70  static void computeSuffixMax(int[] input, int[] suffixMax) {
71    final IntVector _zero = IntVector.zero(SP);
```

```
72
73      int iterations = input.length / (4 * vl);
74      int remainder = input.length % (4 * vl);
75
76      int acc = 0, pos = input.length;
77      while (remainder-- > 0) {
78        acc = Math.max(acc, input[--pos]);
79        suffixMax[pos] = acc;
80      }
81
82      for (int i = 0; i < iterations; i++) {
83        pos -= 4 * vl;
84
85        var _part0 = IntVector.fromArray(SP, input, pos + 0 * vl);
86        var _part1 = IntVector.fromArray(SP, input, pos + 1 * vl);
87        var _part2 = IntVector.fromArray(SP, input, pos + 2 * vl);
88        var _part3 = IntVector.fromArray(SP, input, pos + 3 * vl);
89
90        for (int step = 1; step < vl; step <<= 1) {
91          var _shifted3 = _part3.slice(step, _zero);
92          var _shifted2 = _part2.slice(step, _zero);
93          var _shifted1 = _part1.slice(step, _zero);
94          var _shifted0 = _part0.slice(step, _zero);
95          _part3 = _part3.max(_shifted3);
96          _part2 = _part2.max(_shifted2);
97          _part1 = _part1.max(_shifted1);
98          _part0 = _part0.max(_shifted0);
99        }
100
101       var _accV = IntVector.broadcast(SP, acc);
102       _part3 = _part3.max(_accV);
103       _accV = IntVector.broadcast(SP, _part3.lane(0));
104       _part2 = _part2.max(_accV);
105       _accV = IntVector.broadcast(SP, _part2.lane(0));
106       _part1 = _part1.max(_accV);
```

```
107            _accV = IntVector.broadcast(SP, _part1.lane(0));
108            _part0 = _part0.max(_accV);
109
110        acc = _part0.lane(0);
111
112            _part0.intoArray(suffixMax, pos + 0 * vl);
113            _part1.intoArray(suffixMax, pos + 1 * vl);
114            _part2.intoArray(suffixMax, pos + 2 * vl);
115            _part3.intoArray(suffixMax, pos + 3 * vl);
116        }
117      }
118    }
119
```

Look more carefully at how the unrolled suffix maximum calculation works.

- Lines 85–88 load four vectors. There is no data dependency.

- Lines 91–94 shift the vectors in a loop, again independently of each other.

- Lines 95–98 compute the maximums; these operations are independent and may execute in parallel.

- Lines 101–108 perform suffix sum correction. Essentially, this is another suffix sum, but now between vectors. This second pass is the price for parallel execution of vector scans. Unfortunately, operations must execute sequentially.

- Lines 112–115 store results into the array.

Optimal Vector Scan

The previous algorithm added instruction-level parallelism to the vector scan. Next, we tackle the second problem: inefficient register usage. Guy Blelloch (Blelloch, 1989) proposed a work-optimal parallel scan algorithm. Consider the modified algorithm shown in Figure 10-2, where only the cells indicated by arrows are in computation.

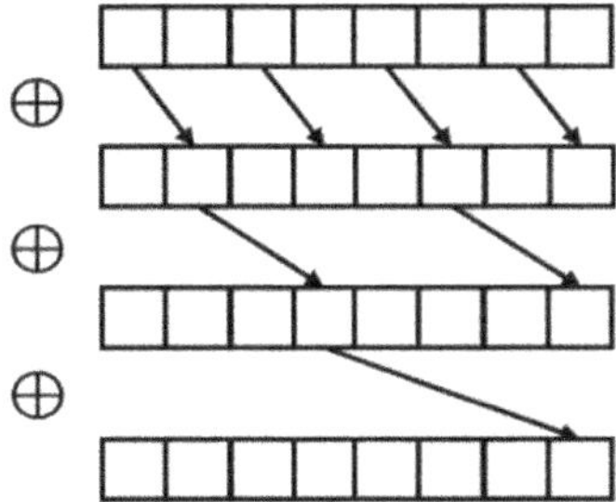

Figure 10-2. *Blelloch's work-optimal scan: upsweep phase*

After the first pass through the vector, that Blelloch calls the **upsweep**, all elements in power-of-two positions (counting elements starting at one, not at zero as we programmers do) have the correct final values.

Consider the path to the element at position 2^k. At the first step, this element receives the sum with its neighbor (positions $2^k - 1$ and 2^k). At the second step, it forms the sum with the pair to the left (positions $2^k - 3$ and $2^k - 2$); now it contains the sum of four elements. At each step i, a block of 2^{i-1} elements from the left is added. After k steps, position 2^k accumulates all 2^k elements to its left, and this is the correct prefix sum value.

This means the last element of the vector contains the sum of all elements. The upsweep is thus equivalent to a vector reduction. The second pass (**downsweep**), shown in Figure 10-3, cleans up values located between positions corresponding to powers of two.

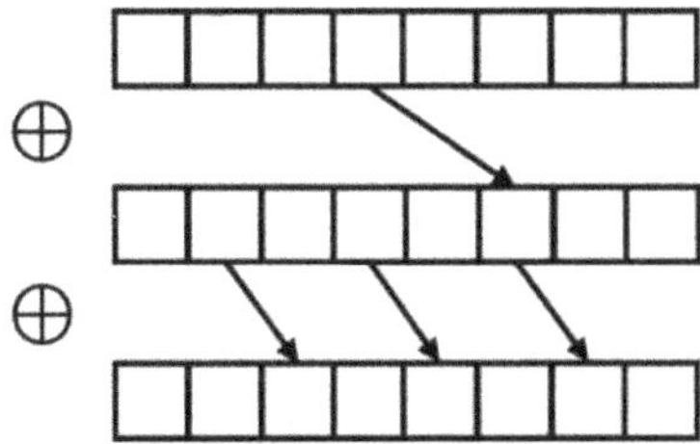

Figure 10-3. *Blelloch's work-optimal scan: downsweep phase*

The number of parallel steps has nearly doubled, yet the total count of operations performed has reached the minimum.

The challenge is operating on only the required elements of the vector. Masking is not a viable solution since it definitely leaves some elements underutilized.

The elegant solution is to transpose the four vectors from the unrolled vector scan (see Figure 10-4), that is, redistribute the data so that instead of rows, data is stored in columns.

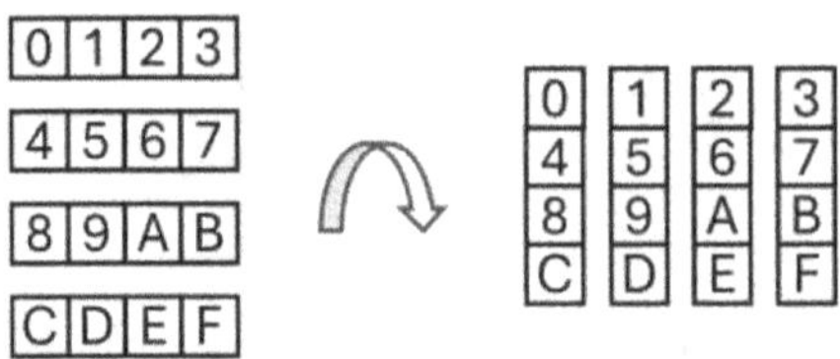

Figure 10-4. *Vector transposition*

Then, imagining columns as elements of some "super-vector"—who said "tensor"?—we can compute an element-wise optimal scan.

Consider how transposition solves the problem. Before transposition, each vector contains sequential elements of the array, and scan within the vector leaves elements at boundaries unused (as shown earlier, $W - 1$ elements per vector). After transposition, each vector contains elements with the same positions from four different array sections. Now Blelloch's work-optimal scan applies element-wise: for each position within the vector, a scan is independently computed over four values from different sections. This fully utilizes all vector elements without waste, since operations apply to all elements in parallel.

For vector transposition, we need **zip** and **unzip** operations.

The **zip0** operation (Figure 10-5) interleaves data from the first halves of two vectors.

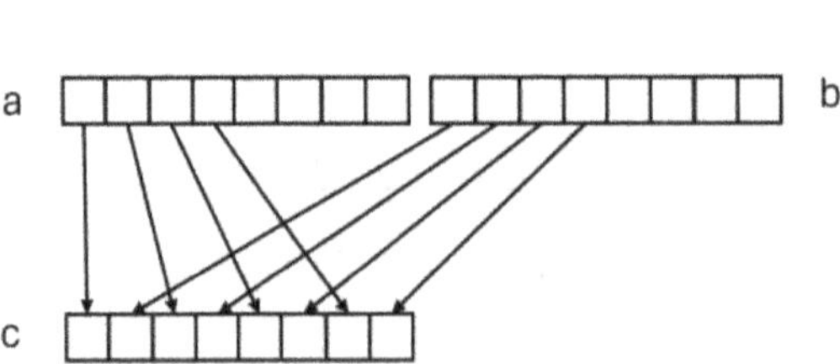

Figure 10-5. *The zip0 operation*

Similarly, the **zip1** operation (Figure 10-6) interleaves data from the second halves of two vectors.

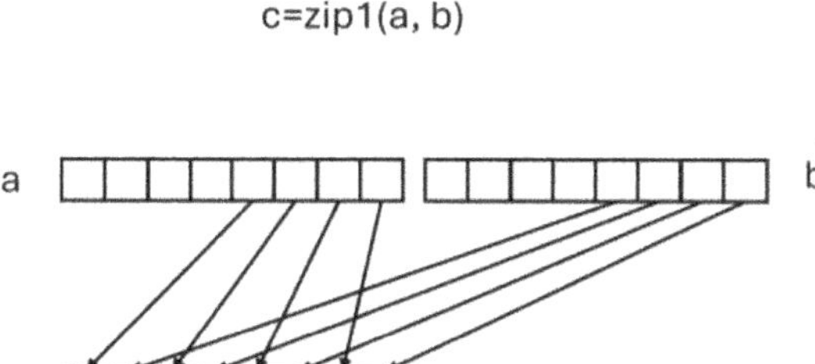

Figure 10-6. *The zip1 operation*

The **unzip0** operation (Figure 10-7) is the inverse of **zip0**; it sequentially selects even elements from a pair of vectors.

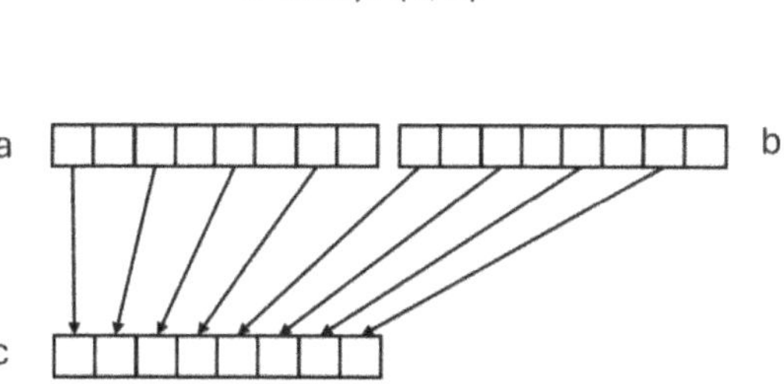

Figure 10-7. *The unzip0 operation*

Finally, **unzip1** (Figure 10-8) sequentially selects odd elements from a pair of vectors.

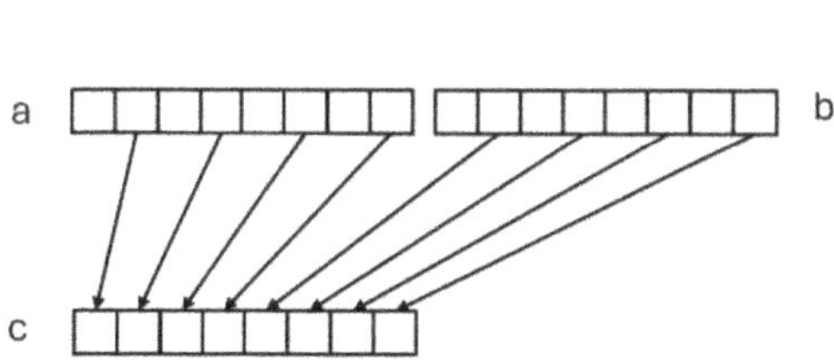

Figure 10-8. *The unzip1 operation*

In the Java Vector API, these useful operations are implemented in two steps. First, you need to create an index vector that correctly describes the operation for the current vector length. Second, use the universal **rearrange** instruction that selects elements from two vectors according to specified indices. Let us implement these ideas.

```java
 1    package com.nonpareilcoder.realleetcode;
 2
 3    import jdk.incubator.vector.*;
 4
 5    public class TrappingRainWaterTransposedX4 {
 6      public static int trap(int[] input) {
 7        int[] prefixMax = new int[input.length];
 8        int[] suffixMax = new int[input.length];
 9
10        computePrefixMax(input, prefixMax);
11        computeSuffixMax(input, suffixMax);
12
13        return TrappingRainWaterHorizontal
14          .reduceHeights(input, prefixMax, suffixMax);
15      }
16
17      static final VectorSpecies<Integer> SP =
18        IntVector.SPECIES_PREFERRED;
19      static final int vl = SP.length();
20
21      static final IntVector _zero = IntVector.broadcast(SP, 0);
22
23      static final VectorShuffle<Integer> _zip0 =
24        VectorShuffle.makeZip(SP, 0);
25      static final VectorShuffle<Integer> _zip1 =
26        VectorShuffle.makeZip(SP, 1);
27      static final VectorShuffle<Integer> _uzp0 =
28        VectorShuffle.makeUnzip(SP, 0);
29      static final VectorShuffle<Integer> _uzp1 =
30        VectorShuffle.makeUnzip(SP, 1);
31
32      static void computePrefixMax(int[] input, int[] prefixMax) {
33        int iterations = input.length / (4 * vl);
34        int remainder = input.length % (4 * vl);
35
```

```
36      int acc = 0, pos = 0;
37      for (int i = 0; i < iterations; i++) {
38        IntVector _part0 = IntVector.fromArray(SP, input, pos);
39        IntVector _part1 =
40          IntVector.fromArray(SP, input, pos + vl);
41        IntVector _part2 =
42          IntVector.fromArray(SP, input, pos + 2 * vl);
43        IntVector _part3 =
44          IntVector.fromArray(SP, input, pos + 3 * vl);
45
46        IntVector _t0 = _part0;
47        _part0 = _part0.rearrange(_uzp0, _part1);
48        _part1 = _t0.rearrange(_uzp1, _part1);
49        IntVector _t1 = _part2;
50        _part2 = _part2.rearrange(_uzp0, _part3);
51        _part3 = _t1.rearrange(_uzp1, _part3);
52
53        _t0 = _part0;
54        _part0 = _part0.rearrange(_uzp0, _part2);
55        _t1 = _part1;
56        _part1 = _part1.rearrange(_uzp0, _part3);
57        _part2 = _t0.rearrange(_uzp1, _part2);
58        _part3 = _t1.rearrange(_uzp1, _part3);
59
60        _part1 = _part1.max(_part0);
61        _part3 = _part3.max(_part2);
62
63        _part3 = _part3.max(_part1);
64
65        _part2 = _part2.max(_part1);
66
67        IntVector _prev = IntVector.broadcast(SP, acc);
68
69        IntVector _partZ = _prev.slice(vl - 1, _part3);
70
```

```
71          for (int step = 1; step < vl; step <<= 1) {
72            IntVector _shifted = _zero.slice(vl - step, _partZ);
73            _partZ = _partZ.max(_shifted);
74          }
75
76          _part0 = _part0.max(_partZ);
77          _part1 = _part1.max(_partZ);
78          _part2 = _part2.max(_partZ);
79          _part3 = _part3.max(_partZ);
80
81          acc = _part3.lane(vl - 1);
82
83          _t0 = _part0;
84          _part0 = _part0.rearrange(_zip0, _part2);
85          _t1 = _part1;
86          _part1 = _part1.rearrange(_zip0, _part3);
87          _part2 = _t0.rearrange(_zip1, _part2);
88          _part3 = _t1.rearrange(_zip1, _part3);
89
90          _t0 = _part0;
91          _part0 = _part0.rearrange(_zip0, _part1);
92          _part1 = _t0.rearrange(_zip1, _part1);
93          _t1 = _part2;
94          _part2 = _part2.rearrange(_zip0, _part3);
95          _part3 = _t1.rearrange(_zip1, _part3);
96
97          _part0.intoArray(prefixMax, pos);
98          _part1.intoArray(prefixMax, pos + vl);
99          _part2.intoArray(prefixMax, pos + 2 * vl);
100         _part3.intoArray(prefixMax, pos + 3 * vl);
101
102         pos += 4 * vl;
103       }
104
105       while (remainder-- > 0) {
```

154

```
106        acc = Math.max(acc, input[pos]);
107        prefixMax[pos++] = acc;
108      }
109    }
110
111    static void computeSuffixMax(int[] input, int[] suffixMax) {
112      int iterations = input.length / (4 * vl);
113      int remainder = input.length % (4 * vl);
114
115      int acc = 0, pos = input.length;
116      while (remainder-- > 0) {
117        acc = Math.max(acc, input[--pos]);
118        suffixMax[pos] = acc;
119      }
120
121      IntVector _prev = IntVector.broadcast(SP, acc);
122
123      for (int i = 0; i < iterations; i++) {
124        pos -= 4 * vl;
125
126        IntVector _part0 = IntVector.fromArray(SP, input, pos);
127        IntVector _part1 =
128          IntVector.fromArray(SP, input, pos + vl);
129        IntVector _part2 =
130          IntVector.fromArray(SP, input, pos + 2 * vl);
131        IntVector _part3 =
132          IntVector.fromArray(SP, input, pos + 3 * vl);
133
134        IntVector _t0 = _part0;
135        _part0 = _part0.rearrange(_uzp0, _part1);
136        _part1 = _t0.rearrange(_uzp1, _part1);
137        IntVector _t1 = _part2;
138        _part2 = _part2.rearrange(_uzp0, _part3);
139        _part3 = _t1.rearrange(_uzp1, _part3);
140
```

```
141        _t0 = _part0;
142        _part0 = _part0.rearrange(_uzp0, _part2);
143        _t1 = _part1;
144        _part1 = _part1.rearrange(_uzp0, _part3);
145        _part2 = _t0.rearrange(_uzp1, _part2);
146        _part3 = _t1.rearrange(_uzp1, _part3);
147
148        _part2 = _part2.max(_part3);
149        _part0 = _part0.max(_part1);
150
151        _part0 = _part0.max(_part2);
152
153        _part1 = _part1.max(_part2);
154
155     IntVector _partZ = _part0.slice(1, _prev);
156
157     for (int step = 1; step < vl; step <<= 1) {
158       IntVector _shifted = _partZ.slice(step, _zero);
159       _partZ = _partZ.max(_shifted);
160     }
161
162     _part3 = _part3.max(_partZ);
163     _part2 = _part2.max(_partZ);
164     _part1 = _part1.max(_partZ);
165     _part0 = _part0.max(_partZ);
166
167     _prev = _part0;
168
169     _t0 = _part0;
170     _part0 = _part0.rearrange(_zip0, _part2);
171     _t1 = _part1;
172     _part1 = _part1.rearrange(_zip0, _part3);
173     _part2 = _t0.rearrange(_zip1, _part2);
174     _part3 = _t1.rearrange(_zip1, _part3);
175
```

```
176            _t0 = _part0;
177            _part0 = _part0.rearrange(_zip0, _part1);
178            _part1 = _t0.rearrange(_zip1, _part1);
179            _t1 = _part2;
180            _part2 = _part2.rearrange(_zip0, _part3);
181            _part3 = _t1.rearrange(_zip1, _part3);
182
183            _part0.intoArray(suffixMax, pos);
184            _part1.intoArray(suffixMax, pos + vl);
185            _part2.intoArray(suffixMax, pos + 2 * vl);
186            _part3.intoArray(suffixMax, pos + 3 * vl);
187        }
188    }
189 }
190
```

As usual, we analyze the suffix maximum computation.

- Lines 126–132 load four vectors.

- Lines 134–146 perform data transformation. If each register has four elements (i.e., we are performing transposition in the mathematical sense), then **zip** and **unzip** operations are interchangeable. For a vector-length-agnostic algorithm, specifically **unzip** is suitable, and we will use the more general term "vector pivot" to describe the transformation procedure.

- Lines 148–153 perform the upsweep.

- Line 155 cleans up data at positions between powers of two.

- Lines 157–165 perform suffix sum correction. Now, correction has become a true horizontal vector scan in lines 157–160, followed by a series of operations in lines 162–165.

- Lines 169–181 pivot the data back, this time using the **zip** operation.

- Lines 183–186 store the results into the array.

Accelerating Optimal Scan

The advantages of parallel scan manifest stronger as the length of the cumulative sum increases. Since modern vector architectures have 32 registers, we can dedicate 16 of them to data for the unrolled scan. The remaining registers will be used for storing intermediate data and constants. We just need to write code for pivoting 16 vectors that is vector-length agnostic.

We can further reduce the number of unrolled scan operations by swapping the cleanup and cumulative sum correction. Then we can correct only the vectors whose values formed during the upsweep, and the remaining vectors will automatically be corrected during downsweep.

The mechanism of this optimization can be clarified as follows. After the upsweep, only vectors at power-of-two positions have correct values (e.g., with a scan over 16, these are vectors 1, 2, 4, 8, 16). If we first perform correction for these $log_2 W$ vectors (add the previous block's sum to them), then run the downsweep, the cleanup phase automatically propagates the corrected values to intermediate positions. This happens because downsweep combines already-corrected values from power-of-two positions with local partial sums. Thus, instead of correcting all W vectors, it is sufficient to correct only $log_2 W$ vectors.

```java
1    package com.nonpareilcoder.realleetcode;
2
3    import jdk.incubator.vector.*;
4
5    public class TrappingRainWaterTransposedX16 {
6      public static int trap(int[] input) {
7        int[] prefixMax = new int[input.length];
8        int[] suffixMax = new int[input.length];
9
10       computePrefixMax(input, prefixMax);
11       computeSuffixMax(input, suffixMax);
12
13       return TrappingRainWaterHorizontal
14          .reduceHeights(input, prefixMax, suffixMax);
15     }
16
```

```
17    static final VectorSpecies<Integer> SP =
18      IntVector.SPECIES_PREFERRED;
19
20    static final int vl = SP.length();
21
22    static final IntVector _zero = IntVector.broadcast(SP, 0);
23
24    static final VectorShuffle<Integer> _zip0 =
25      VectorShuffle.makeZip(SP, 0);
26    static final VectorShuffle<Integer> _zip1 =
27      VectorShuffle.makeZip(SP, 1);
28    static final VectorShuffle<Integer> _uzp0 =
29      VectorShuffle.makeUnzip(SP, 0);
30    static final VectorShuffle<Integer> _uzp1 =
31      VectorShuffle.makeUnzip(SP, 1);
32
33    static void computePrefixMax(int[] input, int[] prefixMax) {
34      int iterations = input.length / (16 * vl);
35      int remainder = input.length % (16 * vl);
36
37      IntVector _prev = _zero;
38
39      int pos = 0;
40      for (int i = 0; i < iterations; i++) {
41        IntVector _part0 = IntVector.fromArray(SP, input, pos);
42        IntVector _part1 = IntVector.fromArray(SP, input, pos + vl);
43        IntVector _part2 =
44          IntVector.fromArray(SP, input, pos + 2 * vl);
45        IntVector _part3 =
46          IntVector.fromArray(SP, input, pos + 3 * vl);
47        IntVector _part4 =
48          IntVector.fromArray(SP, input, pos + 4 * vl);
49        IntVector _part5 =
50          IntVector.fromArray(SP, input, pos + 5 * vl);
51        IntVector _part6 =
```

```
52          IntVector.fromArray(SP, input, pos + 6 * vl);
53      IntVector _part7 =
54          IntVector.fromArray(SP, input, pos + 7 * vl);
55      IntVector _part8 =
56          IntVector.fromArray(SP, input, pos + 8 * vl);
57      IntVector _part9 =
58          IntVector.fromArray(SP, input, pos + 9 * vl);
59      IntVector _partA =
60          IntVector.fromArray(SP, input, pos + 10 * vl);
61      IntVector _partB =
62          IntVector.fromArray(SP, input, pos + 11 * vl);
63      IntVector _partC =
64          IntVector.fromArray(SP, input, pos + 12 * vl);
65      IntVector _partD =
66          IntVector.fromArray(SP, input, pos + 13 * vl);
67      IntVector _partE =
68          IntVector.fromArray(SP, input, pos + 14 * vl);
69      IntVector _partF =
70          IntVector.fromArray(SP, input, pos + 15 * vl);
71
72      IntVector _t0 = _part0;
73      _part0 = _part0.rearrange(_uzp0, _part1);
74      _part1 = _t0.rearrange(_uzp1, _part1);
75      IntVector _t1 = _part2;
76      _part2 = _part2.rearrange(_uzp0, _part3);
77      _part3 = _t1.rearrange(_uzp1, _part3);
78      IntVector _t2 = _part4;
79      _part4 = _part4.rearrange(_uzp0, _part5);
80      _part5 = _t2.rearrange(_uzp1, _part5);
81      IntVector _t3 = _part6;
82      _part6 = _part6.rearrange(_uzp0, _part7);
83      _part7 = _t3.rearrange(_uzp1, _part7);
84      IntVector _t4 = _part8;
85      _part8 = _part8.rearrange(_uzp0, _part9);
86      _part9 = _t4.rearrange(_uzp1, _part9);
```

```
87      IntVector _t5 = _partA;
88      _partA = _partA.rearrange(_uzp0, _partB);
89      _partB = _t5.rearrange(_uzp1, _partB);
90      IntVector _t6 = _partC;
91      _partC = _partC.rearrange(_uzp0, _partD);
92      _partD = _t6.rearrange(_uzp1, _partD);
93      IntVector _t7 = _partE;
94      _partE = _partE.rearrange(_uzp0, _partF);
95      _partF = _t7.rearrange(_uzp1, _partF);
96
97      _t0 = _part0;
98      _part0 = _part0.rearrange(_uzp0, _part2);
99      _t1 = _part1;
100     _part1 = _part1.rearrange(_uzp0, _part3);
101     _part2 = _t0.rearrange(_uzp1, _part2);
102     _part3 = _t1.rearrange(_uzp1, _part3);
103     _t2 = _part4;
104     _part4 = _part4.rearrange(_uzp0, _part6);
105     _t3 = _part5;
106     _part5 = _part5.rearrange(_uzp0, _part7);
107     _part6 = _t2.rearrange(_uzp1, _part6);
108     _part7 = _t3.rearrange(_uzp1, _part7);
109     _t4 = _part8;
110     _part8 = _part8.rearrange(_uzp0, _partA);
111     _t5 = _part9;
112     _part9 = _part9.rearrange(_uzp0, _partB);
113     _partA = _t4.rearrange(_uzp1, _partA);
114     _partB = _t5.rearrange(_uzp1, _partB);
115     _t6 = _partC;
116     _partC = _partC.rearrange(_uzp0, _partE);
117     _t7 = _partD;
118     _partD = _partD.rearrange(_uzp0, _partF);
119     _partE = _t6.rearrange(_uzp1, _partE);
120     _partF = _t7.rearrange(_uzp1, _partF);
121
```

```
122             _t0 = _part0;
123             _part0 = _part0.rearrange(_uzp0, _part4);
124             _t1 = _part1;
125             _part1 = _part1.rearrange(_uzp0, _part5);
126             _t2 = _part2;
127             _part2 = _part2.rearrange(_uzp0, _part6);
128             _t3 = _part3;
129             _part3 = _part3.rearrange(_uzp0, _part7);
130             _part4 = _t0.rearrange(_uzp1, _part4);
131             _part5 = _t1.rearrange(_uzp1, _part5);
132             _part6 = _t2.rearrange(_uzp1, _part6);
133             _part7 = _t3.rearrange(_uzp1, _part7);
134             _t4 = _part8;
135             _part8 = _part8.rearrange(_uzp0, _partC);
136             _t5 = _part9;
137             _part9 = _part9.rearrange(_uzp0, _partD);
138             _t6 = _partA;
139             _partA = _partA.rearrange(_uzp0, _partE);
140             _t7 = _partB;
141             _partB = _partB.rearrange(_uzp0, _partF);
142             _partC = _t4.rearrange(_uzp1, _partC);
143             _partD = _t5.rearrange(_uzp1, _partD);
144             _partE = _t6.rearrange(_uzp1, _partE);
145             _partF = _t7.rearrange(_uzp1, _partF);
146
147             _t0 = _part0;
148             _part0 = _part0.rearrange(_uzp0, _part8);
149             _t1 = _part1;
150             _part1 = _part1.rearrange(_uzp0, _part9);
151             _t2 = _part2;
152             _part2 = _part2.rearrange(_uzp0, _partA);
153             _t3 = _part3;
154             _part3 = _part3.rearrange(_uzp0, _partB);
155             _t4 = _part4;
156             _part4 = _part4.rearrange(_uzp0, _partC);
```

```
157        _t5 = _part5;
158        _part5 = _part5.rearrange(_uzp0, _partD);
159        _t6 = _part6;
160        _part6 = _part6.rearrange(_uzp0, _partE);
161        _t7 = _part7;
162        _part7 = _part7.rearrange(_uzp0, _partF);
163        _part8 = _t0.rearrange(_uzp1, _part8);
164        _part9 = _t1.rearrange(_uzp1, _part9);
165        _partA = _t2.rearrange(_uzp1, _partA);
166        _partB = _t3.rearrange(_uzp1, _partB);
167        _partC = _t4.rearrange(_uzp1, _partC);
168        _partD = _t5.rearrange(_uzp1, _partD);
169        _partE = _t6.rearrange(_uzp1, _partE);
170        _partF = _t7.rearrange(_uzp1, _partF);
171
172        _part1 = _part1.max(_part0);
173        _part3 = _part3.max(_part2);
174        _part5 = _part5.max(_part4);
175        _part7 = _part7.max(_part6);
176        _part9 = _part9.max(_part8);
177        _partB = _partB.max(_partA);
178        _partD = _partD.max(_partC);
179        _partF = _partF.max(_partE);
180
181        _part3 = _part3.max(_part1);
182        _part7 = _part7.max(_part5);
183        _partB = _partB.max(_part9);
184        _partF = _partF.max(_partD);
185
186        _part7 = _part7.max(_part3);
187        _partF = _partF.max(_partB);
188
189    _partF = _partF.max(_part7);
190
191    IntVector _partZ = _prev.slice(vl - 1, _partF);
```

```
192
193          for (int step = 1; step < vl; step <<= 1) {
194            IntVector _shifted = _zero.slice(vl - step, _partZ);
195            _partZ = _partZ.max(_shifted);
196          }
197
198          _part0 = _part0.max(_partZ);
199          _part1 = _part1.max(_partZ);
200          _part3 = _part3.max(_partZ);
201          _part7 = _part7.max(_partZ);
202          _partF = _partF.max(_partZ);
203
204          _partB = _partB.max(_part7);
205
206          _part5 = _part5.max(_part3);
207          _part9 = _part9.max(_part7);
208          _partD = _partD.max(_partB);
209
210          _part2 = _part2.max(_part1);
211          _part4 = _part4.max(_part3);
212          _part6 = _part6.max(_part5);
213          _part8 = _part8.max(_part7);
214          _partA = _partA.max(_part9);
215          _partC = _partC.max(_partB);
216          _partE = _partE.max(_partD);
217
218          _prev = _partF;
219
220          _t0 = _part0;
221          _part0 = _part0.rearrange(_zip0, _part8);
222          _t1 = _part1;
223          _part1 = _part1.rearrange(_zip0, _part9);
224          _t2 = _part2;
225          _part2 = _part2.rearrange(_zip0, _partA);
226          _t3 = _part3;
```

```
227        _part3 = _part3.rearrange(_zip0, _partB);
228        _t4 = _part4;
229        _part4 = _part4.rearrange(_zip0, _partC);
230        _t5 = _part5;
231        _part5 = _part5.rearrange(_zip0, _partD);
232        _t6 = _part6;
233        _part6 = _part6.rearrange(_zip0, _partE);
234        _t7 = _part7;
235        _part7 = _part7.rearrange(_zip0, _partF);
236        _part8 = _t0.rearrange(_zip1, _part8);
237        _part9 = _t1.rearrange(_zip1, _part9);
238        _partA = _t2.rearrange(_zip1, _partA);
239        _partB = _t3.rearrange(_zip1, _partB);
240        _partC = _t4.rearrange(_zip1, _partC);
241        _partD = _t5.rearrange(_zip1, _partD);
242        _partE = _t6.rearrange(_zip1, _partE);
243        _partF = _t7.rearrange(_zip1, _partF);
244
245        _t0 = _part0;
246        _part0 = _part0.rearrange(_zip0, _part4);
247        _t1 = _part1;
248        _part1 = _part1.rearrange(_zip0, _part5);
249        _t2 = _part2;
250        _part2 = _part2.rearrange(_zip0, _part6);
251        _t3 = _part3;
252        _part3 = _part3.rearrange(_zip0, _part7);
253        _part4 = _t0.rearrange(_zip1, _part4);
254        _part5 = _t1.rearrange(_zip1, _part5);
255        _part6 = _t2.rearrange(_zip1, _part6);
256        _part7 = _t3.rearrange(_zip1, _part7);
257        _t4 = _part8;
258        _part8 = _part8.rearrange(_zip0, _partC);
259        _t5 = _part9;
260        _part9 = _part9.rearrange(_zip0, _partD);
261        _t6 = _partA;
```

```
262        _partA = _partA.rearrange(_zip0, _partE);
263        _t7 = _partB;
264        _partB = _partB.rearrange(_zip0, _partF);
265        _partC = _t4.rearrange(_zip1, _partC);
266        _partD = _t5.rearrange(_zip1, _partD);
267        _partE = _t6.rearrange(_zip1, _partE);
268        _partF = _t7.rearrange(_zip1, _partF);
269
270        _t0 = _part0;
271        _part0 = _part0.rearrange(_zip0, _part2);
272        _t1 = _part1;
273        _part1 = _part1.rearrange(_zip0, _part3);
274        _part2 = _t0.rearrange(_zip1, _part2);
275        _part3 = _t1.rearrange(_zip1, _part3);
276        _t2 = _part4;
277        _part4 = _part4.rearrange(_zip0, _part6);
278        _t3 = _part5;
279        _part5 = _part5.rearrange(_zip0, _part7);
280        _part6 = _t2.rearrange(_zip1, _part6);
281        _part7 = _t3.rearrange(_zip1, _part7);
282        _t4 = _part8;
283        _part8 = _part8.rearrange(_zip0, _partA);
284        _t5 = _part9;
285        _part9 = _part9.rearrange(_zip0, _partB);
286        _partA = _t4.rearrange(_zip1, _partA);
287        _partB = _t5.rearrange(_zip1, _partB);
288        _t6 = _partC;
289        _partC = _partC.rearrange(_zip0, _partE);
290        _t7 = _partD;
291        _partD = _partD.rearrange(_zip0, _partF);
292        _partE = _t6.rearrange(_zip1, _partE);
293        _partF = _t7.rearrange(_zip1, _partF);
294
295        _t0 = _part0;
296        _part0 = _part0.rearrange(_zip0, _part1);
```

```
297        _part1 = _t0.rearrange(_zip1, _part1);
298        _t1 = _part2;
299        _part2 = _part2.rearrange(_zip0, _part3);
300        _part3 = _t1.rearrange(_zip1, _part3);
301        _t2 = _part4;
302        _part4 = _part4.rearrange(_zip0, _part5);
303        _part5 = _t2.rearrange(_zip1, _part5);
304        _t3 = _part6;
305        _part6 = _part6.rearrange(_zip0, _part7);
306        _part7 = _t3.rearrange(_zip1, _part7);
307        _t4 = _part8;
308        _part8 = _part8.rearrange(_zip0, _part9);
309        _part9 = _t4.rearrange(_zip1, _part9);
310        _t5 = _partA;
311        _partA = _partA.rearrange(_zip0, _partB);
312        _partB = _t5.rearrange(_zip1, _partB);
313        _t6 = _partC;
314        _partC = _partC.rearrange(_zip0, _partD);
315        _partD = _t6.rearrange(_zip1, _partD);
316        _t7 = _partE;
317        _partE = _partE.rearrange(_zip0, _partF);
318        _partF = _t7.rearrange(_zip1, _partF);
319
320        _part0.intoArray(prefixMax, pos);
321        _part1.intoArray(prefixMax, pos + vl);
322        _part2.intoArray(prefixMax, pos + 2 * vl);
323        _part3.intoArray(prefixMax, pos + 3 * vl);
324        _part4.intoArray(prefixMax, pos + 4 * vl);
325        _part5.intoArray(prefixMax, pos + 5 * vl);
326        _part6.intoArray(prefixMax, pos + 6 * vl);
327        _part7.intoArray(prefixMax, pos + 7 * vl);
328        _part8.intoArray(prefixMax, pos + 8 * vl);
329        _part9.intoArray(prefixMax, pos + 9 * vl);
330        _partA.intoArray(prefixMax, pos + 10 * vl);
331        _partB.intoArray(prefixMax, pos + 11 * vl);
```

```
332        _partC.intoArray(prefixMax, pos + 12 * vl);
333        _partD.intoArray(prefixMax, pos + 13 * vl);
334        _partE.intoArray(prefixMax, pos + 14 * vl);
335        _partF.intoArray(prefixMax, pos + 15 * vl);
336
337      pos += 16 * vl;
338    }
339
340    int acc = _prev.lane(vl - 1);
341    ;
342
343    while (remainder-- > 0) {
344      acc += input[pos];
345      prefixMax[pos++] = acc;
346    }
347  }
348
349  static void computeSuffixMax(int[] input, int[] suffixMax) {
350    int iterations = input.length / (16 * vl);
351    int remainder = input.length % (16 * vl);
352
353    int acc = 0, pos = input.length;
354    while (remainder-- > 0) {
355      acc = Math.max(acc, input[--pos]);
356      suffixMax[pos] = acc;
357    }
358
359    IntVector _prev = IntVector.broadcast(SP, acc);
360
361    for (int i = 0; i < iterations; i++) {
362      pos -= 16 * vl;
363
364      IntVector _part0 = IntVector.fromArray(SP, input, pos);
365      IntVector _part1 =
366        IntVector.fromArray(SP, input, pos + vl);
```

```
367        IntVector _part2 =
368          IntVector.fromArray(SP, input, pos + 2 * vl);
369        IntVector _part3 =
370          IntVector.fromArray(SP, input, pos + 3 * vl);
371        IntVector _part4 =
372          IntVector.fromArray(SP, input, pos + 4 * vl);
373        IntVector _part5 =
374          IntVector.fromArray(SP, input, pos + 5 * vl);
375        IntVector _part6 =
376          IntVector.fromArray(SP, input, pos + 6 * vl);
377        IntVector _part7 =
378          IntVector.fromArray(SP, input, pos + 7 * vl);
379        IntVector _part8 =
380          IntVector.fromArray(SP, input, pos + 8 * vl);
381        IntVector _part9 =
382          IntVector.fromArray(SP, input, pos + 9 * vl);
383        IntVector _partA =
384          IntVector.fromArray(SP, input, pos + 10 * vl);
385        IntVector _partB =
386          IntVector.fromArray(SP, input, pos + 11 * vl);
387        IntVector _partC =
388          IntVector.fromArray(SP, input, pos + 12 * vl);
389        IntVector _partD =
390          IntVector.fromArray(SP, input, pos + 13 * vl);
391        IntVector _partE =
392          IntVector.fromArray(SP, input, pos + 14 * vl);
393        IntVector _partF =
394          IntVector.fromArray(SP, input, pos + 15 * vl);
395
396        IntVector _t0 = _part0;
397        _part0 = _part0.rearrange(_uzp0, _part1);
398        _part1 = _t0.rearrange(_uzp1, _part1);
399        IntVector _t1 = _part2;
400        _part2 = _part2.rearrange(_uzp0, _part3);
401        _part3 = _t1.rearrange(_uzp1, _part3);
```

```
402         IntVector _t2 = _part4;
403         _part4 = _part4.rearrange(_uzp0, _part5);
404         _part5 = _t2.rearrange(_uzp1, _part5);
405         IntVector _t3 = _part6;
406         _part6 = _part6.rearrange(_uzp0, _part7);
407         _part7 = _t3.rearrange(_uzp1, _part7);
408         IntVector _t4 = _part8;
409         _part8 = _part8.rearrange(_uzp0, _part9);
410         _part9 = _t4.rearrange(_uzp1, _part9);
411         IntVector _t5 = _partA;
412         _partA = _partA.rearrange(_uzp0, _partB);
413         _partB = _t5.rearrange(_uzp1, _partB);
414         IntVector _t6 = _partC;
415         _partC = _partC.rearrange(_uzp0, _partD);
416         _partD = _t6.rearrange(_uzp1, _partD);
417         IntVector _t7 = _partE;
418         _partE = _partE.rearrange(_uzp0, _partF);
419         _partF = _t7.rearrange(_uzp1, _partF);
420
421         _t0 = _part0;
422         _part0 = _part0.rearrange(_uzp0, _part2);
423         _t1 = _part1;
424         _part1 = _part1.rearrange(_uzp0, _part3);
425         _part2 = _t0.rearrange(_uzp1, _part2);
426         _part3 = _t1.rearrange(_uzp1, _part3);
427         _t2 = _part4;
428         _part4 = _part4.rearrange(_uzp0, _part6);
429         _t3 = _part5;
430         _part5 = _part5.rearrange(_uzp0, _part7);
431         _part6 = _t2.rearrange(_uzp1, _part6);
432         _part7 = _t3.rearrange(_uzp1, _part7);
433         _t4 = _part8;
434         _part8 = _part8.rearrange(_uzp0, _partA);
435         _t5 = _part9;
436         _part9 = _part9.rearrange(_uzp0, _partB);
```

```
437          _partA = _t4.rearrange(_uzp1, _partA);
438          _partB = _t5.rearrange(_uzp1, _partB);
439          _t6 = _partC;
440          _partC = _partC.rearrange(_uzp0, _partE);
441          _t7 = _partD;
442          _partD = _partD.rearrange(_uzp0, _partF);
443          _partE = _t6.rearrange(_uzp1, _partE);
444          _partF = _t7.rearrange(_uzp1, _partF);
445
446          _t0 = _part0;
447          _part0 = _part0.rearrange(_uzp0, _part4);
448          _t1 = _part1;
449          _part1 = _part1.rearrange(_uzp0, _part5);
450          _t2 = _part2;
451          _part2 = _part2.rearrange(_uzp0, _part6);
452          _t3 = _part3;
453          _part3 = _part3.rearrange(_uzp0, _part7);
454          _part4 = _t0.rearrange(_uzp1, _part4);
455          _part5 = _t1.rearrange(_uzp1, _part5);
456          _part6 = _t2.rearrange(_uzp1, _part6);
457          _part7 = _t3.rearrange(_uzp1, _part7);
458          _t4 = _part8;
459          _part8 = _part8.rearrange(_uzp0, _partC);
460          _t5 = _part9;
461          _part9 = _part9.rearrange(_uzp0, _partD);
462          _t6 = _partA;
463          _partA = _partA.rearrange(_uzp0, _partE);
464          _t7 = _partB;
465          _partB = _partB.rearrange(_uzp0, _partF);
466          _partC = _t4.rearrange(_uzp1, _partC);
467          _partD = _t5.rearrange(_uzp1, _partD);
468          _partE = _t6.rearrange(_uzp1, _partE);
469          _partF = _t7.rearrange(_uzp1, _partF);
470
471          _t0 = _part0;
```

```
472            _part0 = _part0.rearrange(_uzp0, _part8);
473            _t1 = _part1;
474            _part1 = _part1.rearrange(_uzp0, _part9);
475            _t2 = _part2;
476            _part2 = _part2.rearrange(_uzp0, _partA);
477            _t3 = _part3;
478            _part3 = _part3.rearrange(_uzp0, _partB);
479            _t4 = _part4;
480            _part4 = _part4.rearrange(_uzp0, _partC);
481            _t5 = _part5;
482            _part5 = _part5.rearrange(_uzp0, _partD);
483            _t6 = _part6;
484            _part6 = _part6.rearrange(_uzp0, _partE);
485            _t7 = _part7;
486            _part7 = _part7.rearrange(_uzp0, _partF);
487            _part8 = _t0.rearrange(_uzp1, _part8);
488            _part9 = _t1.rearrange(_uzp1, _part9);
489            _partA = _t2.rearrange(_uzp1, _partA);
490            _partB = _t3.rearrange(_uzp1, _partB);
491            _partC = _t4.rearrange(_uzp1, _partC);
492            _partD = _t5.rearrange(_uzp1, _partD);
493            _partE = _t6.rearrange(_uzp1, _partE);
494            _partF = _t7.rearrange(_uzp1, _partF);
495
496            _partE = _partE.max(_partF);
497            _partC = _partC.max(_partD);
498            _partA = _partA.max(_partB);
499            _part8 = _part8.max(_part9);
500            _part6 = _part6.max(_part7);
501            _part4 = _part4.max(_part5);
502            _part2 = _part2.max(_part3);
503            _part0 = _part0.max(_part1);
504
505            _partC = _partC.max(_partE);
506            _part8 = _part8.max(_partA);
```

```
507       _part4 = _part4.max(_part6);
508       _part0 = _part0.max(_part2);
509
510       _part8 = _part8.max(_partC);
511       _part0 = _part0.max(_part4);
512
513       _part0 = _part0.max(_part8);
514
515       IntVector _partZ = _part0.slice(1, _prev);
516
517       for (int step = 1; step < vl; step <<= 1) {
518         IntVector _shifted = _partZ.slice(step, _zero);
519         _partZ = _partZ.max(_shifted);
520       }
521
522       _part0 = _part0.max(_partZ);
523       _part8 = _part8.max(_partZ);
524       _partC = _partC.max(_partZ);
525       _partE = _partE.max(_partZ);
526       _partF = _partF.max(_partZ);
527
528       _part4 = _part4.max(_part8);
529
530       _partA = _partA.max(_partC);
531       _part6 = _part6.max(_part8);
532       _part2 = _part2.max(_part4);
533
534       _partD = _partD.max(_partE);
535       _partB = _partB.max(_partC);
536       _part9 = _part9.max(_partA);
537       _part7 = _part7.max(_part8);
538       _part5 = _part5.max(_part6);
539       _part3 = _part3.max(_part4);
540       _part1 = _part1.max(_part2);
541
```

```
542            _prev = _part0;
543
544            _t0 = _part0;
545            _part0 = _part0.rearrange(_zip0, _part8);
546            _t1 = _part1;
547            _part1 = _part1.rearrange(_zip0, _part9);
548            _t2 = _part2;
549            _part2 = _part2.rearrange(_zip0, _partA);
550            _t3 = _part3;
551            _part3 = _part3.rearrange(_zip0, _partB);
552            _t4 = _part4;
553            _part4 = _part4.rearrange(_zip0, _partC);
554            _t5 = _part5;
555            _part5 = _part5.rearrange(_zip0, _partD);
556            _t6 = _part6;
557            _part6 = _part6.rearrange(_zip0, _partE);
558            _t7 = _part7;
559            _part7 = _part7.rearrange(_zip0, _partF);
560            _part8 = _t0.rearrange(_zip1, _part8);
561            _part9 = _t1.rearrange(_zip1, _part9);
562            _partA = _t2.rearrange(_zip1, _partA);
563            _partB = _t3.rearrange(_zip1, _partB);
564            _partC = _t4.rearrange(_zip1, _partC);
565            _partD = _t5.rearrange(_zip1, _partD);
566            _partE = _t6.rearrange(_zip1, _partE);
567            _partF = _t7.rearrange(_zip1, _partF);
568
569            _t0 = _part0;
570            _part0 = _part0.rearrange(_zip0, _part4);
571            _t1 = _part1;
572            _part1 = _part1.rearrange(_zip0, _part5);
573            _t2 = _part2;
574            _part2 = _part2.rearrange(_zip0, _part6);
575            _t3 = _part3;
576            _part3 = _part3.rearrange(_zip0, _part7);
```

```
577        _part4 = _t0.rearrange(_zip1, _part4);
578        _part5 = _t1.rearrange(_zip1, _part5);
579        _part6 = _t2.rearrange(_zip1, _part6);
580        _part7 = _t3.rearrange(_zip1, _part7);
581        _t4 = _part8;
582        _part8 = _part8.rearrange(_zip0, _partC);
583        _t5 = _part9;
584        _part9 = _part9.rearrange(_zip0, _partD);
585        _t6 = _partA;
586        _partA = _partA.rearrange(_zip0, _partE);
587        _t7 = _partB;
588        _partB = _partB.rearrange(_zip0, _partF);
589        _partC = _t4.rearrange(_zip1, _partC);
590        _partD = _t5.rearrange(_zip1, _partD);
591        _partE = _t6.rearrange(_zip1, _partE);
592        _partF = _t7.rearrange(_zip1, _partF);
593
594        _t0 = _part0;
595        _part0 = _part0.rearrange(_zip0, _part2);
596        _t1 = _part1;
597        _part1 = _part1.rearrange(_zip0, _part3);
598        _part2 = _t0.rearrange(_zip1, _part2);
599        _part3 = _t1.rearrange(_zip1, _part3);
600        _t2 = _part4;
601        _part4 = _part4.rearrange(_zip0, _part6);
602        _t3 = _part5;
603        _part5 = _part5.rearrange(_zip0, _part7);
604        _part6 = _t2.rearrange(_zip1, _part6);
605        _part7 = _t3.rearrange(_zip1, _part7);
606        _t4 = _part8;
607        _part8 = _part8.rearrange(_zip0, _partA);
608        _t5 = _part9;
609        _part9 = _part9.rearrange(_zip0, _partB);
610        _partA = _t4.rearrange(_zip1, _partA);
611        _partB = _t5.rearrange(_zip1, _partB);
```

```
612            _t6 = _partC;
613            _partC = _partC.rearrange(_zip0, _partE);
614            _t7 = _partD;
615            _partD = _partD.rearrange(_zip0, _partF);
616            _partE = _t6.rearrange(_zip1, _partE);
617            _partF = _t7.rearrange(_zip1, _partF);
618
619            _t0 = _part0;
620            _part0 = _part0.rearrange(_zip0, _part1);
621            _part1 = _t0.rearrange(_zip1, _part1);
622            _t1 = _part2;
623            _part2 = _part2.rearrange(_zip0, _part3);
624            _part3 = _t1.rearrange(_zip1, _part3);
625            _t2 = _part4;
626            _part4 = _part4.rearrange(_zip0, _part5);
627            _part5 = _t2.rearrange(_zip1, _part5);
628            _t3 = _part6;
629            _part6 = _part6.rearrange(_zip0, _part7);
630            _part7 = _t3.rearrange(_zip1, _part7);
631            _t4 = _part8;
632            _part8 = _part8.rearrange(_zip0, _part9);
633            _part9 = _t4.rearrange(_zip1, _part9);
634            _t5 = _partA;
635            _partA = _partA.rearrange(_zip0, _partB);
636            _partB = _t5.rearrange(_zip1, _partB);
637            _t6 = _partC;
638            _partC = _partC.rearrange(_zip0, _partD);
639            _partD = _t6.rearrange(_zip1, _partD);
640            _t7 = _partE;
641            _partE = _partE.rearrange(_zip0, _partF);
642            _partF = _t7.rearrange(_zip1, _partF);
643
644            _part0.intoArray(suffixMax, pos);
645            _part1.intoArray(suffixMax, pos + vl);
646            _part2.intoArray(suffixMax, pos + 2 * vl);
```

```
647            _part3.intoArray(suffixMax, pos + 3 * vl);
648            _part4.intoArray(suffixMax, pos + 4 * vl);
649            _part5.intoArray(suffixMax, pos + 5 * vl);
650            _part6.intoArray(suffixMax, pos + 6 * vl);
651            _part7.intoArray(suffixMax, pos + 7 * vl);
652            _part8.intoArray(suffixMax, pos + 8 * vl);
653            _part9.intoArray(suffixMax, pos + 9 * vl);
654            _partA.intoArray(suffixMax, pos + 10 * vl);
655            _partB.intoArray(suffixMax, pos + 11 * vl);
656            _partC.intoArray(suffixMax, pos + 12 * vl);
657            _partD.intoArray(suffixMax, pos + 13 * vl);
658            _partE.intoArray(suffixMax, pos + 14 * vl);
659            _partF.intoArray(suffixMax, pos + 15 * vl);
660        }
661      }
662    }
663
```

- Lines 364–394 load 16 vectors.

- Lines 396–494 pivot the 16 vectors.

- Lines 496–513 perform the upsweep.

- Lines 517–526 perform suffix sum correction at power-of-two positions.

- Lines 528–540 clean up data at positions between powers of two.

- Lines 544–642 pivot the data back.

- Lines 644–659 store the results into the array.

Memoization

The 16-way unrolled optimal scan is impressive. The scan itself uses so few operations that it is lost against the backdrop of the code performing vector pivot. Since now the pivot consumes most of the program's time and energy, we need to optimize it.

- After pivoting vectors on the program's first pass, we save the pivot result to memory. Then on the second pass, instead of re-pivoting the original vectors, we simply load the already-pivoted vectors from memory. This technique of saving intermediate computation results for reuse is called **memoization**—caching computed results.

- The cumulative sum computation result does not need to be pivoted at all. The third pass result does not depend on data order, as long as all three components—source data, prefix sum, and suffix sum—are loaded in the same order. We obtained pivoted source data through memoization, so we can leave the cumulative sums in pivoted form as well.

- Since memoization somewhat increased memory load, we can compensate for it by merging the second and third passes. Thus, the suffix sum will not be written to memory and then read from there at all, but will be immediately used in computations.

```
1    package com.nonpareilcoder.realleetcode;
2
3    import jdk.incubator.vector.*;
4
5    import static jdk.incubator.vector.VectorOperators.*;
6
7    public class TrappingRainWaterMemoizedX16 {
8      public static int trap(int[] input) {
9        int[] prefixMax = new int[input.length];
10       int[] pivotedInput = new int[input.length];
11
12       computePrefixMax(input, pivotedInput, prefixMax);
13       return computeSuffixMaxFused(pivotedInput, prefixMax);
14     }
15
16     static final VectorSpecies<Integer> SP =
17       IntVector.SPECIES_PREFERRED;
18     static final int vl = SP.length();
19
```

```
20    static final IntVector _zero = IntVector.broadcast(SP, 0);
21
22    static final VectorShuffle<Integer> _uzp0 =
23      VectorShuffle.makeUnzip(SP, 0);
24    static final VectorShuffle<Integer> _uzp1 =
25      VectorShuffle.makeUnzip(SP, 1);
26
27    static void computePrefixMax(
28      int[] input, int[] pivotedInput, int[] prefixMax) {
29      int iterations = input.length / (16 * vl);
30      int remainder = input.length % (16 * vl);
31
32      var _prev = _zero;
33
34      int pos = 0;
35      for (int i = 0; i < iterations; i++) {
36        var _part0 = IntVector.fromArray(SP, input, pos);
37        var _part1 = IntVector.fromArray(SP, input, pos + vl);
38        var _part2 = IntVector.fromArray(SP, input, pos + 2 * vl);
39        var _part3 = IntVector.fromArray(SP, input, pos + 3 * vl);
40        var _part4 = IntVector.fromArray(SP, input, pos + 4 * vl);
41        var _part5 = IntVector.fromArray(SP, input, pos + 5 * vl);
42        var _part6 = IntVector.fromArray(SP, input, pos + 6 * vl);
43        var _part7 = IntVector.fromArray(SP, input, pos + 7 * vl);
44        var _part8 = IntVector.fromArray(SP, input, pos + 8 * vl);
45        var _part9 = IntVector.fromArray(SP, input, pos + 9 * vl);
46        var _partA = IntVector.fromArray(SP, input, pos + 10 * vl);
47        var _partB = IntVector.fromArray(SP, input, pos + 11 * vl);
48        var _partC = IntVector.fromArray(SP, input, pos + 12 * vl);
49        var _partD = IntVector.fromArray(SP, input, pos + 13 * vl);
50        var _partE = IntVector.fromArray(SP, input, pos + 14 * vl);
51        var _partF = IntVector.fromArray(SP, input, pos + 15 * vl);
52
53        var _t0 = _part0;
54        _part0 = _part0.rearrange(_uzp0, _part1);
```

```
55        _part1 = _t0.rearrange(_uzp1, _part1);
56        var _t1 = _part2;
57        _part2 = _part2.rearrange(_uzp0, _part3);
58        _part3 = _t1.rearrange(_uzp1, _part3);
59        var _t2 = _part4;
60        _part4 = _part4.rearrange(_uzp0, _part5);
61        _part5 = _t2.rearrange(_uzp1, _part5);
62        var _t3 = _part6;
63        _part6 = _part6.rearrange(_uzp0, _part7);
64        _part7 = _t3.rearrange(_uzp1, _part7);
65        var _t4 = _part8;
66        _part8 = _part8.rearrange(_uzp0, _part9);
67        _part9 = _t4.rearrange(_uzp1, _part9);
68        var _t5 = _partA;
69        _partA = _partA.rearrange(_uzp0, _partB);
70        _partB = _t5.rearrange(_uzp1, _partB);
71        var _t6 = _partC;
72        _partC = _partC.rearrange(_uzp0, _partD);
73        _partD = _t6.rearrange(_uzp1, _partD);
74        var _t7 = _partE;
75        _partE = _partE.rearrange(_uzp0, _partF);
76        _partF = _t7.rearrange(_uzp1, _partF);
77
78        _t0 = _part0;
79        _part0 = _part0.rearrange(_uzp0, _part2);
80        _t1 = _part1;
81        _part1 = _part1.rearrange(_uzp0, _part3);
82        _part2 = _t0.rearrange(_uzp1, _part2);
83        _part3 = _t1.rearrange(_uzp1, _part3);
84        _t2 = _part4;
85        _part4 = _part4.rearrange(_uzp0, _part6);
86        _t3 = _part5;
87        _part5 = _part5.rearrange(_uzp0, _part7);
88        _part6 = _t2.rearrange(_uzp1, _part6);
89        _part7 = _t3.rearrange(_uzp1, _part7);
```

```
 90         _t4 = _part8;
 91         _part8 = _part8.rearrange(_uzp0, _partA);
 92         _t5 = _part9;
 93         _part9 = _part9.rearrange(_uzp0, _partB);
 94         _partA = _t4.rearrange(_uzp1, _partA);
 95         _partB = _t5.rearrange(_uzp1, _partB);
 96         _t6 = _partC;
 97         _partC = _partC.rearrange(_uzp0, _partE);
 98         _t7 = _partD;
 99         _partD = _partD.rearrange(_uzp0, _partF);
100         _partE = _t6.rearrange(_uzp1, _partE);
101         _partF = _t7.rearrange(_uzp1, _partF);
102
103         _t0 = _part0;
104         _part0 = _part0.rearrange(_uzp0, _part4);
105         _t1 = _part1;
106         _part1 = _part1.rearrange(_uzp0, _part5);
107         _t2 = _part2;
108         _part2 = _part2.rearrange(_uzp0, _part6);
109         _t3 = _part3;
110         _part3 = _part3.rearrange(_uzp0, _part7);
111         _part4 = _t0.rearrange(_uzp1, _part4);
112         _part5 = _t1.rearrange(_uzp1, _part5);
113         _part6 = _t2.rearrange(_uzp1, _part6);
114         _part7 = _t3.rearrange(_uzp1, _part7);
115         _t4 = _part8;
116         _part8 = _part8.rearrange(_uzp0, _partC);
117         _t5 = _part9;
118         _part9 = _part9.rearrange(_uzp0, _partD);
119         _t6 = _partA;
120         _partA = _partA.rearrange(_uzp0, _partE);
121         _t7 = _partB;
122         _partB = _partB.rearrange(_uzp0, _partF);
123         _partC = _t4.rearrange(_uzp1, _partC);
124         _partD = _t5.rearrange(_uzp1, _partD);
```

```
125             _partE = _t6.rearrange(_uzp1, _partE);
126             _partF = _t7.rearrange(_uzp1, _partF);
127
128             _t0 = _part0;
129             _part0 = _part0.rearrange(_uzp0, _part8);
130             _t1 = _part1;
131             _part1 = _part1.rearrange(_uzp0, _part9);
132             _t2 = _part2;
133             _part2 = _part2.rearrange(_uzp0, _partA);
134             _t3 = _part3;
135             _part3 = _part3.rearrange(_uzp0, _partB);
136             _t4 = _part4;
137             _part4 = _part4.rearrange(_uzp0, _partC);
138             _t5 = _part5;
139             _part5 = _part5.rearrange(_uzp0, _partD);
140             _t6 = _part6;
141             _part6 = _part6.rearrange(_uzp0, _partE);
142             _t7 = _part7;
143             _part7 = _part7.rearrange(_uzp0, _partF);
144             _part8 = _t0.rearrange(_uzp1, _part8);
145             _part9 = _t1.rearrange(_uzp1, _part9);
146             _partA = _t2.rearrange(_uzp1, _partA);
147             _partB = _t3.rearrange(_uzp1, _partB);
148             _partC = _t4.rearrange(_uzp1, _partC);
149             _partD = _t5.rearrange(_uzp1, _partD);
150             _partE = _t6.rearrange(_uzp1, _partE);
151             _partF = _t7.rearrange(_uzp1, _partF);
152
153             _part0.intoArray(pivotedInput, pos);
154             _part1.intoArray(pivotedInput, pos + vl);
155             _part2.intoArray(pivotedInput, pos + 2 * vl);
156             _part3.intoArray(pivotedInput, pos + 3 * vl);
157             _part4.intoArray(pivotedInput, pos + 4 * vl);
158             _part5.intoArray(pivotedInput, pos + 5 * vl);
159             _part6.intoArray(pivotedInput, pos + 6 * vl);
```

```
160        _part7.intoArray(pivotedInput, pos + 7 * vl);
161        _part8.intoArray(pivotedInput, pos + 8 * vl);
162        _part9.intoArray(pivotedInput, pos + 9 * vl);
163        _partA.intoArray(pivotedInput, pos + 10 * vl);
164        _partB.intoArray(pivotedInput, pos + 11 * vl);
165        _partC.intoArray(pivotedInput, pos + 12 * vl);
166        _partD.intoArray(pivotedInput, pos + 13 * vl);
167        _partE.intoArray(pivotedInput, pos + 14 * vl);
168        _partF.intoArray(pivotedInput, pos + 15 * vl);
169
170        _part1 = _part1.max(_part0);
171        _part3 = _part3.max(_part2);
172        _part5 = _part5.max(_part4);
173        _part7 = _part7.max(_part6);
174        _part9 = _part9.max(_part8);
175        _partB = _partB.max(_partA);
176        _partD = _partD.max(_partC);
177        _partF = _partF.max(_partE);
178
179        _part3 = _part3.max(_part1);
180        _part7 = _part7.max(_part5);
181        _partB = _partB.max(_part9);
182        _partF = _partF.max(_partD);
183
184        _part7 = _part7.max(_part3);
185        _partF = _partF.max(_partB);
186
187        _partF = _partF.max(_part7);
188
189      var _partZ = _prev.slice(vl - 1, _partF);
190
191      for (int step = 1; step < vl; step <<= 1) {
192        var _shifted = _zero.slice(vl - step, _partZ);
193        _partZ = _partZ.max(_shifted);
194      }
```

```
195
196            _part0 = _part0.max(_partZ);
197            _part1 = _part1.max(_partZ);
198            _part3 = _part3.max(_partZ);
199            _part7 = _part7.max(_partZ);
200            _partF = _partF.max(_partZ);
201
202            _partB = _partB.max(_part7);
203
204            _part5 = _part5.max(_part3);
205            _part9 = _part9.max(_part7);
206            _partD = _partD.max(_partB);
207
208            _part2 = _part2.max(_part1);
209            _part4 = _part4.max(_part3);
210            _part6 = _part6.max(_part5);
211            _part8 = _part8.max(_part7);
212            _partA = _partA.max(_part9);
213            _partC = _partC.max(_partB);
214            _partE = _partE.max(_partD);
215
216            _prev = _partF;
217
218            _part0.intoArray(prefixMax, pos);
219            _part1.intoArray(prefixMax, pos + vl);
220            _part2.intoArray(prefixMax, pos + 2 * vl);
221            _part3.intoArray(prefixMax, pos + 3 * vl);
222            _part4.intoArray(prefixMax, pos + 4 * vl);
223            _part5.intoArray(prefixMax, pos + 5 * vl);
224            _part6.intoArray(prefixMax, pos + 6 * vl);
225            _part7.intoArray(prefixMax, pos + 7 * vl);
226            _part8.intoArray(prefixMax, pos + 8 * vl);
227            _part9.intoArray(prefixMax, pos + 9 * vl);
228            _partA.intoArray(prefixMax, pos + 10 * vl);
229            _partB.intoArray(prefixMax, pos + 11 * vl);
```

```
230        _partC.intoArray(prefixMax, pos + 12 * vl);
231        _partD.intoArray(prefixMax, pos + 13 * vl);
232        _partE.intoArray(prefixMax, pos + 14 * vl);
233        _partF.intoArray(prefixMax, pos + 15 * vl);
234
235      pos += 16 * vl;
236    }
237
238    int acc = _prev.lane(vl - 1);
239    ;
240
241    while (remainder-- > 0) {
242      pivotedInput[pos] = input[pos];
243      acc += input[pos];
244      prefixMax[pos++] = acc;
245    }
246  }
247
248  static int computeSuffixMaxFused(
249    int[] pivotedInput, int[] prefixMax) {
250    int iterations = pivotedInput.length / (16 * vl);
251    int remainder = pivotedInput.length % (16 * vl);
252
253    int trapped = 0, acc = 0;
254    int pos = pivotedInput.length;
255    while (remainder-- > 0) {
256      acc = Math.max(acc, pivotedInput[--pos]);
257      int minVal = Math.min(prefixMax[pos], acc);
258      trapped += minVal - pivotedInput[pos];
259    }
260
261    var _trapped = IntVector.zero(SP);
262    var _prev = IntVector.broadcast(SP, acc);
263
264    for (int i = 0; i < iterations; i++) {
```

```
265            pos -= 16 * vl;
266
267            int[] pi = pivotedInput;
268            var _part0 = IntVector.fromArray(SP, pi, pos);
269            var _part1 = IntVector.fromArray(SP, pi, pos + vl);
270            var _part2 = IntVector.fromArray(SP, pi, pos + 2 * vl);
271            var _part3 = IntVector.fromArray(SP, pi, pos + 3 * vl);
272            var _part4 = IntVector.fromArray(SP, pi, pos + 4 * vl);
273            var _part5 = IntVector.fromArray(SP, pi, pos + 5 * vl);
274            var _part6 = IntVector.fromArray(SP, pi, pos + 6 * vl);
275            var _part7 = IntVector.fromArray(SP, pi, pos + 7 * vl);
276            var _part8 = IntVector.fromArray(SP, pi, pos + 8 * vl);
277            var _part9 = IntVector.fromArray(SP, pi, pos + 9 * vl);
278            var _partA = IntVector.fromArray(SP, pi, pos + 10 * vl);
279            var _partB = IntVector.fromArray(SP, pi, pos + 11 * vl);
280            var _partC = IntVector.fromArray(SP, pi, pos + 12 * vl);
281            var _partD = IntVector.fromArray(SP, pi, pos + 13 * vl);
282            var _partE = IntVector.fromArray(SP, pi, pos + 14 * vl);
283            var _partF = IntVector.fromArray(SP, pi, pos + 15 * vl);
284
285            _partE = _partE.max(_partF);
286            _partC = _partC.max(_partD);
287            _partA = _partA.max(_partB);
288            _part8 = _part8.max(_part9);
289            _part6 = _part6.max(_part7);
290            _part4 = _part4.max(_part5);
291            _part2 = _part2.max(_part3);
292            _part0 = _part0.max(_part1);
293
294            _partC = _partC.max(_partE);
295            _part8 = _part8.max(_partA);
296            _part4 = _part4.max(_part6);
297            _part0 = _part0.max(_part2);
298
299            _part8 = _part8.max(_partC);
```

```
300          _part0 = _part0.max(_part4);

301

302          _part0 = _part0.max(_part8);

303

304          var _partZ = _part0.slice(1, _prev);

305

306          for (int step = 1; step < vl; step <<= 1) {
307            var _shifted = _partZ.slice(step, _zero);
308            _partZ = _partZ.max(_shifted);
309          }

310

311          _part0 = _part0.max(_partZ);
312          _part8 = _part8.max(_partZ);
313          _partC = _partC.max(_partZ);
314          _partE = _partE.max(_partZ);
315          _partF = _partF.max(_partZ);

316

317          _part4 = _part4.max(_part8);

318

319          _partA = _partA.max(_partC);
320          _part6 = _part6.max(_part8);
321          _part2 = _part2.max(_part4);

322

323          _partD = _partD.max(_partE);
324          _partB = _partB.max(_partC);
325          _part9 = _part9.max(_partA);
326          _part7 = _part7.max(_part8);
327          _part5 = _part5.max(_part6);
328          _part3 = _part3.max(_part4);
329          _part1 = _part1.max(_part2);

330

331          _prev = _part0;

332

333          var _pf0 = IntVector.fromArray(SP, prefixMax, pos);
334          var _pf1 = IntVector.fromArray(SP, prefixMax, pos + vl);
```

```
335        var _pf2 = IntVector.fromArray(SP, prefixMax, pos + 2 * vl);
336        var _pf3 = IntVector.fromArray(SP, prefixMax, pos + 3 * vl);
337        var _pf4 = IntVector.fromArray(SP, prefixMax, pos + 4 * vl);
338        var _pf5 = IntVector.fromArray(SP, prefixMax, pos + 5 * vl);
339        var _pf6 = IntVector.fromArray(SP, prefixMax, pos + 6 * vl);
340        var _pf7 = IntVector.fromArray(SP, prefixMax, pos + 7 * vl);
341        var _pf8 = IntVector.fromArray(SP, prefixMax, pos + 8 * vl);
342        var _pf9 = IntVector.fromArray(SP, prefixMax, pos + 9 * vl);
343        var _pfA = IntVector.fromArray(SP, prefixMax, pos + 10 * vl);
344        var _pfB = IntVector.fromArray(SP, prefixMax, pos + 11 * vl);
345        var _pfC = IntVector.fromArray(SP, prefixMax, pos + 12 * vl);
346        var _pfD = IntVector.fromArray(SP, prefixMax, pos + 13 * vl);
347        var _pfE = IntVector.fromArray(SP, prefixMax, pos + 14 * vl);
348        var _pfF = IntVector.fromArray(SP, prefixMax, pos + 15 * vl);
349
350        var _pv0 = IntVector.fromArray(SP, pi, pos);
351        var _pv1 = IntVector.fromArray(SP, pi, pos + vl);
352        var _pv2 = IntVector.fromArray(SP, pi, pos + 2 * vl);
353        var _pv3 = IntVector.fromArray(SP, pi, pos + 3 * vl);
354        var _pv4 = IntVector.fromArray(SP, pi, pos + 4 * vl);
355        var _pv5 = IntVector.fromArray(SP, pi, pos + 5 * vl);
356        var _pv6 = IntVector.fromArray(SP, pi, pos + 6 * vl);
357        var _pv7 = IntVector.fromArray(SP, pi, pos + 7 * vl);
358        var _pv8 = IntVector.fromArray(SP, pi, pos + 8 * vl);
359        var _pv9 = IntVector.fromArray(SP, pi, pos + 9 * vl);
360        var _pvA = IntVector.fromArray(SP, pi, pos + 10 * vl);
361        var _pvB = IntVector.fromArray(SP, pi, pos + 11 * vl);
362        var _pvC = IntVector.fromArray(SP, pi, pos + 12 * vl);
363        var _pvD = IntVector.fromArray(SP, pi, pos + 13 * vl);
364        var _pvE = IntVector.fromArray(SP, pi, pos + 14 * vl);
365        var _pvF = IntVector.fromArray(SP, pi, pos + 15 * vl);
366
367    _part0 = _part0.min(_pf0).sub(_pv0);
368    _part1 = _part1.min(_pf1).sub(_pv1);
369    _part2 = _part2.min(_pf2).sub(_pv2);
```

```
370        _part3 = _part3.min(_pf3).sub(_pv3);
371        _part4 = _part4.min(_pf4).sub(_pv4);
372        _part5 = _part5.min(_pf5).sub(_pv5);
373        _part6 = _part6.min(_pf6).sub(_pv6);
374        _part7 = _part7.min(_pf7).sub(_pv7);
375        _part8 = _part8.min(_pf8).sub(_pv8);
376        _part9 = _part9.min(_pf9).sub(_pv9);
377        _partA = _partA.min(_pfA).sub(_pvA);
378        _partB = _partB.min(_pfB).sub(_pvB);
379        _partC = _partC.min(_pfC).sub(_pvC);
380        _partD = _partD.min(_pfD).sub(_pvD);
381        _partE = _partE.min(_pfE).sub(_pvE);
382        _partF = _partF.min(_pfF).sub(_pvF);
383
384        _part0 = _part0.add(_part1);
385        _part2 = _part2.add(_part3);
386        _part4 = _part4.add(_part5);
387        _part6 = _part6.add(_part7);
388        _part8 = _part8.add(_part9);
389        _partA = _partA.add(_partB);
390        _partC = _partC.add(_partD);
391        _partE = _partE.add(_partF);
392
393        _part0 = _part0.add(_part2);
394        _part4 = _part4.add(_part6);
395        _part8 = _part8.add(_partA);
396        _partC = _partC.add(_partE);
397
398        _part0 = _part0.add(_part4);
399        _part8 = _part8.add(_partC);
400
401        _trapped = _trapped.add(_part0);
402        _trapped = _trapped.add(_part8);
403    }
404
405    trapped += _trapped.reduceLanes(ADD);
```

```
406
407        return trapped;
408      }
409    }
410
```

- Lines 36–51 load 16 vectors of source data.

- Lines 53–151 pivot all 16 vectors.

- Lines 153–168 save the pivoted vectors to memory for reuse. This is memoization proper.

- Lines 170–214 optimally compute the prefix sum.

- Lines 218–233 store the prefix sum to memory still in pivoted format.

- Lines 267–283 load the pivoted source data.

- Lines 285–329 compute the suffix sum without any preprocessing.

- Lines 333–402 are essentially the third pass through the array, unrolled by 16 and merged with the second pass, the suffix sum computation. Notice how, with unrolling, the addition operation turned into a reduction in lines 384–402.

Memoization allowed us to reduce four vector pivots to just one. The code turned out fast and beautiful in its own way, though somewhat bulky. When writing real code, one must often find a balance between code readability and efficiency. I choose efficiency, unafraid of applying additional intellectual effort.

Mini Algorithm

The universal vector pivot algorithm is complex. If you are working with short vectors of fixed length, a lightweight variant of the algorithm can be used. Here is a variation for 128 bits.

```
1    package com.nonpareilcoder.realleetcode;
2
3    import jdk.incubator.vector.*;
4
```

```
 5   import static jdk.incubator.vector.VectorOperators.*;
 6
 7   public class TrappingRainWater128X16 {
 8     public static int trap(int[] input) {
 9       int[] prefixMax = new int[input.length];
10       int[] pivotedInput = new int[input.length];
11
12       computePrefixMax(input, pivotedInput, prefixMax);
13       return computeSuffixMaxFused(pivotedInput, prefixMax);
14     }
15
16     static final VectorSpecies<Integer> SP =
17       IntVector.SPECIES_128;
18     static final int vl = SP.length();
19
20     static final IntVector _zero = IntVector.broadcast(SP, 0);
21
22     static final VectorShuffle<Integer> _zip0 =
23       VectorShuffle.makeZip(SP, 0);
24     static final VectorShuffle<Integer> _zip1 =
25       VectorShuffle.makeZip(SP, 1);
26
27     static void computePrefixMax(
28       int[] input, int[] pivotedInput, int[] prefixMax) {
29       int iterations = input.length / (16 * vl);
30       int remainder = input.length % (16 * vl);
31
32       var _prev = _zero;
33
34       int pos = 0;
35       for (int i = 0; i < iterations; i++) {
36         var _part0 = IntVector.fromArray(SP, input, pos + 0 * vl);
37         var _part1 = IntVector.fromArray(SP, input, pos + 1 * vl);
38         var _part2 = IntVector.fromArray(SP, input, pos + 2 * vl);
39         var _part3 = IntVector.fromArray(SP, input, pos + 3 * vl);
```

```
40        var _part4 = IntVector.fromArray(SP, input, pos + 4 * vl);
41        var _part5 = IntVector.fromArray(SP, input, pos + 5 * vl);
42        var _part6 = IntVector.fromArray(SP, input, pos + 6 * vl);
43        var _part7 = IntVector.fromArray(SP, input, pos + 7 * vl);
44        var _part8 = IntVector.fromArray(SP, input, pos + 8 * vl);
45        var _part9 = IntVector.fromArray(SP, input, pos + 9 * vl);
46        var _partA = IntVector.fromArray(SP, input, pos + 10 * vl);
47        var _partB = IntVector.fromArray(SP, input, pos + 11 * vl);
48        var _partC = IntVector.fromArray(SP, input, pos + 12 * vl);
49        var _partD = IntVector.fromArray(SP, input, pos + 13 * vl);
50        var _partE = IntVector.fromArray(SP, input, pos + 14 * vl);
51        var _partF = IntVector.fromArray(SP, input, pos + 15 * vl);
52
53
54        var _t0 = _part0;
55        _part0 = _part0.rearrange(_zip0, _part8);
56        _part8 = _t0.rearrange(_zip1, _part8);
57        var _t1 = _part1;
58        _part1 = _part1.rearrange(_zip0, _part9);
59        _part9 = _t1.rearrange(_zip1, _part9);
60        var _t2 = _part2;
61        _part2 = _part2.rearrange(_zip0, _partA);
62        _partA = _t2.rearrange(_zip1, _partA);
63        var _t3 = _part3;
64        _part3 = _part3.rearrange(_zip0, _partB);
65        _partB = _t3.rearrange(_zip1, _partB);
66        var _t4 = _part4;
67        _part4 = _part4.rearrange(_zip0, _partC);
68        _partC = _t4.rearrange(_zip1, _partC);
69        var _t5 = _part5;
70        _part5 = _part5.rearrange(_zip0, _partD);
71        _partD = _t5.rearrange(_zip1, _partD);
72        var _t6 = _part6;
73        _part6 = _part6.rearrange(_zip0, _partE);
74        _partE = _t6.rearrange(_zip1, _partE);
```

```
75        var _t7 = _part7;
76        _part7 = _part7.rearrange(_zip0, _partF);
77        _partF = _t7.rearrange(_zip1, _partF);
78
79
80        _t0 = _part0;
81        _t1 = _part1;
82        _t2 = _part2;
83        _t3 = _part3;
84        _t4 = _part8;
85        _t5 = _part9;
86        _t6 = _partA;
87        _t7 = _partB;
88        var _t8 = _part7;
89
90        _part0 = _t0.rearrange(_zip0, _part4);
91        _part1 = _t0.rearrange(_zip1, _part4);
92
93        _part4 = _t1.rearrange(_zip0, _part5);
94        _part5 = _t1.rearrange(_zip1, _part5);
95
96        _part2 = _t4.rearrange(_zip0, _partC);
97        _part3 = _t4.rearrange(_zip1, _partC);
98
99        _part8 = _t2.rearrange(_zip0, _part6);
100       _part9 = _t2.rearrange(_zip1, _part6);
101
102       _part6 = _t5.rearrange(_zip0, _partD);
103       _part7 = _t5.rearrange(_zip1, _partD);
104
105       _partC = _t3.rearrange(_zip0, _t8);
106       _partD = _t3.rearrange(_zip1, _t8);
107
108       _partA = _t6.rearrange(_zip0, _partE);
109       _partB = _t6.rearrange(_zip1, _partE);
```

```
110
111            _partE = _t7.rearrange(_zip0, _partF);
112            _partF = _t7.rearrange(_zip1, _partF);
113
114
115            _part0.intoArray(pivotedInput, pos + 0 * vl);
116            _part1.intoArray(pivotedInput, pos + 1 * vl);
117            _part2.intoArray(pivotedInput, pos + 2 * vl);
118            _part3.intoArray(pivotedInput, pos + 3 * vl);
119            _part4.intoArray(pivotedInput, pos + 4 * vl);
120            _part5.intoArray(pivotedInput, pos + 5 * vl);
121            _part6.intoArray(pivotedInput, pos + 6 * vl);
122            _part7.intoArray(pivotedInput, pos + 7 * vl);
123            _part8.intoArray(pivotedInput, pos + 8 * vl);
124            _part9.intoArray(pivotedInput, pos + 9 * vl);
125            _partA.intoArray(pivotedInput, pos + 10 * vl);
126            _partB.intoArray(pivotedInput, pos + 11 * vl);
127            _partC.intoArray(pivotedInput, pos + 12 * vl);
128            _partD.intoArray(pivotedInput, pos + 13 * vl);
129            _partE.intoArray(pivotedInput, pos + 14 * vl);
130            _partF.intoArray(pivotedInput, pos + 15 * vl);
131
132
133            _part1 = _part1.max(_part0);
134            _part3 = _part3.max(_part2);
135            _part5 = _part5.max(_part4);
136            _part7 = _part7.max(_part6);
137            _part9 = _part9.max(_part8);
138            _partB = _partB.max(_partA);
139            _partD = _partD.max(_partC);
140            _partF = _partF.max(_partE);
141
142            _part3 = _part3.max(_part1);
143            _part7 = _part7.max(_part5);
144            _partB = _partB.max(_part9);
```

```
145          _partF = _partF.max(_partD);
146
147          _part7 = _part7.max(_part3);
148          _partF = _partF.max(_partB);
149
150          _partF = _partF.max(_part7);
151
152          var _partZ = _prev.slice(3, _partF);
153
154          var _shifted = _zero.slice(3, _partZ);
155          _partZ = _partZ.max(_shifted);
156
157          _shifted = _zero.slice(2, _partZ);
158          _partZ = _partZ.max(_shifted);
159
160          _part0 = _part0.max(_partZ);
161          _part1 = _part1.max(_partZ);
162          _part3 = _part3.max(_partZ);
163          _part7 = _part7.max(_partZ);
164          _partF = _partF.max(_partZ);
165
166          _partB = _partB.max(_part7);
167
168          _part5 = _part5.max(_part3);
169          _part9 = _part9.max(_part7);
170          _partD = _partD.max(_partB);
171
172          _part2 = _part2.max(_part1);
173          _part4 = _part4.max(_part3);
174          _part6 = _part6.max(_part5);
175          _part8 = _part8.max(_part7);
176          _partA = _partA.max(_part9);
177          _partC = _partC.max(_partB);
178          _partE = _partE.max(_partD);
179
```

```
180            _prev = _partF;
181
182            _part0.intoArray(prefixMax, pos + 0 * vl);
183            _part1.intoArray(prefixMax, pos + 1 * vl);
184            _part2.intoArray(prefixMax, pos + 2 * vl);
185            _part3.intoArray(prefixMax, pos + 3 * vl);
186            _part4.intoArray(prefixMax, pos + 4 * vl);
187            _part5.intoArray(prefixMax, pos + 5 * vl);
188            _part6.intoArray(prefixMax, pos + 6 * vl);
189            _part7.intoArray(prefixMax, pos + 7 * vl);
190            _part8.intoArray(prefixMax, pos + 8 * vl);
191            _part9.intoArray(prefixMax, pos + 9 * vl);
192            _partA.intoArray(prefixMax, pos + 10 * vl);
193            _partB.intoArray(prefixMax, pos + 11 * vl);
194            _partC.intoArray(prefixMax, pos + 12 * vl);
195            _partD.intoArray(prefixMax, pos + 13 * vl);
196            _partE.intoArray(prefixMax, pos + 14 * vl);
197            _partF.intoArray(prefixMax, pos + 15 * vl);
198
199          pos += 16 * vl;
200        }
201
202      int acc = _prev.lane(vl - 1);
203        ;
204
205      while (remainder-- > 0) {
206        pivotedInput[pos] = input[pos];
207        acc += input[pos];
208        prefixMax[pos++] = acc;
209      }
210    }
211
212    static int computeSuffixMaxFused(
213      int[] pivotedInput, int[] prefixMax) {
214      int iterations = pivotedInput.length / (16 * vl);
```

```
215    int remainder = pivotedInput.length % (16 * vl);
216
217    int trapped = 0, acc = 0, pos = pivotedInput.length;
218    while (remainder-- > 0) {
219      acc = Math.max(acc, pivotedInput[--pos]);
220      int minVal = Math.min(prefixMax[pos], acc);
221      trapped += minVal - pivotedInput[pos];
222    }
223
224    var _trapped = IntVector.zero(SP);
225    var _prev = IntVector.broadcast(SP, acc);
226
227    for (int i = 0; i < iterations; i++) {
228      pos -= 16 * vl;
229
230      int[] pi = pivotedInput;
231      var _part0 = IntVector.fromArray(SP, pi, pos + 0 * vl);
232      var _part1 = IntVector.fromArray(SP, pi, pos + 1 * vl);
233      var _part2 = IntVector.fromArray(SP, pi, pos + 2 * vl);
234      var _part3 = IntVector.fromArray(SP, pi, pos + 3 * vl);
235      var _part4 = IntVector.fromArray(SP, pi, pos + 4 * vl);
236      var _part5 = IntVector.fromArray(SP, pi, pos + 5 * vl);
237      var _part6 = IntVector.fromArray(SP, pi, pos + 6 * vl);
238      var _part7 = IntVector.fromArray(SP, pi, pos + 7 * vl);
239      var _part8 = IntVector.fromArray(SP, pi, pos + 8 * vl);
240      var _part9 = IntVector.fromArray(SP, pi, pos + 9 * vl);
241      var _partA = IntVector.fromArray(SP, pi, pos + 10 * vl);
242      var _partB = IntVector.fromArray(SP, pi, pos + 11 * vl);
243      var _partC = IntVector.fromArray(SP, pi, pos + 12 * vl);
244      var _partD = IntVector.fromArray(SP, pi, pos + 13 * vl);
245      var _partE = IntVector.fromArray(SP, pi, pos + 14 * vl);
246      var _partF = IntVector.fromArray(SP, pi, pos + 15 * vl);
247
248      _partE = _partE.max(_partF);
249      _partC = _partC.max(_partD);
```

```
250        _partA = _partA.max(_partB);
251        _part8 = _part8.max(_part9);
252        _part6 = _part6.max(_part7);
253        _part4 = _part4.max(_part5);
254        _part2 = _part2.max(_part3);
255        _part0 = _part0.max(_part1);
256
257        _partC = _partC.max(_partE);
258        _part8 = _part8.max(_partA);
259        _part4 = _part4.max(_part6);
260        _part0 = _part0.max(_part2);
261
262        _part8 = _part8.max(_partC);
263        _part0 = _part0.max(_part4);
264
265        _part0 = _part0.max(_part8);
266
267        var _partZ = _part0.slice(1, _prev);
268
269        var _shifted = _partZ.slice(1, _zero);
270        _partZ = _partZ.max(_shifted);
271
272        _shifted = _partZ.slice(2, _zero);
273        _partZ = _partZ.max(_shifted);
274
275        _part0 = _part0.max(_partZ);
276        _part8 = _part8.max(_partZ);
277        _partC = _partC.max(_partZ);
278        _partE = _partE.max(_partZ);
279        _partF = _partF.max(_partZ);
280
281        _part4 = _part4.max(_part8);
282
283        _partA = _partA.max(_partC);
284        _part6 = _part6.max(_part8);
```

```
285         _part2 = _part2.max(_part4);
286
287         _partD = _partD.max(_partE);
288         _partB = _partB.max(_partC);
289         _part9 = _part9.max(_partA);
290         _part7 = _part7.max(_part8);
291         _part5 = _part5.max(_part6);
292         _part3 = _part3.max(_part4);
293         _part1 = _part1.max(_part2);
294
295         _prev = _part0;
296
297         var _pf0 = IntVector.fromArray(SP, prefixMax, pos);
298         var _pf1 = IntVector.fromArray(SP, prefixMax, pos + 1 * vl);
299         var _pf2 = IntVector.fromArray(SP, prefixMax, pos + 2 * vl);
300         var _pf3 = IntVector.fromArray(SP, prefixMax, pos + 3 * vl);
301         var _pf4 = IntVector.fromArray(SP, prefixMax, pos + 4 * vl);
302         var _pf5 = IntVector.fromArray(SP, prefixMax, pos + 5 * vl);
303         var _pf6 = IntVector.fromArray(SP, prefixMax, pos + 6 * vl);
304         var _pf7 = IntVector.fromArray(SP, prefixMax, pos + 7 * vl);
305         var _pf8 = IntVector.fromArray(SP, prefixMax, pos + 8 * vl);
306         var _pf9 = IntVector.fromArray(SP, prefixMax, pos + 9 * vl);
307         var _pfA = IntVector.fromArray(SP, prefixMax, pos + 10 * vl);
308         var _pfB = IntVector.fromArray(SP, prefixMax, pos + 11 * vl);
309         var _pfC = IntVector.fromArray(SP, prefixMax, pos + 12 * vl);
310         var _pfD = IntVector.fromArray(SP, prefixMax, pos + 13 * vl);
311         var _pfE = IntVector.fromArray(SP, prefixMax, pos + 14 * vl);
312         var _pfF = IntVector.fromArray(SP, prefixMax, pos + 15 * vl);
313
314         var _pv0 = IntVector.fromArray(SP, pivotedInput, pos);
315         var _pv1 = IntVector.fromArray(SP, pivotedInput, pos + 1 * vl);
316         var _pv2 = IntVector.fromArray(SP, pivotedInput, pos + 2 * vl);
317         var _pv3 = IntVector.fromArray(SP, pivotedInput, pos + 3 * vl);
318         var _pv4 = IntVector.fromArray(SP, pivotedInput, pos + 4 * vl);
319         var _pv5 = IntVector.fromArray(SP, pivotedInput, pos + 5 * vl);
```

```
320            var _pv6 = IntVector.fromArray(SP, pivotedInput, pos + 6 * vl);
321            var _pv7 = IntVector.fromArray(SP, pivotedInput, pos + 7 * vl);
322            var _pv8 = IntVector.fromArray(SP, pivotedInput, pos + 8 * vl);
323            var _pv9 = IntVector.fromArray(SP, pivotedInput, pos + 9 * vl);
324            var _pvA = IntVector.fromArray(SP, pivotedInput, pos +
10 * vl);
325            var _pvB = IntVector.fromArray(SP, pivotedInput, pos +
11 * vl);
326            var _pvC = IntVector.fromArray(SP, pivotedInput, pos +
12 * vl);
327            var _pvD = IntVector.fromArray(SP, pivotedInput, pos +
13 * vl);
328            var _pvE = IntVector.fromArray(SP, pivotedInput, pos +
14 * vl);
329            var _pvF = IntVector.fromArray(SP, pivotedInput, pos +
15 * vl);
330
331            _part0 = _part0.min(_pf0).sub(_pv0);
332            _part1 = _part1.min(_pf1).sub(_pv1);
333            _part2 = _part2.min(_pf2).sub(_pv2);
334            _part3 = _part3.min(_pf3).sub(_pv3);
335            _part4 = _part4.min(_pf4).sub(_pv4);
336            _part5 = _part5.min(_pf5).sub(_pv5);
337            _part6 = _part6.min(_pf6).sub(_pv6);
338            _part7 = _part7.min(_pf7).sub(_pv7);
339            _part8 = _part8.min(_pf8).sub(_pv8);
340            _part9 = _part9.min(_pf9).sub(_pv9);
341            _partA = _partA.min(_pfA).sub(_pvA);
342            _partB = _partB.min(_pfB).sub(_pvB);
343            _partC = _partC.min(_pfC).sub(_pvC);
344            _partD = _partD.min(_pfD).sub(_pvD);
345            _partE = _partE.min(_pfE).sub(_pvE);
346            _partF = _partF.min(_pfF).sub(_pvF);
347
348            _part0 = _part0.add(_part1);
```

```
349            _part2 = _part2.add(_part3);
350            _part4 = _part4.add(_part5);
351            _part6 = _part6.add(_part7);
352            _part8 = _part8.add(_part9);
353            _partA = _partA.add(_partB);
354            _partC = _partC.add(_partD);
355            _partE = _partE.add(_partF);
356
357            _part0 = _part0.add(_part2);
358            _part4 = _part4.add(_part6);
359            _part8 = _part8.add(_partA);
360            _partC = _partC.add(_partE);
361
362            _part0 = _part0.add(_part4);
363            _part8 = _part8.add(_partC);
364
365            _trapped = _trapped.add(_part0);
366            _trapped = _trapped.add(_part8);
367        }
368
369     trapped += _trapped.reduceLanes(ADD);
370
371     return trapped;
372    }
373  }
374
```

- Lines 36–51 load 16 vectors of source data.

- Lines 54–112 pivot all 16 vectors. Note that now they are pivoted "in the opposite direction"—using the **zip** operation.

- In line 88, an additional variable breaks a cyclic dependency.

- Lines 154–158 fully unroll the horizontal prefix scan loop, which also provides a small performance contribution.

- Similarly, lines 269–273 unroll the horizontal suffix scan loop.

Benchmarks

Table 10-1 and Table 10-2 compare the trapping rainwater algorithm implementations.

Table 10-1. *Single-core speedup on x86 platforms (higher is better)*

Variant	GL	Z2	IL	SR	Z5
horizontal	0.08	0.81	0.92	1.02	1.10
horizontalX4	0.10	1.10	1.29	1.12	1.79
memoizedX16	0.07	1.01	1.58	1.33	2.29
scalar	1.00	1.00	1.00	1.00	1.00
shortX16	0.17	1.37	1.56	1.33	2.50
transposedX16	0.02	0.60	1.03	0.95	1.58
transposedX4	0.05	0.86	1.18	1.09	1.84

The X86 benchmark results demonstrate that optimal scan implementations require careful matching of algorithm complexity to hardware capabilities. Z5 (AMD Turin) shows the strongest performance, with shortX16 achieving 2.50× and memoizedX16 reaching 2.29× speedup—showcasing the benefits of modern AVX-512 implementations with excellent out-of-order execution.

The transposedX16 variant underperforms on Z2 (AMD Rome) at 0.60x, indicating that the 16-way unrolled pivot operations exert excessive register pressure, causing register spills to memory. Memoization provides significant benefits on wider-vector platforms (1.58× on IL (Intel Ice Lake), 2.29× on Z5) by reducing redundant pivot computations, validating the optimization strategy. Interestingly, the shortX16 variant—optimized for 128-bit vectors—paradoxically excels on 512-bit platforms, suggesting that its simpler structure enables better instruction-level parallelism than the complex transposed algorithms.

Table 10-2. *Single-core speedup on ARM platforms (higher is better)*

Variant	M4	O6	CO	NV	G3
horizontal	0.11	0.48	0.55	0.63	0.65
horizontalX4	0.21	0.75	0.75	0.66	0.71
memoizedX16	0.64	0.65	0.98	0.99	0.58
scalar	1.00	1.00	1.00	1.00	1.00
shortX16	0.99	0.66	1.06	1.04	1.04
transposedX16	0.15	0.43	0.45	0.60	0.19
transposedX4	0.20	0.49	0.53	0.80	0.34

The ARM benchmark results reveal that the advanced scan algorithms struggle severely on this architecture, with most variants producing significant slowdowns. G3 (Amazon Graviton 3) is a surprising outlier: despite having 256-bit SVE support, its transposedX16 performance drops to just 0.19×, indicating that the 16-way pivot operations create excessive register pressure or memory traffic on this platform. Memoization, which helped significantly on X86, provides no benefit on ARM (0.58–0.99×), suggesting that memory access patterns optimized for X86 caches do not transfer well to ARM.

Overall, these results indicate that for the trapping rainwater problem on ARM, either the scalar algorithm or the lightweight shortX16 variant should be preferred. This makes 128-bit vectors a safe and reasonably performant choice across all platforms.

What's Next

We return to Project Euler with a problem that pushes vectorization to its limits: computing convergents of the mathematical constant e. The next chapter ventures into BigInteger territory, exploring Strassen's and Karatsuba's algorithms for fast multiplication, and introduces the curious gigenary number system for representing impossibly large numbers.

CHAPTER 11

Convergents of e

Project Euler. Problem 65.

The square root of two can be represented as an infinite continued fraction:

$$\sqrt{2} = 1 + \cfrac{1}{2 + \cfrac{1}{2 + \cfrac{1}{2 + \cfrac{1}{2 + \cdots}}}}$$

An infinite continued fraction can be written as $\sqrt{2} = \left[1;(2)\right]$, where (2) denotes infinite repetition. Similarly, $\sqrt{23} = \left[4;(1,3,1,8)\right]$. It turns out that partial values of continued fractions give the best approximations of roots as simple fractions. For example, convergents of $\sqrt{2}$:

$$1 + \cfrac{1}{2} = \cfrac{3}{2}$$

$$1 + \cfrac{1}{2 + \cfrac{1}{2}} = \cfrac{7}{5}$$

$$1 + \cfrac{1}{2 + \cfrac{1}{2 + \cfrac{1}{2}}} = \cfrac{17}{12}$$

$$1 + \cfrac{1}{2 + \cfrac{1}{2 + \cfrac{1}{2 + \cfrac{1}{2}}}} = \cfrac{41}{29}$$

© Roman Snytsar 2026

R. Snytsar, *Mastering SIMD with Java Vector API*, https://doi.org/10.1007/979-8-8688-2676-4_11

Thus, the sequence of the first ten convergents of the square root of two:

$$1; \frac{3}{2}; \frac{7}{5}; \frac{17}{12}; \frac{41}{29}; \frac{99}{70}; \frac{239}{169}; \frac{577}{408}; \frac{1393}{985}; \frac{3363}{2378}; \ldots$$

The ubiquitous constant e can be represented as a continued fraction:

$$e = [2;1;2;1;1;4;1;1;6;1;\ldots;1;2k;1;\ldots]$$

Hence, the first ten convergents of e:

$$2;3; \frac{8}{3}; \frac{11}{4}; \frac{19}{7}; \frac{87}{32}; \frac{106}{39}; \frac{193}{71}; \frac{1264}{465}; \frac{1457}{536}; \ldots$$

The sum of digits in the numerator of the tenth convergent is $1 + 4 + 5 + 7 = 17$. Find the sum of digits in the numerator of the 100th convergent of e.

In This Chapter

1. Strassen's and Karatsuba's algorithms for fast matrix multiplication

2. Exploiting Hankel matrix structure to reduce multiplication count

3. The gigenary number system for vectorizing BigInteger operations

4. How to match algorithm complexity to vector width

Scalar Solution

We start with mathematics.

Given a continued fraction

$$Q = [q_0; q_1; q_2; q_3; \ldots; q_n; \ldots]$$

we set initial values for the numerator and the denominator:

$$A_{-1} = 1, \quad A_0 = q_0,$$
$$B_{-1} = 0, \quad B_0 = 1$$

Then, the n-th convergent can be computed by the formula

$$Q_n = \frac{A_n}{B_n}$$

where

$$A_n = q_n A_{n-1} + A_{n-2}$$
$$B_n = q_n B_{n-1} + B_{n-2}$$

The justification for these formulas follows. The key observation is that the n-th convergent

$$Q_n = [q_0; q_1, \ldots, q_{n-1}, q_n]$$

can be obtained from the $(n-1)$-th convergent

$$Q_{n-1} = [q_0; q_1, \ldots, q_{n-1}]$$

by replacing q_{n-1} with $q_{n-1} + \dfrac{1}{q_n}$.

Since $A_{n-1} = q_{n-1} A_{n-2} + A_{n-3}$ depends linearly on q_{n-1}, making this substitution yields

$$A'_{n-1} = \left(q_{n-1} + \frac{1}{q_n} \right) A_{n-2} + A_{n-3} = A_{n-1} + \frac{A_{n-2}}{q_n}$$

Similarly for the denominator:

$$B'_{n-1} = B_{n-1} + \frac{B_{n-2}}{q_n}$$

Therefore:

$$Q_n = \frac{A'_{n-1}}{B'_{n-1}} = \frac{A_{n-1} + \dfrac{A_{n-2}}{q_n}}{B_{n-1} + \dfrac{B_{n-2}}{q_n}} = \frac{q_n A_{n-1} + A_{n-2}}{q_n B_{n-1} + B_{n-2}} = \frac{A_n}{B_n}$$

This confirms that the recurrence relations hold.

These formulas resemble the recurrence formulas for computing Fibonacci numbers that we encountered earlier. Indeed, ratios of consecutive Fibonacci numbers are convergents of φ, the golden ratio, described by the elementary continued fraction

$$\phi = \left[(1) \right]$$

The analogy with Fibonacci numbers suggests a method for solving this problem.

First, numerators and denominators of convergents grow no slower than Fibonacci numbers—meaning exponentially, nearly doubling at each step. It follows that the sought numerator of the 100th convergent will exceed 2^{100}, so it will not fit in Int format, whose unsigned values cannot exceed 2^{32}, nor in Long format, limited to 2^{64}. Fortunately, we are working in a high-level language that offers a data type for arbitrary-precision integers: BigInteger. We will use the capabilities of the BigInteger class for a scalar solution.

```
1    package com.nonpareilcoder.projecteuler;
2
3    import java.math.BigInteger;
4
5    public class ConvergentsOfEScalar {
6      public static long compute() {
7        BigInteger p0 = BigInteger.ONE;
8        BigInteger p1 = BigInteger.TWO;
9
10       for (long k = 0; k++ < 33; ) {
11         BigInteger tmp = p1.add(p0);
12         p0 = tmp.multiply(BigInteger.valueOf(2 * k)).add(p1);
13         p1 = p0.add(tmp);
14       }
15
16       long sum = 0;
17
18       while (p1.compareTo(BigInteger.ZERO) != 0) {
19         var divRem = p1.divideAndRemainder(BigInteger.TEN);
20         sum += divRem[1].longValue();
21         p1 = divRem[0];
```

```
22        }
23
24      return sum;
25    }
26  }
27
```

- The loop in lines 10–14 somewhat resembles the leaping loop for computing even Fibonacci numbers. It even advances with the same three-position jumps. Indeed, our continued fraction consists of triples of the form $[1, 2k, 1]$. To get from convergent number 1 to convergent number 100 requires 99 iterations—exactly 33 triples.

- In the loop located in lines 18–22, the sum of digits of the sought number accumulates, obtained as remainders from successive division by 10.

Horizontal Vector Solution

For a vector solution, we will again use the analogy with computing Fibonacci numbers. We can represent the two previous sequence terms as a two-component vector. Then, the recursive formula can be written as

$$\begin{bmatrix} A_{n+1} \\ A_n \end{bmatrix} = \begin{bmatrix} q_n & 1 \\ 1 & 0 \end{bmatrix} \begin{bmatrix} A_n \\ A_{n-1} \end{bmatrix}$$

To prove the correctness of this formula, consider the following. Let vector $[A_n; A_{n-1}]$ contain two consecutive convergent numerators. Performing the multiplication:

$$\begin{bmatrix} q_n & 1 \\ 1 & 0 \end{bmatrix} \begin{bmatrix} A_n \\ A_{n-1} \end{bmatrix} = \begin{bmatrix} q_n A_n + A_{n-1} \\ A_n \end{bmatrix} = \begin{bmatrix} A_{n+1} \\ A_n \end{bmatrix}$$

Indeed, the first component of the result equals $q_n A_n + A_{n-1} = A_{n+1}$ by the recurrence formula (considering that in the next step q_n becomes the coefficient for A_n), while the second component contains A_n. The formula works similarly for denominators B_n.

Then, for a three-position jump to compute convergents of e, we get

$$\begin{bmatrix} A_{n+3} \\ A_{n+2} \end{bmatrix} = \begin{bmatrix} 1 & 1 \\ 1 & 0 \end{bmatrix}\begin{bmatrix} 2k & 1 \\ 1 & 0 \end{bmatrix}\begin{bmatrix} 1 & 1 \\ 1 & 0 \end{bmatrix}\begin{bmatrix} A_n \\ A_{n-1} \end{bmatrix}$$

Computing this matrix product step by step yields the following. First, multiply the last two matrices:

$$\begin{bmatrix} 2k & 1 \\ 1 & 0 \end{bmatrix}\begin{bmatrix} 1 & 1 \\ 1 & 0 \end{bmatrix} = \begin{bmatrix} 2k+1 & 2k \\ 1 & 1 \end{bmatrix}$$

Then multiply the result by the first matrix:

$$\begin{bmatrix} 1 & 1 \\ 1 & 0 \end{bmatrix}\begin{bmatrix} 2k+1 & 2k \\ 1 & 1 \end{bmatrix} = \begin{bmatrix} 2k+2 & 2k+1 \\ 2k+1 & 2k \end{bmatrix}$$

Thus, the final formula for a three-position jump:

$$\begin{bmatrix} A_{n+3} \\ A_{n+2} \end{bmatrix} = \begin{bmatrix} 2k+2 & 2k+1 \\ 2k+1 & 2k \end{bmatrix}\begin{bmatrix} A_n \\ A_{n-1} \end{bmatrix}$$

The following code implements computations using this formula.

```
1    package com.nonpareilcoder.projecteuler;
2
3    import jdk.incubator.vector.*;
4
5    import java.math.BigInteger;
6
7    public class ConvergentsOfEHorizontal {
8      static final VectorSpecies<Long> SP =
9        LongVector.SPECIES_PREFERRED;
10
11     public static long compute() {
12       BigInteger p0 = BigInteger.TWO;
13       BigInteger p1 = BigInteger.ONE;
14
15       var v4 = BigInteger.valueOf(4);
```

```
16      var v3 = BigInteger.valueOf(3);
17      var tmp = p0.multiply(v4).add(p1.multiply(v3));
18      p1 = p0.multiply(v3).add(p1.multiply(BigInteger.TWO));
19      p0 = tmp;
20
21      final int vl = SP.length();
22      var _idx = VectorShuffle.iota(SP, vl - 1, -1, false)
23        .toVector().reinterpretAsLongs().add(2L);
24
25      final var _zero = LongVector.zero(SP);
26      final var _one = LongVector.broadcast(SP, 1L);
27
28      for (long k = 0; k < 32; k += vl) {
29        var _a11 = _idx.add(_idx);
30        var _a10 = _a11.add(1);
31        var _a01 = _a10;
32        var _a00 = _a11.add(2);
33
34        for (int step = 1; step < vl; step <<= 1) {
35          var _b00 = _a00.slice(step, _one);
36          var _b01 = _a01.slice(step, _zero);
37          var _b10 = _a10.slice(step, _zero);
38          var _b11 = _a11.slice(step, _one);
39
40          var _c00 = _a00.mul(_b00).add(_a01.mul(_b10));
41          var _c01 = _a00.mul(_b01).add(_a01.mul(_b11));
42          var _c10 = _a10.mul(_b00).add(_a11.mul(_b10));
43          var _c11 = _a10.mul(_b01).add(_a11.mul(_b11));
44
45          _a00 = _c00;
46          _a01 = _c01;
47          _a10 = _c10;
48          _a11 = _c11;
49        }
50
```

```
51          var a00 = BigInteger.valueOf(_a00.lane(0));
52          var a01 = BigInteger.valueOf(_a01.lane(0));
53          var a10 = BigInteger.valueOf(_a10.lane(0));
54          var a11 = BigInteger.valueOf(_a11.lane(0));
55          tmp = p0.multiply(a00).add(p1.multiply(a01));
56          p1 = p0.multiply(a10).add(p1.multiply(a11));
57          p0 = tmp;
58
59          _idx = _idx.add(vl);
60        }
61
62      long sum = 0;
63
64      while (p0.compareTo(BigInteger.ZERO) != 0) {
65        var divRem = p0.divideAndRemainder(BigInteger.TEN);
66        sum += divRem[1].longValue();
67        p0 = divRem[0];
68      }
69
70      return sum;
71    }
72  }
73
```

- Lines 15–19 perform multiplication by the matrix corresponding to the first triple. This leaves 32 triples—a round number, definitely divisible by the vector size. This way, we avoid dealing with the last outer loop iteration with an incomplete vector.

- In the loop located in lines 34–49, an upsweep with respect to matrix multiplication is computed.

- In lines 51–57, the resulting matrix is multiplied by a BigInteger vector, and this concludes the outer loop iteration.

- In lines 64–68, digits of the sought number are computed through successive scalar division.

Vertical Vector Solution

We are already familiar with the drawbacks of horizontal upsweep: suboptimal use of vector resources and lack of instruction-level parallelism due to data dependencies between instructions, which in this case is compensated by component-wise storage of matrices in four different vectors. The solution is also known: vector reversal. Since all source matrices are generated from vector _idx, reversing just requires adjusting this vector.

```
1    package com.nonpareilcoder.projecteuler;
2
3    import jdk.incubator.vector.*;
4
5    import java.math.BigInteger;
6
7    public class ConvergentsOfEVertical {
8      static final VectorSpecies<Long> SP =
9        LongVector.SPECIES_PREFERRED;
10
11     public static long compute() {
12       BigInteger p0 = BigInteger.TWO;
13       BigInteger p1 = BigInteger.ONE;
14
15       var v4 = BigInteger.valueOf(4);
16       var v3 = BigInteger.valueOf(3);
17       var tmp = p0.multiply(v4).add(p1.multiply(v3));
18       p1 = p0.multiply(v3).add(p1.multiply(BigInteger.TWO));
19       p0 = tmp;
20
21       final int vl = SP.length();
22       var _idx = VectorShuffle.iota(SP, 0, 1, false)
23         .toVector().reinterpretAsLongs().mul(4L).add(1);
24
25       for (long k = 0; k < 32; k += 4 * vl) {
26         _idx = _idx.add(1);
27
```

```
28        var _a11 = _idx.add(_idx);
29        var _a10 = _a11.add(1);
30        var _a01 = _a10;
31        var _a00 = _a11.add(2);
32
33        for (int i = 1; i < 4; i++) {
34          _idx = _idx.add(1);
35
36          var _b11 = _idx.add(_idx);
37          var _b10 = _b11.add(1);
38          var _b01 = _b10;
39          var _b00 = _b11.add(2);
40
41          var _c00 = _b00.mul(_a00).add(_b01.mul(_a10));
42          var _c01 = _b00.mul(_a01).add(_b01.mul(_a11));
43          var _c10 = _b10.mul(_a00).add(_b11.mul(_a10));
44          var _c11 = _b10.mul(_a01).add(_b11.mul(_a11));
45
46          _a00 = _c00;
47          _a01 = _c01;
48          _a10 = _c10;
49          _a11 = _c11;
50        }
51
52        for (int i = 0; i < vl; i++) {
53          var a00 = BigInteger.valueOf(_a00.lane(i));
54          var a01 = BigInteger.valueOf(_a01.lane(i));
55          var a10 = BigInteger.valueOf(_a10.lane(i));
56          var a11 = BigInteger.valueOf(_a11.lane(i));
57          tmp = p0.multiply(a00).add(p1.multiply(a01));
58          p1 = p0.multiply(a10).add(p1.multiply(a11));
59          p0 = tmp;
60        }
61
62        _idx = _idx.add(4L * (vl - 1));
```

```
63          }
64
65      long sum = 0;
66
67      while (p0.compareTo(BigInteger.ZERO) != 0) {
68        var divRem = p0.divideAndRemainder(BigInteger.TEN);
69        sum += divRem[1].longValue();
70        p0 = divRem[0];
71      }
72
73      return sum;
74    }
75  }
76
```

- In lines 21-23, _idx initialization now happens with a stride of four.

- In the inner loop located in lines 33-50, a vertical upsweep with respect to matrix multiplication is computed.

- In lines 52-60, the resulting matrices are sequentially multiplied by a BigInteger vector, and this concludes the outer loop iteration.

- In lines 67-70, digits of the sought number are computed, still through successive scalar division.

Strassen Algorithm

Multiplying 2×2 matrices the classical textbook way requires eight multiplications: two per component. Mathematician Volker Strassen (Strassen, 1969) proposed a method requiring only seven multiplications. If we need to multiply matrices

$$C = B \times A = \begin{bmatrix} b_{00} & b_{01} \\ b_{10} & b_{11} \end{bmatrix} \times \begin{bmatrix} a_{00} & a_{01} \\ a_{10} & a_{11} \end{bmatrix}$$

we compute seven intermediate products:

$$m_1 = \left(b_{00} + b_{11}\right) \times \left(a_{00} + a_{11}\right)$$

$$m_2 = \left(b_{10} + b_{11}\right) \times a_{00}$$

$$m_3 = b_{00} \times \left(a_{01} - a_{11}\right)$$

$$m_4 = b_{11} \times \left(a_{10} - a_{00}\right)$$

$$m_5 = \left(b_{00} + b_{01}\right) \times a_{11}$$

$$m_6 = \left(b_{10} - b_{00}\right) \times \left(a_{00} + a_{01}\right)$$

$$m_7 = \left(b_{01} - b_{11}\right) \times \left(a_{10} + a_{11}\right)$$

Then, the product elements are computed by the formulas:

$$c_{00} = m_1 + m_4 - m_5 + m_7$$

$$c_{01} = m_3 + m_5$$

$$c_{10} = m_2 + m_4$$

$$c_{11} = m_1 - m_2 + m_3 + m_6$$

The following code implements this:

```
1   package com.nonpareilcoder.projecteuler;
2
3   import jdk.incubator.vector.*;
4
5   import java.math.BigInteger;
6
7   public class ConvergentsOfEStrassen {
8     static final VectorSpecies<Long> SP =
9       LongVector.SPECIES_PREFERRED;
10
11    public static long compute() {
12      BigInteger p0 = BigInteger.TWO;
13      BigInteger p1 = BigInteger.ONE;
```

```
14
15      var tmp = p0.multiply(BigInteger.valueOf(4))
16        .add(p1.multiply(BigInteger.valueOf(3)));
17      p1 = p0.multiply(BigInteger.valueOf(3))
18        .add(p1.multiply(BigInteger.TWO));
19      p0 = tmp;
20
21      LongVector _idx =
22        VectorShuffle.iota(SP, 0, 1, false)
23          .toVector().reinterpretAsLongs().mul(4L).add(1);
24
25      for (long k = 0; k < 32; k += 4 * SP.length()) {
26        _idx = _idx.add(1);
27
28        LongVector _a11 = _idx.add(_idx);
29        LongVector _a10 = _a11.add(1);
30        LongVector _a01 = _a10;
31        LongVector _a00 = _a11.add(2);
32
33        for (int i = 1; i < 4; i++) {
34          _idx = _idx.add(1);
35
36          LongVector _b11 = _idx.add(_idx);
37          LongVector _b10 = _b11.add(1);
38          LongVector _b01 = _b10;
39          LongVector _b00 = _b11.add(2);
40
41          LongVector _m1 = _b00.add(_b11).mul(_a00.add(_a11));
42          LongVector _m2 = _b10.add(_b11).mul(_a00);
43          LongVector _m3 = _a01.sub(_a11).mul(_b00);
44          LongVector _m4 = _a10.sub(_a00).mul(_b11);
45          LongVector _m5 = _b00.add(_b01).mul(_a11);
46          LongVector _m6 = _b10.sub(_b00).mul(_a00.add(_a01));
47          LongVector _m7 = _b01.sub(_b11).mul(_a10.add(_a11));
48
```

```
49              _a00 = _m1.add(_m4).sub(_m5).add(_m7);
50              _a01 = _m3.add(_m5);
51              _a10 = _m2.add(_m4);
52              _a11 = _m1.sub(_m2).add(_m3).add(_m6);
53          }
54
55        var vl = SP.length();
56        for (int i = 0; i < vl; i++) {
57          tmp = p0.multiply(BigInteger.valueOf(
58            _a00.lane(i))).add(p1.multiply(
59            BigInteger.valueOf(_a01.lane(i))));
60          p1 = p0.multiply(BigInteger.valueOf(
61            _a10.lane(i))).add(p1.multiply(
62            BigInteger.valueOf(_a11.lane(i))));
63          p0 = tmp;
64        }
65
66        _idx = _idx.add(4L * (vl - 1));
67      }
68
69      long sum = 0;
70
71      while (p0.compareTo(BigInteger.ZERO) != 0) {
72        var divRem = p0.divideAndRemainder(BigInteger.TEN);
73        sum += divRem[1].longValue();
74        p0 = divRem[0];
75      }
76
77      return sum;
78    }
79  }
80
```

- Lines 41–47 compute the intermediate products.

- Lines 49–52 form the matrix elements.

Nowadays, the Strassen algorithm is mainly of historical interest. In modern processors, multiplications are not much slower than additions, which are required in greater quantity than in classical formulas. Moreover, for matrices consisting of floating-point numbers, additions lead to rounding errors, and multiplications rapidly increase the scale of errors. All this leads to numerical instability of the algorithm.

The value of the Strassen algorithm is that it sparked a surge of interest in finding fast matrix multiplication algorithms, widely used in artificial intelligence systems. Interestingly, neural networks helped discover a new class of such algorithms, thus closing the circle.

Karatsuba Algorithm

Consider whether we can further reduce the number of multiplications for 2×2 matrices. For the general case, the answer is negative. But in our case, matrices B have the form:

$$\begin{bmatrix} 2k+2 & 2k+1 \\ 2k+1 & 2k \end{bmatrix}$$

Elements located on the antidiagonal are equal. Such matrices are called **Hankel matrices**. For multiplying a 2×2 Hankel matrix by a vector, we can apply a variant of the algorithm invented by Anatoly Karatsuba (Karatsuba & Ofman, 1963) originally for multiplying large numbers—the very BigIntegers we use here.

To obtain vector

$$\begin{bmatrix} c_0 \\ c_1 \end{bmatrix} = \begin{bmatrix} b_0 & b_1 \\ b_1 & b_2 \end{bmatrix} \times \begin{bmatrix} a_0 \\ a_1 \end{bmatrix}$$

we compute three intermediate products:

$$p_1 = b_1 \times (a_0 + a_1)$$

$$p_2 = (b_0 - b_1) \times a_0$$

$$p_3 = (b_2 - b_1) \times a_1$$

Then, the product elements are computed by the formulas:

$$c_0 = p_1 + p_2$$

$$c_1 = p_1 + p_3$$

To verify the correctness of these formulas, expand the expression for c_0:

$$c_0 = p_1 + p_2$$

$$= b_1(a_0 + a_1) + (b_0 - b_1)a_0$$

$$= b_1 a_0 + b_1 a_1 + b_0 a_0 - b_1 a_0$$

$$= b_0 a_0 + b_1 a_1$$

Similarly for c_1:

$$c_1 = p_1 + p_3$$

$$= b_1(a_0 + a_1) + (b_2 - b_1)a_1$$

$$= b_1 a_0 + b_1 a_1 + b_2 a_1 - b_1 a_1$$

$$= b_1 a_0 + b_2 a_1$$

These expressions exactly match direct matrix-vector multiplication, confirming the algorithm's correctness.

In total, multiplying a Hankel matrix by a vector required three multiplications. Since a matrix consists of two vectors, multiplying a Hankel matrix by an arbitrary matrix takes six multiplications.

But that is not all. For our matrix B, we have:

$$b_0 - b_1 = (2k+2) - (2k+1) = 1$$

$$b_2 - b_1 = 2k - (2k+1) = -1$$

Since $b_0 - b_1 = 1$, the multiplication $(b_0 - b_1) \times a_{00}$ becomes simply a_{00}, requiring no multiplication operation. Similarly, $b_2 - b_1 = -1$ turns the product into $-a_{10}$. Thus, instead of six multiplications for matrix-matrix product, only two remain: $p_0 = b_1 \times (a_{00} + a_{10})$ and $p_1 = b_1 \times (a_{01} + a_{11})$. All other operations are addition and subtraction. Then, the matrix multiplication formulas become

$$p_0 = b_1 \times \left(a_{00} + a_{10} \right)$$

$$p_1 = b_1 \times \left(a_{01} + a_{11} \right)$$

$$c_{00} = p_0 + a_{00}$$

$$c_{10} = p_0 - a_{10}$$

$$c_{01} = p_1 + a_{01}$$

$$c_{11} = p_1 - a_{11}$$

This became possible thanks to the special structure of our matrices, where elements differ from each other by exactly one.

We have reduced the required number of multiplications to two!

```
 1   package com.nonpareilcoder.projecteuler;
 2
 3   import jdk.incubator.vector.*;
 4
 5   import java.math.BigInteger;
 6
 7   public class ConvergentsOfEKaratsuba {
 8     static final VectorSpecies<Long> SP =
 9       LongVector.SPECIES_PREFERRED;
10
11     public static long compute() {
12       BigInteger p0 = BigInteger.TWO;
13       BigInteger p1 = BigInteger.ONE;
14
15       var tmp = p0.multiply(BigInteger.valueOf(4))
16         .add(p1.multiply(BigInteger.valueOf(3)));
17       p1 = p0.multiply(BigInteger.valueOf(3))
18         .add(p1.multiply(BigInteger.TWO));
19       p0 = tmp;
20
21       LongVector _idx =
22         VectorShuffle.iota(SP, 0, 1, false)
```

```
23              .toVector().reinterpretAsLongs().mul(8L).add(3);
24
25        for (long k = 0; k < 32; k += 4 * SP.length()) {
26          _idx = _idx.add(2);
27
28          LongVector _a00 = _idx.add(1L);
29          LongVector _a01 = _idx;
30          LongVector _a10 = _a01;
31          LongVector _a11 = _idx.sub(1L);
32
33          for (int i = 1; i < 4; i++) {
34            _idx = _idx.add(2);
35
36            LongVector _p0 = _a00.add(_a10).mul(_idx);
37            LongVector _p1 = _a01.add(_a11).mul(_idx);
38
39            _a00 = _p0.add(_a00);
40            _a10 = _p0.sub(_a10);
41            _a01 = _p1.add(_a01);
42            _a11 = _p1.sub(_a11);
43          }
44
45          var vl = SP.length();
46          for (int i = 0; i < vl; i++) {
47            tmp = p0.multiply(BigInteger.valueOf(
48              _a00.lane(i))).add(p1.multiply(
49              BigInteger.valueOf(_a01.lane(i))));
50            p1 = p0.multiply(BigInteger.valueOf(
51              _a10.lane(i))).add(p1.multiply(
52              BigInteger.valueOf(_a11.lane(i))));
53            p0 = tmp;
54          }
55
56          _idx = _idx.add(8L * (vl - 1));
57        }
```

```
58
59        long sum = 0;
60
61        while (p0.compareTo(BigInteger.ZERO) != 0) {
62          var divRem = p0.divideAndRemainder(BigInteger.TEN);
63          sum += divRem[1].longValue();
64          p0 = divRem[0];
65        }
66
67        return sum;
68      }
69    }
70
```

- Lines 36–37 contain all two multiplications of the inner loop.

- Lines 39–42 form the matrix elements.

The Billionaire Algorithm

The numerator of the 100th convergent now computes lightning-fast. The lion's share of program execution time goes to sequential division of BigInteger format numbers in lines 61–65. To vectorize this loop, you need to think like a billionaire. Why billionaires? Because they naturally count in billions rather than individual dollars. We will do the same with our digits—instead of extracting decimal digits one at a time, we will work with groups of nine digits at once, treating each group as a single "billion-dollar" unit.

The approach is to convert the original large number to a number system with base one billion (**gigenary** system). As any billionaire will confirm, counting in billions is convenient. First, there will be a few gigenary digits: nine times fewer than decimal ones. Second, since a billion is a power of ten, the decimal digits describing gigenary places are the same as in the original decimal representation. Third, although a billion is an impressive number, it is not too large and fits in 32 binary digits. This means we can extract decimal digits from each gigenary place in parallel using the vector division-by-constant algorithm we already know.

The key advantage for vectorization: BigInteger does not allow direct vectorization of operations due to variable number length and complex internal structure. However, after splitting into gigenary digits, we get an array of ordinary 32-bit integers of fixed size that are handled efficiently by the vector instructions. Each gigenary digit is processed independently, which is ideal for parallel processing.

```
1    package com.nonpareilcoder.projecteuler;
2
3    import jdk.incubator.vector.*;
4
5    import static jdk.incubator.vector.VectorOperators.*;
6
7    import java.math.BigInteger;
8
9    public class ConvergentsOfEBillionaire256 {
10     static final VectorSpecies<Long> SP =
11       LongVector.SPECIES_256;
12
13     static final long c10 = 0x1999999AL;
14     static final long lowPart = 0xFFFFFFFFL;
15
16     public static long compute() {
17       LongVector _idx =
18         VectorShuffle.iota(SP, 0, 1, false)
19           .toVector().reinterpretAsLongs().mul(16L).add(3);
20
21       var _a00 = LongVector.broadcast(SP, 1).withLane(0, 4L);
22       var _a01 = LongVector.zero(SP).withLane(0, 3L);
23       LongVector _a10 = _a01;
24       var _a11 = LongVector.broadcast(SP, 1).withLane(0, 2L);
25
26       for (int i = 0; i < 8; i++) {
27         _idx = _idx.add(2L);
28
29           LongVector _p0 = _a00.add(_a10).mul(_idx);
30           LongVector _p1 = _a01.add(_a11).mul(_idx);
```

```
31
32       _a00 = _p0.add(_a00);
33       _a10 = _p0.sub(_a10);
34       _a01 = _p1.add(_a01);
35       _a11 = _p1.sub(_a11);
36     }
37
38     BigInteger p0 = BigInteger.TWO;
39     BigInteger p1 = BigInteger.ONE;
40
41     var vl = SP.length();
42     for (int i = 0; i < vl; i++) {
43       var tmp =
44         p0.multiply(BigInteger.valueOf(_a00.lane(i)))
45         .add(p1.multiply(BigInteger.valueOf(_a01.lane(i))));
46       p1 = p0.multiply(BigInteger.valueOf(
47         _a10.lane(i))).add(p1.multiply(
48         BigInteger.valueOf(_a11.lane(i))));
49       p0 = tmp;
50     }
51
52     long[] billions = new long[8];
53
54     final var billion = BigInteger.valueOf(1_000_000_000L);
55
56     for (int i = 0; i < 8; i++) {
57       BigInteger[] divRem = p0.divideAndRemainder(billion);
58       billions[i] = divRem[1].longValue();
59       p0 = divRem[0];
60     }
61
62     LongVector _sum = LongVector.zero(SP);
63
64     LongVector _bil0 = LongVector.fromArray(SP, billions, 0);
65     LongVector _bil1 = LongVector.fromArray(SP, billions, 4);
66
```

```
67        for (int i = 0; i < 9; i++) {
68          LongVector _div0 = _bil0.mul(c10);
69          LongVector _div1 = _bil1.mul(c10);
70          var _rem0 = _div0.and(lowPart).mul(10L).lanewise(LSHR, 32);
71          var _rem1 = _div1.and(lowPart).mul(10L).lanewise(LSHR, 32);
72          _sum = _sum.add(_rem0).add(_rem1);
73          _bil0 = _div0.lanewise(LSHR, 32);
74          _bil1 = _div1.lanewise(LSHR, 32);
75        }
76
77        long sum = _sum.reduceLanes(ADD);
78
79        return sum;
80      }
81    }
82
```

- In line 11, we abandoned arbitrary vector length and requested a configuration with 256-bit vectors. This allows us to use the Karatsuba algorithm most efficiently without overflowing the Long type range. This choice can be explained in more detail. When using the Karatsuba algorithm for multiplying 2×2 matrices by a vector of length W, intermediate results generated are roughly twice as large as the original numbers. With vectors of 512 bits or more, intermediate products might overflow the Long type range (2^{64}), requiring a switch to BigInteger and negating vectorization advantages. A 256-bit vector contains four Long-type elements, allowing efficient vectorization while maintaining sufficient margin before overflow.

- Lines 56–60 split the large number into gigenary places. The code is analogous to splitting into decimal places, just with a different number system base.

- Lines 67–75 extract decimal digits from gigenary places for the final sum.

- Line 77 is the final vector reduction.

Both convergent computation and its digit breakdown are now vectorized. The use of BigInteger, necessary for this problem but slow, has been minimized.

Short Vectors

Choosing 256-bit vector length may lead to performance loss on systems with 128-bit vectors. We modify the billionaire algorithm, trading vector length for an increase in the number of operations.

```
1   package com.nonpareilcoder.projecteuler;
2
3   import jdk.incubator.vector.*;
4
5   import static jdk.incubator.vector.VectorOperators.*;
6
7   import java.math.BigInteger;
8
9   public class ConvergentsOfEBillionaire128 {
10    static final VectorSpecies<Long> SP =
11      LongVector.SPECIES_128;
12
13    static final long c10 = 0x1999999AL;
14    static final long lowPart = 0xFFFFFFFFL;
15
16    public static long compute() {
17      LongVector _idxa =
18        VectorShuffle.iota(SP, 0, 1, false)
19          .toVector().reinterpretAsLongs().mul(32L).add(3L);
20
21      LongVector _idxb =
22        VectorShuffle.iota(SP, 0, 1, false)
23          .toVector().reinterpretAsLongs().mul(32L).add(19L);
24
25      LongVector _b00 = LongVector.broadcast(SP, 1);
26      LongVector _b01 = LongVector.zero(SP);
```

```
27          LongVector _b10 = _b01;
28          LongVector _b11 = LongVector.broadcast(SP, 1);
29
30          LongVector _a00 = _b00.withLane(0, 4L);
31          LongVector _a01 = _b01.withLane(0, 3L);
32          LongVector _a10 = _a01;
33          LongVector _a11 = _b11.withLane(0, 2L);
34
35
36      for (int i = 0; i < 8; i++) {
37        _idxa = _idxa.add(2L);
38
39        LongVector _p0 = _a00.add(_a10).mul(_idxa);
40        LongVector _p1 = _a01.add(_a11).mul(_idxa);
41
42        _a00 = _p0.add(_a00);
43        _a10 = _p0.sub(_a10);
44        _a01 = _p1.add(_a01);
45        _a11 = _p1.sub(_a11);
46
47        _idxb = _idxb.add(2L);
48
49        _p0 = _b00.add(_b10).mul(_idxb);
50        _p1 = _b01.add(_b11).mul(_idxb);
51
52        _b00 = _p0.add(_b00);
53        _b10 = _p0.sub(_b10);
54        _b01 = _p1.add(_b01);
55        _b11 = _p1.sub(_b11);
56      }
57
58      BigInteger p0 = BigInteger.TWO;
59      BigInteger p1 = BigInteger.ONE;
60
61      for (int i = 0; i < SP.length(); i++) {
```

```
62    BigInteger tmp =
63      p0.multiply(BigInteger.valueOf(_a00.lane(i)))
64        .add(p1.multiply(BigInteger.valueOf(_a01.lane(i))));
65    p1 = p0.multiply(BigInteger.valueOf(_a10.lane(i)))
66        .add(p1.multiply(BigInteger.valueOf(_a11.lane(i))));
67    p0 = tmp;
68
69    tmp = p0.multiply(BigInteger.valueOf(_b00.lane(i)))
70        .add(p1.multiply(BigInteger.valueOf(_b01.lane(i))));
71    p1 = p0.multiply(BigInteger.valueOf(_b10.lane(i)))
72        .add(p1.multiply(BigInteger.valueOf(_b11.lane(i))));
73    p0 = tmp;
74  }
75
76  long[] billions = new long[8];
77
78  final BigInteger billion = BigInteger.valueOf(1_000_000_000L);
79
80  for (int i = 0; i < 8; i++) {
81    BigInteger[] divRem = p0.divideAndRemainder(billion);
82    billions[i] = divRem[1].longValue();
83    p0 = divRem[0];
84  }
85
86  LongVector _sum = LongVector.zero(SP);
87
88  LongVector _bil0 = LongVector.fromArray(SP, billions, 0);
89  LongVector _bil1 = LongVector.fromArray(SP, billions, 2);
90  LongVector _bil2 = LongVector.fromArray(SP, billions, 4);
91  LongVector _bil3 = LongVector.fromArray(SP, billions, 6);
92
93  for (int i = 0; i < 9; i++) {
94    LongVector _div0 = _bil0.mul(c10);
95    LongVector _div1 = _bil1.mul(c10);
96    LongVector _div2 = _bil2.mul(c10);
```

```
97           LongVector _div3 = _bil3.mul(c10);
98           var _rem0 = _div0.and(lowPart).mul(10L).lanewise(LSHR, 32);
99           var _rem1 = _div1.and(lowPart).mul(10L).lanewise(LSHR, 32);
100          var _rem2 = _div2.and(lowPart).mul(10L).lanewise(LSHR, 32);
101          var _rem3 = _div3.and(lowPart).mul(10L).lanewise(LSHR, 32);
102          _rem0 = _rem0.add(_rem2);
103          _rem1 = _rem1.add(_rem3);
104          _sum = _sum.add(_rem0).add(_rem1);
105          _bil0 = _div0.lanewise(LSHR, 32);
106          _bil1 = _div1.lanewise(LSHR, 32);
107          _bil2 = _div2.lanewise(LSHR, 32);
108          _bil3 = _div3.lanewise(LSHR, 32);
109        }
110
111      long sum = _sum.reduceLanes(ADD);
112
113      return sum;
114    }
115  }
116
```

- We have touched primarily the code responsible for the matrix products.

- In lines 17–23, two indices are initialized with interleaved values.

- In lines 25–56, two sets of matrix values are computed in parallel.

- The interleaved arrangement of elements allows merging the BigInteger computation loops into one, located in lines 61–74.

- In lines 93–109, work with gigenary places is now unrolled by four.

Benchmarks

Table 11-1 and Table 11-2 compare the convergent computation approaches.

Table 11-1. *Single-core speedup on x86 platforms (higher is better)*

Variant	GL	Z2	IL	SR	Z5
billionaire128	3.67	3.35	3.37	3.98	3.44
billionaire256	1.14	3.90	3.58	3.97	3.38
horizontal	0.55	1.11	1.23	1.44	1.22
karatsuba	1.23	1.11	1.09	1.35	1.19
scalar	1.00	1.00	1.00	1.00	1.00
strassen	1.20	1.10	1.08	1.38	1.21
vertical	1.20	1.11	1.22	1.39	1.22

The X86 benchmark results demonstrate that the billionaire algorithm's vectorized digit extraction provides the dominant performance gain for convergent computation. The billionaire128 variant achieves remarkably consistent speedups of 3.35–3.98× across all platforms, confirming that the gigenary representation effectively parallelizes the digit sum computation. The matrix multiplication optimizations (Karatsuba, Strassen, vertical) provide only modest improvements (1.08–1.44×), as the BigInteger operations dominate overall execution time. Overall, the results validate the billionaire strategy of optimizing the digit-level parallelism rather than the matrix computation.

Table 11-2. *Single-core speedup on ARM platforms (higher is better)*

Variant	M4	O6	CO	NV	G3
billionaire128	3.98	4.26	3.93	4.02	3.82
billionaire256	0.98	0.72	0.91	0.66	3.36
horizontal	0.90	0.92	1.03	0.87	1.18
karatsuba	1.16	1.22	1.22	1.15	1.20
scalar	1.00	1.00	1.00	1.00	1.00
strassen	1.19	1.19	1.36	1.14	1.21
vertical	1.21	1.19	1.33	1.10	1.22

The ARM benchmark results highlight the critical importance of matching vector width to hardware capabilities for the convergent algorithm. The billionaire128 variant achieves excellent speedups of 3.82–4.26× uniformly across all ARM platforms. The billionaire256 variant presents dramatic outliers: NV shows the worst performance at 0.66×, while G3, with its 256-bit SVE, achieves 3.36×, confirming that the algorithm design explicitly requires matching vector width. The matrix multiplication variants provide consistent but modest 1.10–1.36× improvements across ARM, similar to X86 results. The horizontal variant causes slight slowdowns on most platforms (0.87–0.92×), confirming that the vector scan's data dependencies create inefficiencies on ARM's in-order cores. Overall, choosing 128-bit implementation is safe and efficient for both X86 and ARM platforms.

What's Next

From number theory, we turn to a fundamental data processing problem: merging two sorted arrays. The next chapter introduces bitonic sorting, the merge path visualization, and the scatter operation for indexed memory writes—powerful techniques that reveal both the potential and the limitations of vectorized comparison-based algorithms.

CHAPTER 12

Merging Arrays

Consider two integer arrays, input0 and input1, both sorted in non-descending order. The task is to create a new array containing all elements from both source arrays, sorted in non-descending order.

In This Chapter

1. The merge path method for visualizing and parallelizing sorted array merging

2. Bitonic sorting networks for sorting sequences that first increase then decrease

3. How structural hazards limit instruction-level parallelism

4. The scatter operation for indexed memory writes

Three-Pointer Method

The scalar solution resembles the two-pointer method introduced in Chapter 5, but uses three indices: one for each input array and one for the output.

```java
1   package com.nonpareilcoder.realleetcode;
2
3   public class MergeArraysScalar {
4     public static int[] merge(int[] input0, int[] input1) {
5       int[] output = new int[input0.length + input1.length];
6       int i0 = 0, i1 = 0, j = 0;
7
```


© Roman Snytsar 2026
R. Snytsar, *Mastering SIMD with Java Vector API*, https://doi.org/10.1007/979-8-8688-2676-4_12

```
 8        mergeCore(input0, input1, output, i0, i1, j);
 9
10        return output;
11      }
12
13      public static void mergeCore(
14        int[] input0, int[] input1, int[] output,
15        int i0, int i1, int j) {
16        for (; ; ) {
17          if (i0 == input0.length) {
18            while (i1 < input1.length)
19              output[j++] = input1[i1++];
20
21            break;
22          }
23
24          if (i1 == input1.length) {
25            while (i0 < input0.length)
26              output[j++] = input0[i0++];
27
28            break;
29          }
30
31          if (input0[i0] < input1[i1])
32            output[j++] = input0[i0++];
33          else
34            output[j++] = input1[i1++];
35        }
36      }
37    }
38
```

- The algorithm core is in lines 31–34.

- Lines 17–22 handle completion when the first array has been
  exhausted.

- Lines 24–29 similarly handle the situation when the second array has been exhausted.

Merge Path

The merge path method (Odeh, Abdelfattah, & Haga, 2012) allows us to visualize the process of merging two arrays or vectors, as shown in Figure 12-1.

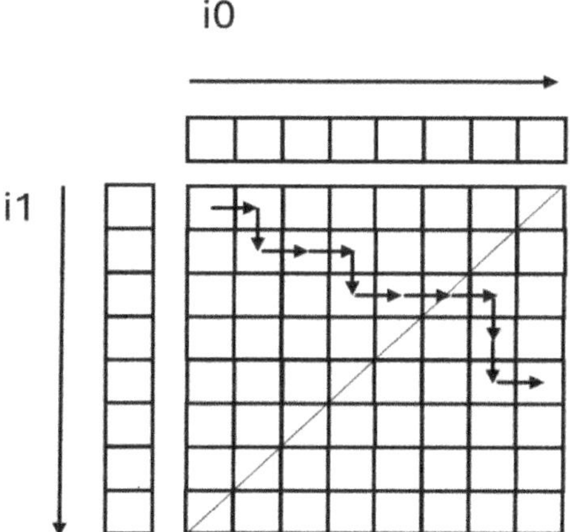

Figure 12-1. *Merge path*

The algorithm state is determined by two indices into the input vectors represented as a cell in a square grid. When comparing, if the current element of the upper vector is less than the corresponding element in the left vector, the upper vector element is written to the output array, and the state (active cell) shifts right. If the current element of the left vector is less than the corresponding element in the upper vector, the left vector element is written to the output array, and the state shifts down. When the trajectory reaches the right or bottom boundary of the square, it is time to load new vectors from memory and restart the algorithm.

Analysis reveals that with vector length W, the longest trajectory has length $2W$ and the shortest has length W. Therefore, when merging two vectors, only the first W elements are guaranteed correct. Elements numbered from $W+1$ to $2W$ may require information from the subsequent vectors.

Any trajectory of length W ends on the square antidiagonal. If the trajectory intersection point with the antidiagonal has coordinates j_0, j_1, this means the guaranteed correct portion of the trajectory includes j_0 elements from the upper vector and j_1 elements from the lower vector. Therefore, to restart the algorithm, we need to read the new upper vector with offset j_0 and the new left vector with offset j_1.

The merge path method provides a way to find j_0 and j_1 without fully merging vectors. Reverse the left vector and compare each element of the upper vector with the corresponding element of the reversed left vector. Count how many times an upper vector element is smaller. This count is the desired number j_0.

The method's correctness can be proven as follows. Suppose the upper vector contains elements $[a_0, a_1, ..., a_{W-1}]$ (an increasing sequence), and the left contains $[b_0, b_1, ..., b_{W-1}]$ (also increasing). After reversal, the left vector becomes $[b_{W-1}, b_{W-2}, ..., b_0]$ (a decreasing sequence). We compare a_i with b_{W-1-i} for all i. The count j_0 of positions i where $a_i < b_{W-1-i}$ equals the number of elements from the upper vector that will enter the first W elements of the result. This is true because element a_i will enter the first W elements if and only if it is less than a sufficient number of elements from the left vector, which is precisely what the comparison with the corresponding reversed vector element checks.

Clearly, $j_1 = W - j_0$. Element-wise comparison can be performed in parallel. Thus, a purely sequential merge path analysis method gave us our first foothold in a parallel algorithm.

Bitonic Sorting

Recall that the upper vector is sorted by definition. In other words, it contains a monotonically increasing sequence. The reversed left vector contains a monotonically decreasing sequence. Both vectors concatenated contain a sequence that first increases and then decreases, that is, a **bitonic** sequence (Knuth, 1998). An interesting parallel algorithm exists for sorting bitonic sequences, illustrated in Figure 12-2 to Figure 12-6.

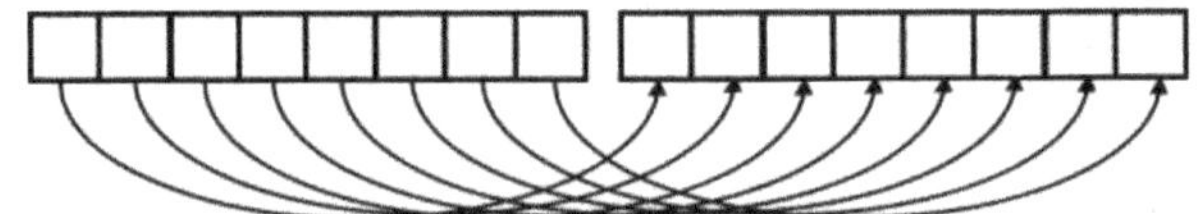

Figure 12-2. *Initial bitonic sequence before sorting*

We split the sequence into two parts and compare each element of the left part with the corresponding element of the right part. If the left element is greater than the right, we swap them. Our sequence consists of two vectors, and the following figure illustrates this operation:

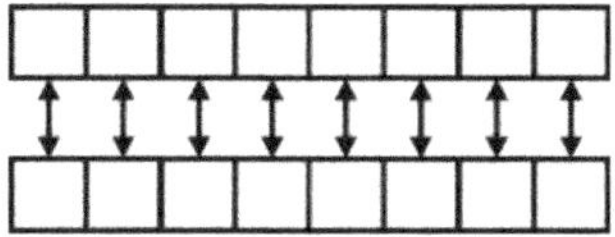

Figure 12-3. *Bitonic sorting step with vector compare-swap operation*

The original bitonic sequence first increases to some maximum point, then decreases. When splitting into two halves and comparing-swapping, element x_i from the left half swaps with element $x_{i+W/2}$ from the right half if $x_i > x_{i+W/2}$. Note that in a bitonic sequence, elements are symmetrically positioned relative to the maximum point. After swapping, each half preserves the "first increasing, then decreasing" property, but now all elements in the left half are guaranteed not to exceed the corresponding elements in the right half. This allows us to recursively sort each half independently.

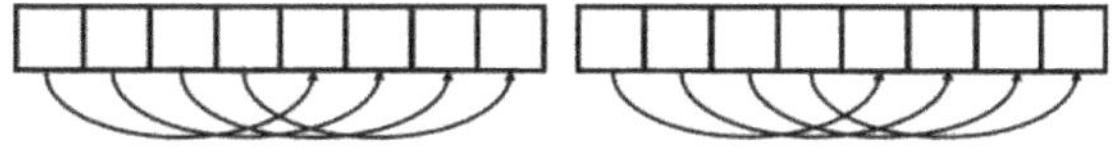

Figure 12-4. *Bitonic sorting: first recursive step*

This continues until we reach sequences of length 1, which are trivially sorted.

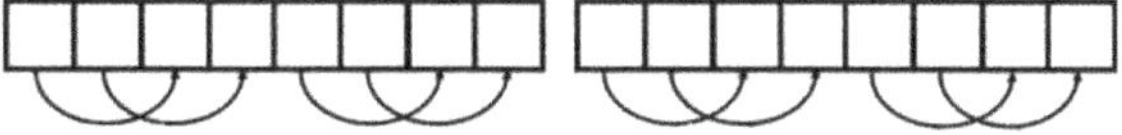

Figure 12-5. *Bitonic sorting: second recursive step*

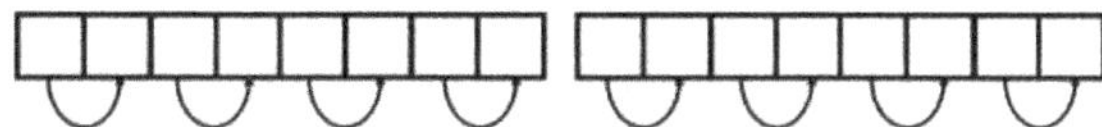

Figure 12-6. *Bitonic sorting: final sorted result*

Note that with vector length W, exactly W comparisons occur at each stage. This means vectors can be used efficiently if we correctly rearrange elements each time. The familiar **zip** operation facilitates this rearrangement.

```java
1    package com.nonpareilcoder.realleetcode;
2
3    import jdk.incubator.vector.*;
4
5    import static jdk.incubator.vector.VectorOperators.*;
6
7    public class MergeArraysBitonic {
8      static final VectorSpecies<Integer> SP =
9        IntVector.SPECIES_PREFERRED;
10     static final int vl = SP.length();
11
12     static final VectorShuffle<Integer> _rev =
13       VectorShuffle.iota(SP, vl - 1, -1, false);
14
15     static final VectorShuffle<Integer> _zip0 =
16       VectorShuffle.makeZip(SP, 0);
17     static final VectorShuffle<Integer> _zip1 =
18       VectorShuffle.makeZip(SP, 1);
19
20     public static int[] merge(int[] input0, int[] input1) {
21       int[] output = new int[input0.length + input1.length];
22
23       int stop0 = input0.length - 2 * vl;
24       int stop1 = input1.length - 2 * vl;
25
26       int i0 = 0, i1 = 0, j = 0;
27       for (; i0 < stop0 && i1 < stop1; ) {
28         var _part0 = IntVector.fromArray(SP, input0, i0);
29         var _part1 = IntVector.fromArray(SP, input0, i0 + vl);
30         var _part3 = IntVector.fromArray(SP, input1, i1);
31         var _part2 = IntVector.fromArray(SP, input1, i1 + vl);
32
33         _part3 = _part3.rearrange(_rev);
34         _part2 = _part2.rearrange(_rev);
35
```

```
36        var _cmp0 = _part0.compare(LT, _part2);
37        var _cmp1 = _part1.compare(LT, _part3);
38
39        _part0 = _part2.blend(_part0, _cmp0);
40        _part1 = _part3.blend(_part1, _cmp1);
41
42        int advance0 = _cmp0.trueCount() + _cmp1.trueCount();
43        int advance1 = 2 * vl - advance0;
44
45        i0 += advance0;
46        i1 += advance1;
47
48        for (int i = 1; i <= vl; i <<= 1) {
49          _cmp0 = _part0.compare(LT, _part1);
50
51          var _t0 = _part0;
52          _part0 = _part1.blend(_part0, _cmp0);
53          _part1 = _t0.blend(_part1, _cmp0);
54
55          _t0 = _part0;
56          _part0 = _part0.rearrange(_zip0, _part1);
57          _part1 = _t0.rearrange(_zip1, _part1);
58        }
59
60        _part0.intoArray(output, j);
61        _part1.intoArray(output, j + vl);
62
63        j += 2 * vl;
64      }
65
66      MergeArraysScalar.mergeCore(input0, input1, output, i0, i1, j);
67
68      return output;
69    }
70  }
71
```

- Lines 28–31 load four vectors.

- Lines 33–34 reverse two of the loaded vectors.

- Lines 36–40 perform the first step of bitonic sorting.

- Since merge path analysis tells us that guaranteed correct results only appear in the first two vectors, the latter two need not be sorted further, reducing computation. The starting indices for the next outer loop iteration are updated in lines 42–46.

- The inner loop in lines 48–58 performs all remaining bitonic sorting steps.

- Lines 60–61 store the sorted vectors into the output array.

- Line 66 merges the remaining short "tails" of the arrays using the scalar algorithm.

Unrolled Loop

Additional performance gains can be obtained by unrolling the outer loop.

```
1    package com.nonpareilcoder.realleetcode;
2
3    import jdk.incubator.vector.*;
4    import static jdk.incubator.vector.VectorOperators.*;
5
6    public class MergeArraysUnrolled {
7      static final VectorSpecies<Integer> SP =
8        IntVector.SPECIES_PREFERRED;
9      static final int vl = SP.length();
10
11     static final VectorShuffle<Integer> _rev =
12       VectorShuffle.iota(SP, vl - 1, -1, false);
13
14     static final VectorShuffle<Integer> _zip0 =
15       VectorShuffle.makeZip(SP, 0);
16     static final VectorShuffle<Integer> _zip1 =
```

```
17        VectorShuffle.makeZip(SP, 1);
18
19    public static int[] merge(int[] input0, int[] input1) {
20      int[] output = new int[input0.length + input1.length];
21
22      int stop0 = input0.length - 4 * vl;
23      int stop1 = input1.length - 4 * vl;
24
25      int i0 = 0, i1 = 0, j = 0;
26      for (; i0 < stop0 && i1 < stop1; ) {
27        var _part0 = IntVector.fromArray(SP, input0, i0);
28        var _part1 = IntVector.fromArray(SP, input0, i0 + vl);
29        var _part3 = IntVector.fromArray(SP, input1, i1);
30        var _part2 = IntVector.fromArray(SP, input1, i1 + vl);
31
32        _part3 = _part3.rearrange(_rev);
33        _part2 = _part2.rearrange(_rev);
34
35        var _cmp0 = _part0.compare(LT, _part2);
36        var _cmp1 = _part1.compare(LT, _part3);
37
38        _part0 = _part2.blend(_part0, _cmp0);
39        _part1 = _part3.blend(_part1, _cmp1);
40
41        int advance0 = _cmp0.trueCount() + _cmp1.trueCount();
42        int advance1 = 2 * vl - advance0;
43
44        i0 += advance0;
45        i1 += advance1;
46
47        var _part4 = IntVector.fromArray(SP, input0, i0);
48        var _part5 = IntVector.fromArray(SP, input0, i0 + vl);
49        var _part7 = IntVector.fromArray(SP, input1, i1);
50        var _part6 = IntVector.fromArray(SP, input1, i1 + vl);
51
52        _part7 = _part7.rearrange(_rev);
```

```
53          _part6 = _part6.rearrange(_rev);
54
55          _cmp0 = _part4.compare(LT, _part6);
56          _cmp1 = _part5.compare(LT, _part7);
57
58          _part4 = _part6.blend(_part4, _cmp0);
59          _part5 = _part7.blend(_part5, _cmp1);
60
61          advance0 = _cmp0.trueCount() + _cmp1.trueCount();
62          advance1 = 2 * vl - advance0;
63
64          i0 += advance0;
65          i1 += advance1;
66
67          for (int i = 1; i <= vl; i <<= 1) {
68            _cmp0 = _part0.compare(LT, _part1);
69
70            var _t0 = _part0;
71            _part0 = _part1.blend(_part0, _cmp0);
72            _part1 = _t0.blend(_part1, _cmp0);
73
74            _cmp1 = _part4.compare(LT, _part5);
75
76            var _t1 = _part4;
77            _part4 = _part5.blend(_part4, _cmp1);
78            _part5 = _t1.blend(_part5, _cmp1);
79
80            _t0 = _part0;
81            _part0 = _part0.rearrange(_zip0, _part1);
82            _part1 = _t0.rearrange(_zip1, _part1);
83
84            _t1 = _part4;
85            _part4 = _part4.rearrange(_zip0, _part5);
86            _part5 = _t1.rearrange(_zip1, _part5);
87          }
88
```

```
 89            _part0.intoArray(output, j);
 90            _part1.intoArray(output, j + vl);
 91            _part4.intoArray(output, j + 2 * vl);
 92            _part5.intoArray(output, j + 3 * vl);
 93
 94          j += 4 * vl;
 95        }
 96
 97      MergeArraysScalar.mergeCore(input0, input1, output, i0, i1, j);
 98
 99      return output;
100    }
101  }
102
```

- Lines 27–30, as before, load four vectors.

- Lines 32–33 reverse two of the loaded vectors.

- Lines 35–39 perform the first step of bitonic sorting.

- Indices are updated in lines 41–45.

- Lines 47–50 load a second quartet of vectors using the new indices.

- Lines 52–53 reverse two vectors from this quartet.

- Lines 55–59 perform the first step of bitonic sorting for the second quartet of vectors.

- The next outer loop iteration's indices are updated in lines 61–65. Everything is ready for the doubled inner loop.

- The loop in lines 67–87 performs all remaining bitonic sorting steps. The compare-swap operations in lines 68–72 and lines 74–78 are data-independent of each other, as they work with different vector pairs. However, both fragments contain identical instructions and therefore require access to the same processor execution unit. This can lead to hardware instruction execution delays.

- Lines 89–92 unload all four sorted vectors into the output array.

Asymmetric Loop

Recall hyperthreading, the technology used in modern processors. Imagine a processor core handling two instruction streams simultaneously. With high probability, instructions from different streams will be different and consequently will execute on different processor subsystems. This results in more efficient processor core utilization.

We now modify the code, creating a software analogue of hyperthreading.

```
 1    package com.nonpareilcoder.realleetcode;
 2
 3    import jdk.incubator.vector.*;
 4
 5    import static jdk.incubator.vector.VectorOperators.*;
 6
 7    public class MergeArraysAsymmetric {
 8      static final VectorSpecies<Integer> SP =
 9        IntVector.SPECIES_PREFERRED;
10      static final int vl = SP.length();
11
12      static final VectorShuffle<Integer> _rev =
13        VectorShuffle.iota(SP, vl - 1, -1, false);
14
15      static final VectorShuffle<Integer> _zip0 =
16        VectorShuffle.makeZip(SP, 0);
17      static final VectorShuffle<Integer> _zip1 =
18        VectorShuffle.makeZip(SP, 1);
19
20      public static int[] merge(int[] input0, int[] input1) {
21        int[] output = new int[input0.length + input1.length];
22
23        int stop0 = input0.length - 4 * vl;
24        int stop1 = input1.length - 4 * vl;
25
26        int i0 = 0, i1 = 0, j = 0;
27        for (; i0 < stop0 && i1 < stop1; ) {
28          var _part0 = IntVector.fromArray(SP, input0, i0);
```

```
29        var _part1 = IntVector.fromArray(SP, input0, i0 + vl);
30        var _part3 = IntVector.fromArray(SP, input1, i1);
31        var _part2 = IntVector.fromArray(SP, input1, i1 + vl);
32
33        _part3 = _part3.rearrange(_rev);
34        _part2 = _part2.rearrange(_rev);
35
36        var _cmp0 = _part0.compare(LT, _part2);
37        var _cmp1 = _part1.compare(LT, _part3);
38
39        int advance0 = _cmp0.trueCount() + _cmp1.trueCount();
40        int advance1 = 2 * vl - advance0;
41
42        i0 += advance0;
43        i1 += advance1;
44
45        _part0 = _part2.blend(_part0, _cmp0);
46        _part1 = _part3.blend(_part1, _cmp1);
47
48        var _part4 = IntVector.fromArray(SP, input0, i0);
49        var _part5 = IntVector.fromArray(SP, input0, i0 + vl);
50        var _part7 = IntVector.fromArray(SP, input1, i1);
51        var _part6 = IntVector.fromArray(SP, input1, i1 + vl);
52
53        _part7 = _part7.rearrange(_rev);
54        _part6 = _part6.rearrange(_rev);
55
56        _cmp0 = _part4.compare(LT, _part6);
57        _cmp1 = _part5.compare(LT, _part7);
58
59        _part4 = _part6.blend(_part4, _cmp0);
60        _part5 = _part7.blend(_part5, _cmp1);
61
62        advance0 = _cmp0.trueCount() + _cmp1.trueCount();
63        advance1 = 2 * vl - advance0;
```

```
64
65            i0 += advance0;
66            i1 += advance1;
67
68            _cmp0 = _part0.compare(LT, _part1);
69
70            var _t0 = _part0;
71            _part0 = _part1.blend(_part0, _cmp0);
72            _part1 = _t0.blend(_part1, _cmp0);
73
74            for (int i = 1; i < vl; i <<= 1) {
75              _t0 = _part0;
76              _part0 = _part0.rearrange(_zip0, _part1);
77              _part1 = _t0.rearrange(_zip1, _part1);
78
79              _cmp1 = _part4.compare(LT, _part5);
80
81              var _t1 = _part4;
82              _part4 = _part5.blend(_part4, _cmp1);
83              _part5 = _t1.blend(_part5, _cmp1);
84
85              _t1 = _part4;
86              _part4 = _part4.rearrange(_zip0, _part5);
87              _part5 = _t1.rearrange(_zip1, _part5);
88
89              _cmp0 = _part0.compare(LT, _part1);
90
91              _t0 = _part0;
92              _part0 = _part1.blend(_part0, _cmp0);
93              _part1 = _t0.blend(_part1, _cmp0);
94            }
95
96         _t0 = _part0;
97         _part0 = _part0.rearrange(_zip0, _part1);
98         _part1 = _t0.rearrange(_zip1, _part1);
99
```

```
100            _cmp1 = _part4.compare(LT, _part5);
101
102         var _t1 = _part4;
103         _part4 = _part5.blend(_part4, _cmp1);
104         _part5 = _t1.blend(_part5, _cmp1);
105
106         _t1 = _part4;
107         _part4 = _part4.rearrange(_zip0, _part5);
108         _part5 = _t1.rearrange(_zip1, _part5);
109
110         _part0.intoArray(output, j);
111         _part1.intoArray(output, j + vl);
112         _part4.intoArray(output, j + 2 * vl);
113         _part5.intoArray(output, j + 3 * vl);
114
115       j += 4 * vl;
116     }
117
118   MergeArraysScalar.mergeCore(input0, input1, output, i0, i1, j);
119
120   return output;
121   }
122 }
123
```

- Preparation of two vector pairs in lines 28–66 does not differ from the previous program.

- Lines 68–72 contain the inner loop's prologue. We essentially pulled the first (or last) loop iteration out of it and placed one of the compare-swap operations before the loop.

- The loop in lines 74–94 performs all remaining bitonic sorting steps except one. The loop appears unusual, as if it does not start from the beginning.

- The asymmetric inner loop, despite seeming illogical, has advantages. The permutations in lines 75–77 are followed by a compare-swap of a different vector pair in lines 79–83. These two fragments are not only data-independent, working with different vector pairs, but also use different instructions that likely execute in different processor subsystems. This increases the probability of out-of-order execution of the second fragment's instructions.

- Similarly, executing fragments in lines 85–87 and lines 89–93 can be accelerated using instruction-level parallelism.

- Note that lines 89–93 already begin the next iteration.

- The remnants of the last iteration, from which we tore the prologue, follow the loop in lines 96–108.

- Lines 110–113 unload all four sorted vectors into the output array.

Writing such an asymmetric loop with a prologue and an epilogue based on intuition is impossible. It contradicts our sense of beauty. But meticulous parallelism analysis allows us to derive a non-trivial solution. Instruction-level parallelism works better when the loop interleaves several independent and maximally dissimilar instruction streams. Since each stream works with its own data set, the critical resource typically becomes the number of available vector registers.

Ranking Elements

Consider the vector merging task from a different point of view. Given two sorted vectors, for each element of these vectors, we can compute its position in the merged vector and then place all elements in their correct positions in one fell swoop. The position of each element x in the final vector equals the count of elements y such that

- y belongs to the first or second source vector;

- $y < x$.

The count of elements belonging to the same source vector as x and less than x is already known: this count equals the index of element x, since the vector is sorted by definition. We deal with the case of equal elements in vectors later.

Since the other vector is also sorted, the count of its elements less than x is easily found using binary search. This yields a simple algorithm.

```
1   package com.nonpareilcoder.realleetcode;
2
3   import jdk.incubator.vector.*;
4   import static jdk.incubator.vector.VectorOperators.*;
5
6   public class MergeArraysScatter {
7     static final VectorSpecies<Integer> SP =
8         IntVector.SPECIES_PREFERRED;
9     static final int vl = SP.length();
10
11    public static int[] merge(int[] input0, int[] input1) {
12      int[] output = new int[input0.length + input1.length];
13
14      int stop0 = input0.length - vl;
15      int stop1 = input1.length - vl;
16
17      IntVector _iota = VectorShuffle.iota(SP, 0, 1, false)
18        .toVector().reinterpretAsInts();
19
20      int[] pos0 = new int[vl];
21      int[] pos1 = new int[vl];
22
23      int i0 = 0, i1 = 0, j = 0;
24      for (; i0 < stop0 && i1 < stop1;) {
25        IntVector _part0 = IntVector.fromArray(SP, input0, i0);
26        IntVector _part1 = IntVector.fromArray(SP, input1, i1);
27
28        IntVector _shift = IntVector.broadcast(SP, vl);
29        IntVector _pos0 = _shift, _pos1 = _shift;
30
31        for (int step = vl; step > 0; step >>= 1) {
32          _shift = _shift.lanewise(ASHR, 1,
33              _shift.compare(GT, 1));
```

```
34
35            IntVector _new0 = _pos0.sub(_shift);
36            IntVector _new1 = _pos1.sub(_shift);
37
38          var _comp0 = _part1.rearrange(_new0.toShuffle())
39              .compare(GT, _part0);
40          var _comp1 = _part0.rearrange(_new1.toShuffle())
41              .compare(GE, _part1);
42
43          _pos0 = _pos0.blend(_new0, _comp0);
44          _pos1 = _pos1.blend(_new1, _comp1);
45        }
46
47        _pos0 = _pos0.add(_iota);
48        _pos1 = _pos1.add(_iota);
49
50        _pos0.intoArray(pos0, 0);
51        _pos1.intoArray(pos1, 0);
52
53        _part0.intoArray(output, j, pos0, 0);
54        _part1.intoArray(output, j, pos1, 0);
55
56        var _cmp = _pos0.compare(LT, vl);
57        int advance0 = _cmp.trueCount();
58        int advance1 = vl - advance0;
59
60        i0 += advance0;
61        i1 += advance1;
62
63        j += vl;
64      }
65
66      MergeArraysScalar.mergeCore(input0, input1, output, i0, i1, j);
67
68      return output;
```

```
69      }
70    }
71
```

- Lines 31–45 perform binary search in parallel for all vector elements. Operations on both vectors are mirror-symmetric, except for lines 38–41. Note that the inequality in line 39 is strict, while in line 41 it is non-strict. This resolves the ambiguity with equal elements.

- Lines 47–48 add the element index within its own vector to the position.

- Lines 50–51 store the resulting indices into auxiliary arrays.

- Lines 53–54 perform selective writing of vectors into the final array at the specified indices.

- Lines 56–58 determine which portion of the result is correct, using a method that does not rely on the merge path.

We encounter here a new variant of the **intoArray** method that writes values to an array at specified indices.

The operation, commonly called **scatter**,

```
vector.intoArray(output, offset, map, mapOffset);
```

means

```
for(int i = 0; i < SP.length(); i++) {
  output[map[i + mapOffset] + offset] = vector[i];
}
```

The operation is powerful but should be used sparingly.

- Unlike sequential writing of array elements to memory, **scatter** writes the vector elements in arbitrary order according to indices. There is no requirement that all write addresses be used. This means the output array may contain cells without data, which can cause problems in subsequent code.

- Conversely, indices may repeat, leading to write conflicts. It is unknown which of the conflicting elements will win (or lose?) the race and be written to memory last, overwriting previous writes.

- The operation is horizontal, since it works sequentially with elements of a single vector. Even worse, accesses to different memory cells occur sequentially, leading to additional delays.

- In the Java Vector API, the operation requires an awkward two-step process. First, you must write indices to an array. Then, with a second function call, store the data at those indices.

Despite its drawbacks, **scatter** is a useful vector programming tool and, at times, irreplaceable.

Benchmarks

Table 12-1 and Table 12-2 compare the various merge algorithms.

Table 12-1. *Single-core speedup on x86 platforms (higher is better)*

Variant	GL	Z2	IL	SR	Z5
asymmetric	0.04	0.86	1.21	1.03	0.98
bitonic	0.04	0.72	1.15	1.04	0.92
scalar	1.00	1.00	1.00	1.00	1.00
scatter	0.02	0.15	0.36	0.45	0.18
unrolled	0.04	0.82	1.09	1.04	0.99

The X86 benchmark results reveal that array merging is a challenging problem for vectorization, with most configurations showing minimal or negative gains. The scatter variant stands out as a severe outlier with catastrophic slowdowns across all platforms, confirming that indexed memory writes are extremely expensive even on modern hardware. IL (Intel Ice Lake) emerges as the best performer, with the asymmetric variant achieving a modest 1.21× speedup, likely benefiting from AVX-512's rich shuffle and permutation instructions. Interestingly, the server processors (Z2, SR, Z5) show performance near or below scalar, suggesting that the data-dependent nature of merging limits vectorization benefits even on powerful hardware. The asymmetric loop optimization provides a small but consistent advantage over the basic bitonic and unrolled variants on processors that can exploit instruction-level parallelism.

Table 12-2. *Single-core speedup on ARM platforms (higher is better)*

Variant	M4	O6	CO	NV	G3
asymmetric	0.52	0.68	0.69	0.58	0.80
bitonic	0.54	0.69	0.68	0.55	0.78
scalar	1.00	1.00	1.00	1.00	1.00
scatter	0.11	0.26	0.25	0.18	0.15
unrolled	0.52	0.65	0.67	0.58	0.75

The ARM benchmark results paint a discouraging picture for vectorized array merging, with every variant producing slowdowns across all tested platforms. The scatter variant is again the worst outlier, demonstrating that indexed memory writes are even more costly on ARM architectures than on X86. G3 (Amazon Graviton 3) achieves the best relative performance at 0.80× for the asymmetric variant, yet still fails to match scalar execution despite having 256-bit SVE support. The consistent slowdowns across diverse ARM implementations indicate that the merge algorithm's irregular data access patterns and conditional logic fundamentally resist vectorization on this architecture. These results suggest that for array merging on ARM platforms, the simple scalar algorithm remains the optimal choice.

What's Next

Having explored merging sorted sequences, we now tackle a different kind of sequence problem: computing sliding window products. The next chapter develops a universal parallel sliding sum algorithm using suffix and prefix products, introducing the gather operation and demonstrating how vertical scan eliminates the inefficiencies of horizontal approaches.

CHAPTER 13

Largest Product in a Series

Project Euler. Problem 8.

The four adjacent digits in the 1000-digit number that have the greatest product are $9 \times 9 \times 8 \times 9 = 5832$.

7316717653133062491922511967442657474235534919493

9698352031277450632623957831801698480186947885184

8586156078911294949545950173795833195285320880551

1254069874715852386305071569329096329522744304355

6689664895044524452316173185640309871112172238311

6222989342338030813533627661428280644448664523874

3035890729629049156044077239071381051585930796086

7017242712188399879790879227492190169972088809377

6572733300105336788122023542180975125454059475224

5258490771167055601360483958644670632441572215539

5369781797784617406495514929086256932197846862248

8397224137565705605749026140797296865241453510047

821663704844031**9989**000889524345065854122758866688

1642717147992444292823086346567481391912316282458

1786645835912456652947654568284891288314260769004

2421902267105562632111110937054421750694165896040

© Roman Snytsar 2026

R. Snytsar, *Mastering SIMD with Java Vector API*, https://doi.org/10.1007/979-8-8688-2676-4_13

07198403850962455444362981230987879927244284909188

84580156166097919133875499200524063689912560717606

05886116467109405077541002256983155200055935729725

71636269561882670428252483600823257530420752963450

Find the thirteen adjacent digits in the 1000-digit number that have the greatest product. What is the value of this product?

In This Chapter

1. The parallel sliding sum algorithm using suffix and prefix products

2. The gather operation for indexed memory loads

3. When scalar algorithmic optimization outperforms vectorization

4. Trade-offs between gather-based loading and explicit vector pivoting

Naive Algorithm

The parallel sliding sum algorithm is, perhaps, my most significant personal contribution to algorithm theory (Snytsar & Turakhia, 2019). The problem can be formulated in general terms as follows. Given a sequence of N elements

$$[x_1; x_2; \ldots; x_k; \ldots; x_N],$$

along with a number $K < N$, called the window size, and some operation $\oplus$.

We need to find a sequence of $N - K + 1$ elements:

$$[x_1 \oplus x_2 \oplus \ldots \oplus x_K; x_2 \oplus x_3 \oplus \ldots \oplus x_{K+1}; \ldots; x_{N-K} \oplus x_{N-K+1} \oplus \ldots \oplus x_N]$$

We can visualize the problem like this: a template with a window size K slides along the array. At each step, the elements visible in the window are reduced using operation $\oplus$, and the result is placed in the output sequence.

Note on terminology: historically, problems of this type are called "sliding sum" (or sliding window sum), even if operation $\oplus$ is not arithmetic addition. This is an established term reflecting the sliding window mechanism, not the specific operation.

In our particular case, $N = 1000$; $K = 13$; $\oplus = \times$. We are computing a sliding product, but we will use the general term "sliding sum" to describe the class of algorithms.

We start with a simple two-nested-loop algorithm that works according to the sliding sum definition.

```
1   package com.nonpareilcoder.projecteuler;
2
3   public class LargestProductInSeriesBaseline {
4     static final String thousandDigits =
5       "73167176531330624919225119674426574742355349194934" +
6         "96983520312774506326239578318016984801869478851843" +
7         "85861560789112949495459501737958331952853208805511" +
8         "12540698747158523863050715693290963295227443043557" +
9         "66896648950445244523161731856403098711121722383113" +
10        "62229893423380308135336276614282806444486645238749" +
11        "30358907296290491560440772390713810515859307960866" +
12        "70172427121883998797908792274921901699720888093776" +
13        "65727333001053367881220235421809751254540594752243" +
14        "52584907711670556013604839586446706324415722155397" +
15        "53697817977846174064955149290862569321978468622482" +
16        "83972241375657056057490261407972968652414535100474" +
17        "82166370484403199890008895243450658541227588666881" +
18        "16427171479924442928230863465674813919123162824586" +
19        "17866458359124566529476545682848912883142607690042" +
20        "24219022671055626321111109370544217506941658960408" +
21        "07198403850962455444362981230987879927244284909188" +
22        "84580156166097919133875499200524063689912560717606" +
23        "05886116467109405077541002256983155200055935729725" +
24        "71636269561882670428252483600823257530420752963450";
25
26    public static long compute() {
27      long maxValue = 0;
28
```

```
29          for (int i = 0; i < 987; i++) {
30            long currentValue = 1;
31            for (int j = 0; j < 13; j++) {
32              int digit = Character
33                  .getNumericValue(thousandDigits.charAt(i + j));
34              currentValue *= digit;
35            }
36
37            if (maxValue < currentValue) {
38              maxValue = currentValue;
39            }
40          }
41
42          return maxValue;
43        }
44      }
45
```

- The inner loop in lines 31–34 computes each new sliding sum value without using results from previous iterations.

- With array length N and window size K, the algorithm requires $O(NK)$ operations.

Sliding Algorithm

If the sliding sum operation has an inverse operation (which we will call subtraction), then the transition from one sliding sum to the next can be simplified, as shown in Figure 13-1.

Figure 13-1. *Sliding window algorithm*

If we have already computed a sliding sum of K elements, we subtract the leftmost element from it and add the element to the right of the window. Then, we shift the window one element to the right. This sliding algorithm runs much faster, requiring only around N operations and N inverse operations. Unfortunately, not every operation has an inverse; examples of non-invertible operations are **max** and **min**.

Clarification: the absence of an inverse operation does not mean an asymptotically efficient solution is impossible. For max and min operations, specialized sliding window algorithms exist (e.g., based on monotonic queues) that run in $O(N)$ time. However, such algorithms are specific to particular operations and lack the universality of the inverse operation approach.

The inverse operation for multiplication is division. The sliding algorithm works, except there is a danger of division by zero. We can convert this flaw into an opportunity for additional speedup. If a zero appears in the sequence, all K products containing this element are obviously equal to zero. There is no need to compute these products. We can immediately jump past zero and restart the algorithm from the element following zero.

```
1    package com.nonpareilcoder.projecteuler;
2
3    public class LargestProductInSeriesSliding {
4      static final String thousandDigits =
5        LargestProductInSeriesBaseline.thousandDigits;
6
7      public static long compute() {
8        long maxValue = 0;
9
10       for (int start = 0, i; start < 1000; start = i) {
11
12         long currentValue = 1;
13
14         for (i = start; i < 1000; i++) {
15           int newDigit = Character
16             .getNumericValue(thousandDigits.charAt(i));
17
18           if (newDigit == 0) {
19             i++;
20             break;
```

```
21            }
22
23            currentValue *= newDigit;
24
25         if (i < start + 12)
26            continue;
27
28         if (maxValue < currentValue) {
29            maxValue = currentValue;
30         }
31
32         int oldDigit = Character
33            .getNumericValue(thousandDigits.charAt(i - 12));
34         currentValue /= oldDigit;
35       }
36     }
37
38    return maxValue;
39   }
40  }
41
```

- Lines 18–21 show the jump over zero.

- Although the program has two nested loops, execution time is linear.

Element-Wise Vector Algorithm

We begin with a vector algorithm that processes input sequence elements one at a time (see Figure 13-2).

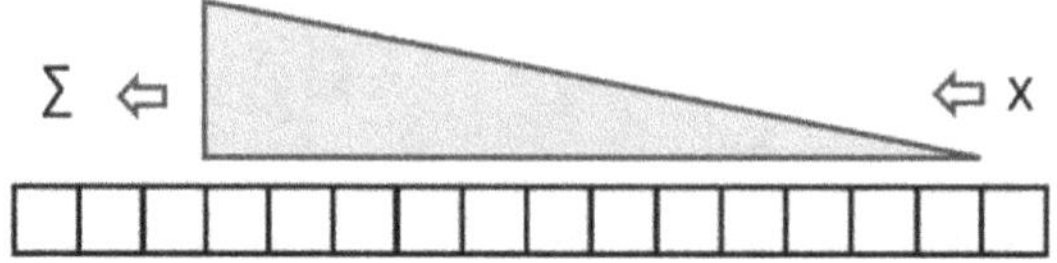

Figure 13-2. *Element-wise vector algorithm with suffix sum*

Suppose the vector contains a suffix sum of the first $K - 1$ sequence terms. The vector can be composite if $K - 1$ is greater than the length of one hardware vector.

The choice of suffix sum specifically requires explanation. Suffix sum means the first (left) vector element contains the sum of all $K - 1$ elements, the second element contains the sum of the last $K - 2$ elements, and so on. When we add a new value x_K to each element of this vector, the first element gets the complete sum of K elements, which is exactly what is needed for the sliding window sum. If we used a prefix sum, the first element would contain only x_1, and adding x_K would not give the needed result without additional permutations.

We add the value of the next sequence term with index K to each vector element. This creates the sum of the first K terms of the original sequence in the very first (left) vector element—the first element of the output sequence. We move this value to the output sequence and shift the vector left, filling the freed right position with the original sequence term at index K.

By repeating the add-shift procedure, we sequentially generate all elements of the output sequence.

```java
1    package com.nonpareilcoder.projecteuler;

2

3    import jdk.incubator.vector.*;

4

5    public class LargestProductInSeriesOnline {
6      static final String thousandDigits =
7        LargestProductInSeriesBaseline.thousandDigits;

8

9      static final VectorSpecies<Long> SP =
10       LongVector.SPECIES_256;

11

12     public static long compute() {
13       LongVector _part0 = LongVector.broadcast(SP, 1L);
14       LongVector _part1 = _part0, _part2 = _part0;

15

16       long maxValue = 0;

17

18       for (int i = 0; i < 1000; i++) {

19
```

```
20          LongVector _currentDigit = LongVector.broadcast(
21            SP, Character.getNumericValue(thousandDigits.charAt(i)));
22
23          _part0 = _part0.mul(_currentDigit);
24          _part1 = _part1.mul(_currentDigit);
25          _part2 = _part2.mul(_currentDigit);
26
27        if (i >= 12) {
28          long currentValue = _part0.lane(0);
29
30          if (maxValue < currentValue) {
31            maxValue = currentValue;
32          }
33        }
34
35          _part0 = _part0.slice(1, _part1);
36          _part1 = _part1.slice(1, _part2);
37          _part2 = _part2.slice(1, _currentDigit);
38      }
39
40      return maxValue;
41    }
42  }
43
```

- We need a vector of 12 Long-type elements. We construct this from three 256-bit vectors. This determines the vector length choice in lines 9–10.

- Lines 23–25 add the next input sequence term to the composite vector.

- Line 28 extracts the newly obtained output sequence term.

- Lines 35–37 shift the composite vector left.

Two-Scan Algorithm

Using suffix sum in the previous algorithm suggests a potentially more efficient parallel approach. We compute a suffix sum of $K - 1$ input sequence terms and a prefix sum of the next $K - 1$ terms (Figure 13-3).

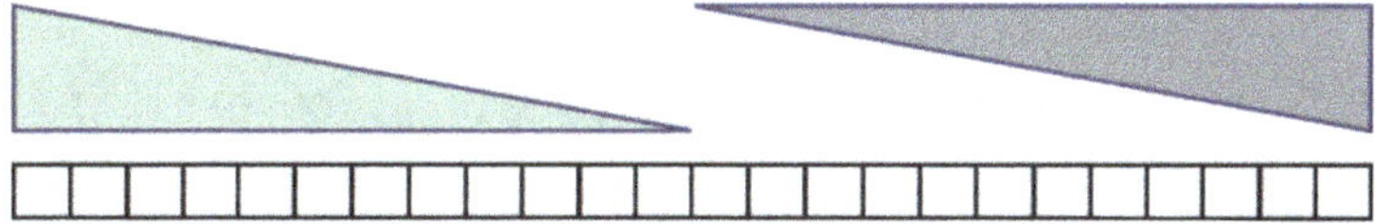

Figure 13-3. *Two-scan algorithm: suffix sum and prefix sum computation*

We add these sums element-wise (Figure 13-4).

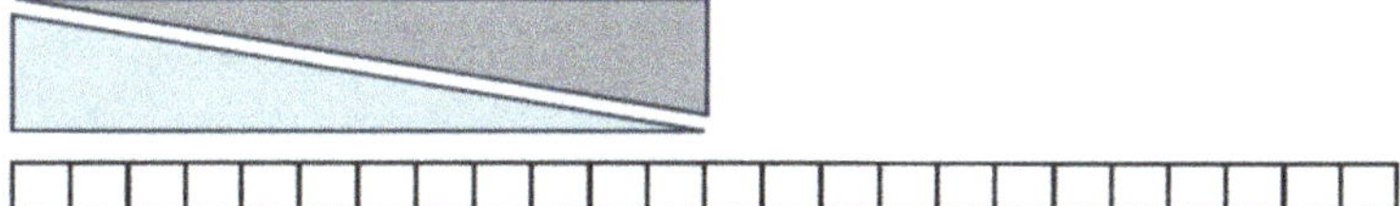

Figure 13-4. *Two-scan algorithm: element-wise addition of suffix and prefix sums*

We immediately get $K - 1$ output sequence terms.

Here is a justification for the correctness of this approach. Suppose the suffix sum contains values $S_i = x_1 \oplus x_2 \oplus \dots \oplus x_i$ for $i = 1, 2, \dots, K - 1$, and the prefix sum contains $P_j = x_K \oplus x_{K+1} \oplus \dots \oplus x_{K+j-1}$ for $j = 1, 2, \dots, K - 1$. Then with element-wise addition, we get:

$$S_i \oplus P_{K-i} = \left(x_1 \oplus \dots \oplus x_i \right) \oplus \left(x_{i+1} \oplus \dots \oplus x_K \right) = x_1 \oplus x_2 \oplus \dots \oplus x_K$$

This is precisely the i-th element of the sliding sum output sequence. Thus, in one iteration, we get $K - 1$ output elements in parallel.

Lastly, the input sequence counter is incremented by $K - 1$, and the procedure is repeated, starting with computing the cumulative sums.

If the sliding sum operation possesses the associative property, cumulative sums can be computed using vector scan. Recall why associativity is critical for vector scan. Vector scan works on the "divide and conquer" principle: at each step, pairs of elements are combined in parallel, then pairs of results are combined again, and so on. For example, to compute $(((a \oplus b) \oplus c) \oplus d)$, the algorithm first computes $(a \oplus b)$

and $(c \oplus d)$ in parallel, then combines the results. This gives the correct result only if $(a \oplus b) \oplus (c \oplus d) = ((a \oplus b) \oplus c) \oplus d$, which is the associative property. In our case, multiplication is associative: $(a \times b) \times c = a \times (b \times c)$, allowing us to apply vector scan.

```java
package com.nonpareilcoder.projecteuler;

import jdk.incubator.vector.*;
import jdk.incubator.vector.VectorOperators.Conversion;

import static jdk.incubator.vector.VectorOperators.*;

public class LargestProductInSeriesHorizontal {
  static final String thousandDigits =
    LargestProductInSeriesBaseline.thousandDigits +
      "00000000000000000000";

  static final VectorSpecies<Long> SP =
    LongVector.SPECIES_256;
  static final int vl = SP.length();
  static final VectorSpecies<Short> CHAR_SPECIES =
    ShortVector.SPECIES_256;
  static final Conversion<Short, Long> CONV =
    Conversion
      .ofCast(short.class, long.class);

  public static long[] preprocess(String chars) {
    var data = chars.toCharArray();

    var digits = new long[data.length];

    final long numBase = '0';
    var _mask = CHAR_SPECIES.indexInRange(0, vl);

    for (int i = 0; i < data.length; i += vl) {
      var shorts = ShortVector.fromCharArray(
        CHAR_SPECIES, data, i, _mask);
```

```
33        var longs = shorts.convertShape(CONV, SP, 0)
34            .reinterpretAsLongs().sub(numBase);
35        longs.intoArray(digits, i);
36      }
37
38     return digits;
39   }
40
41   public static long compute() {
42     var digits = preprocess(thousandDigits);
43
44     final var _one = LongVector.broadcast(SP, 1L);
45
46     var _max = LongVector.zero(SP);
47
48     var _part0 = LongVector.fromArray(SP, digits, 0);
49     var _part1 = LongVector.fromArray(SP, digits, 4);
50     var _part2 = LongVector.fromArray(SP, digits, 8);
51
52     for (int i = 12; i < digits.length; i += 12) {
53       var _prefix3 = LongVector.fromArray(SP, digits, i);
54       var _prefix4 = LongVector.fromArray(SP, digits, i + 4);
55       var _prefix5 = LongVector.fromArray(SP, digits, i + 8);
56
57       var _suffix0 = _part0.slice(1, _part1).mul(_part0);
58       var _suffix1 = _part1.slice(1, _part2).mul(_part1);
59       var _suffix2 = _part2.slice(1, _one).mul(_part2);
60
61       _part0 = _prefix3;
62       _part1 = _prefix4;
63       _part2 = _prefix5;
64
65       _prefix5 = _prefix4.slice(3, _prefix5).mul(_prefix5);
66       _prefix4 = _prefix3.slice(3, _prefix4).mul(_prefix4);
67       _prefix3 = _one.slice(3, _prefix3).mul(_prefix3);
```

```
68
69             _suffix0 = _suffix0.slice(2, _suffix1).mul(_suffix0);
70             _suffix1 = _suffix1.slice(2, _suffix2).mul(_suffix1);
71             _suffix2 = _suffix2.slice(2, _one).mul(_suffix2);
72
73             _prefix5 = _prefix4.slice(2, _prefix5).mul(_prefix5);
74             _prefix4 = _prefix3.slice(2, _prefix4).mul(_prefix4);
75             _prefix3 = _one.slice(2, _prefix3).mul(_prefix3);
76
77             _suffix0 = _suffix1.mul(_suffix0);
78             _suffix1 = _suffix2.mul(_suffix1);
79
80             _prefix5 = _prefix4.mul(_prefix5);
81             _prefix4 = _prefix3.mul(_prefix4);
82
83             _suffix0 = _suffix2.mul(_suffix0);
84
85             _prefix5 = _prefix3.mul(_prefix5);
86
87             _suffix0 = _suffix0.mul(_prefix3);
88             _suffix1 = _suffix1.mul(_prefix4);
89             _suffix2 = _suffix2.mul(_prefix5);
90
91          _max = _max.max(_suffix0);
92          _max = _max.max(_suffix1);
93          _max = _max.max(_suffix2);
94        }
95
96     long maxValue = _max.reduceLanes(MAX);
97
98     return maxValue;
99   }
100  }
101
```

- Input data conversion to Long format is extracted to a separate method in lines 22–39. This avoids cluttering the main loop with secondary details.

- Lines 48–50 contain the main loop prologue, which loads the first composite vector.

- Lines 53–55 load the second composite vector.

- Lines 57–89 compute two cumulative products in parallel. Since vector size is fixed, the vector scan loop is fully unrolled.

- Lines 87–89 multiply the cumulative products together.

Vertical Algorithm

The specifics of vertical scan were discussed in Chapters 10 and 12. The price for the scan's optimality is the cost of pivoting 12 vectors.

```
 1    package com.nonpareilcoder.projecteuler;
 2
 3    import jdk.incubator.vector.*;
 4
 5    import static jdk.incubator.vector.VectorOperators.*;
 6
 7    public class LargestProductInSeriesVertical {
 8      static final String thousandDigits =
 9        LargestProductInSeriesBaseline.thousandDigits +
10          "00000000000000000000";
11
12      static final VectorSpecies<Long> SP =
13        LongVector.SPECIES_256;
14
15      public static long compute() {
16        var digits =
17          LargestProductInSeriesHorizontal.preprocess(thousandDigits);
18
19        final var _zero = LongVector.zero(SP);
```

```
20
21        var _max = _zero;
22
23        final var _uzp0 = VectorShuffle.makeUnzip(SP, 0);
24        final var _uzp1 = VectorShuffle.makeUnzip(SP, 1);
25
26        for (int i = 0; i < 972; i += 36) {
27          var _part0 = LongVector.fromArray(SP, digits, i);
28          var _part1 = LongVector.fromArray(SP, digits, i + 4);
29          var _part2 = LongVector.fromArray(SP, digits, i + 8);
30          var _part3 = LongVector.fromArray(SP, digits, i + 12);
31          var _part4 = LongVector.fromArray(SP, digits, i + 16);
32          var _part5 = LongVector.fromArray(SP, digits, i + 20);
33          var _part6 = LongVector.fromArray(SP, digits, i + 24);
34          var _part7 = LongVector.fromArray(SP, digits, i + 28);
35          var _part8 = LongVector.fromArray(SP, digits, i + 32);
36          var _part9 = LongVector.fromArray(SP, digits, i + 36);
37          var _partA = LongVector.fromArray(SP, digits, i + 40);
38          var _partB = LongVector.fromArray(SP, digits, i + 44);
39
40          var _t0 = _part0.rearrange(_uzp0, _part3);
41          var _t1 = _part1.rearrange(_uzp0, _part4);
42          var _t2 = _part2.rearrange(_uzp0, _part5);
43          var _t3 = _part0.rearrange(_uzp1, _part3);
44          var _t4 = _part1.rearrange(_uzp1, _part4);
45          var _t5 = _part2.rearrange(_uzp1, _part5);
46          var _t6 = _part6.rearrange(_uzp0, _part9);
47          var _t7 = _part7.rearrange(_uzp0, _partA);
48          var _t8 = _part8.rearrange(_uzp0, _partB);
49          var _t9 = _part6.rearrange(_uzp1, _part9);
50          var _tA = _part7.rearrange(_uzp1, _partA);
51          var _tB = _part8.rearrange(_uzp1, _partB);
52
53          _part0 = _t0.rearrange(_uzp0, _t6);
54          _part1 = _t3.rearrange(_uzp0, _t9);
```

```
55        _part2 = _t0.rearrange(_uzp1, _t6);
56        _part3 = _t3.rearrange(_uzp1, _t9);
57        _part4 = _t1.rearrange(_uzp0, _t7);
58        _part5 = _t4.rearrange(_uzp0, _tA);
59        _part6 = _t1.rearrange(_uzp1, _t7);
60        _part7 = _t4.rearrange(_uzp1, _tA);
61        _part8 = _t2.rearrange(_uzp0, _t8);
62        _part9 = _t5.rearrange(_uzp0, _tB);
63        _partA = _t2.rearrange(_uzp1, _t8);
64        _partB = _t5.rearrange(_uzp1, _tB);
65
66        var _suffix0 = _part0.mul(_part1);
67        var _suffix2 = _part2.mul(_part3);
68        var _suffix4 = _part4.mul(_part5);
69        var _suffix6 = _part6.mul(_part7);
70        var _suffix8 = _part8.mul(_part9);
71        var _suffixA = _partA.mul(_partB);
72
73        var _prefix1 = _part1.mul(_part0);
74        var _prefix3 = _part3.mul(_part2);
75        var _prefix5 = _part5.mul(_part4);
76        var _prefix7 = _part7.mul(_part6);
77        var _prefix9 = _part9.mul(_part8);
78        var _prefixB = _partB.mul(_partA);
79
80        _suffix0 = _suffix0.mul(_suffix2);
81        _suffix4 = _suffix4.mul(_suffix6);
82        _suffix8 = _suffix8.mul(_suffixA);
83
84        _prefix3 = _prefix3.mul(_prefix1);
85        _prefix7 = _prefix7.mul(_prefix5);
86        _prefixB = _prefixB.mul(_prefix9);
87
88        _suffix4 = _suffix4.mul(_suffix8);
89
```

```
90          _prefix7 = _prefix7.mul(_prefix3);
91
92          _suffix0 = _suffix0.mul(_suffix4);
93
94          _prefixB = _prefixB.mul(_prefix7);
95
96          _suffix2 = _suffix2.mul(_suffix4);
97          _suffix6 = _suffix6.mul(_suffix8);
98
99          _prefix5 = _prefix5.mul(_prefix3);
100         _prefix9 = _prefix9.mul(_prefix7);
101
102         var _r0 = _part0.slice(1, _zero).mul(_suffix0);
103         _max = _r0.max(_max);
104
105         var _suffix1 = _part1.mul(_suffix2);
106         var _r1 = _prefix1.slice(1, _zero).mul(_suffix1);
107         _max = _r1.max(_max);
108
109         var _prefix2 = _part2.mul(_prefix1);
110         var _r2 = _prefix2.slice(1, _zero).mul(_suffix2);
111         _max = _r2.max(_max);
112
113         var _suffix3 = _part3.mul(_suffix4);
114         var _r3 = _prefix3.slice(1, _zero).mul(_suffix3);
115         _max = _r3.max(_max);
116
117         var _prefix4 = _part4.mul(_prefix3);
118         var _r4 = _prefix4.slice(1, _zero).mul(_suffix4);
119         _max = _r4.max(_max);
120
121         var _suffix5 = _part5.mul(_suffix6);
122         var _r5 = _prefix5.slice(1, _zero).mul(_suffix5);
123         _max = _r5.max(_max);
124
```

```
125        var _prefix6 = _part6.mul(_prefix5);
126        var _r6 = _prefix6.slice(1, _zero).mul(_suffix6);
127        _max = _r6.max(_max);
128
129        var _suffix7 = _part7.mul(_suffix8);
130        var _r7 = _prefix7.slice(1, _zero).mul(_suffix7);
131        _max = _r7.max(_max);
132
133        var _prefix8 = _part8.mul(_prefix7);
134        var _r8 = _prefix8.slice(1, _zero).mul(_suffix8);
135        _max = _r8.max(_max);
136
137        var _suffix9 = _part9.mul(_suffixA);
138        var _r9 = _prefix9.slice(1, _zero).mul(_suffix9);
139        _max = _r9.max(_max);
140
141        var _prefixA = _partA.mul(_prefix9);
142        var _rA = _prefixA.slice(1, _zero).mul(_suffixA);
143        _max = _rA.max(_max);
144
145        _max = _prefixB.slice(1, _zero).mul(_partB).max(_max);
146    }
147
148    long maxValue = _max.reduceLanes(MAX);
149
150    return maxValue;
151    }
152 }
153
```

- Lines 27–38 load 12 vectors.

- Lines 40–64 reverse the vectors.

- Lines 66–100 compute two cumulative products in parallel.

- Lines 102–145 multiply the cumulative products together.

Universal Algorithm

Previous vector algorithms worked with 256-bit vectors. We would like to move to an algorithm independent of vector length. For this, we "merely" need to make the pivoting code universal. As we saw earlier, such code becomes bulky and complex. We will take a different path and use indexed loading (**gather**) to fetch data from memory in already-pivoted form.

Indexed load operation (**gather**)

```
vector = LongVector.fromArray(SP, input, offset, map, mapOffset);
```

is the inverse of **scatter**:

```
for(int i = 0; i < SP.length(); i++) {
  vector[i] = input[map[i + mapOffset] + offset];
}
```

```
 1    package com.nonpareilcoder.projecteuler;
 2
 3    import jdk.incubator.vector.*;
 4
 5    import static jdk.incubator.vector.VectorOperators.*;
 6
 7    public class LargestProductInSeriesGather {
 8      static final String thousandDigits =
 9        LargestProductInSeriesBaseline.thousandDigits +
10          "00000000000000000000000000000";
11
12      static final VectorSpecies<Long> SP =
13        LongVector.SPECIES_256;
14      static final int vl = SP.length();
15
16      public static long compute() {
17        var digits =
18          LargestProductInSeriesHorizontal.preprocess(thousandDigits);
19
20        final var _zero = LongVector.zero(SP);
21
```

```
22        var _max = _zero;
23
24        var strides = new int[vl];
25        for (int i = 0; i < vl; i++)
26          strides[i] = i * 12;
27
28        for (int i = 0; i < 1000; i += 12 * (vl - 1)) {
29          var _part0 = LongVector
30            .fromArray(SP, digits, i, strides, 0);
31          var _part1 = LongVector
32            .fromArray(SP, digits, i + 1, strides, 0);
33          var _part2 = LongVector
34            .fromArray(SP, digits, i + 2, strides, 0);
35          var _part3 = LongVector
36            .fromArray(SP, digits, i + 3, strides, 0);
37          var _part4 = LongVector
38            .fromArray(SP, digits, i + 4, strides, 0);
39          var _part5 = LongVector
40            .fromArray(SP, digits, i + 5, strides, 0);
41          var _part6 = LongVector
42            .fromArray(SP, digits, i + 6, strides, 0);
43          var _part7 = LongVector
44            .fromArray(SP, digits, i + 7, strides, 0);
45          var _part8 = LongVector
46            .fromArray(SP, digits, i + 8, strides, 0);
47          var _part9 = LongVector
48            .fromArray(SP, digits, i + 9, strides, 0);
49          var _partA = LongVector
50            .fromArray(SP, digits, i + 10, strides, 0);
51          var _partB = LongVector
52            .fromArray(SP, digits, i + 11, strides, 0);
53
54          var _suffix2 = _part2.mul(_part3);
55          var _suffix6 = _part6.mul(_part7);
56          var _suffixA = _partA.mul(_partB);
```

```
57
58              var _prefix1 = _part1.mul(_part0);
59              var _prefix5 = _part5.mul(_part4);
60              var _prefix9 = _part9.mul(_part8);
61
62              var _suffix0 = _prefix1.mul(_suffix2);
63              var _suffix4 = _prefix5.mul(_suffix6);
64              var _suffix8 = _prefix9.mul(_suffixA);
65
66              var _prefix3 = _suffix2.mul(_prefix1);
67              var _prefix7 = _suffix6.mul(_prefix5);
68              var _prefixB = _suffixA.mul(_prefix9);
69
70          _suffix4 = _suffix4.mul(_suffix8);
71
72          _prefix7 = _prefix7.mul(_prefix3);
73
74          _suffix0 = _suffix0.mul(_suffix4);
75
76          _prefixB = _prefixB.mul(_prefix7);
77
78          _suffix2 = _suffix2.mul(_suffix4);
79          _suffix6 = _suffix6.mul(_suffix8);
80
81          _prefix5 = _prefix5.mul(_prefix3);
82          _prefix9 = _prefix9.mul(_prefix7);
83
84          var _r0 = _part0.slice(1, _zero).mul(_suffix0);
85          _max = _r0.max(_max);
86
87          var _suffix1 = _part1.mul(_suffix2);
88          var _r1 = _prefix1.slice(1, _zero).mul(_suffix1);
89          _max = _r1.max(_max);
90
91              var _prefix2 = _part2.mul(_prefix1);
```

```
 92        var _r2 = _prefix2.slice(1, _zero).mul(_suffix2);
 93        _max = _r2.max(_max);
 94
 95        var _suffix3 = _part3.mul(_suffix4);
 96        var _r3 = _prefix3.slice(1, _zero).mul(_suffix3);
 97        _max = _r3.max(_max);
 98
 99        var _prefix4 = _part4.mul(_prefix3);
100        var _r4 = _prefix4.slice(1, _zero).mul(_suffix4);
101        _max = _r4.max(_max);
102
103        var _suffix5 = _part5.mul(_suffix6);
104        var _r5 = _prefix5.slice(1, _zero).mul(_suffix5);
105        _max = _r5.max(_max);
106
107        var _prefix6 = _part6.mul(_prefix5);
108        var _r6 = _prefix6.slice(1, _zero).mul(_suffix6);
109        _max = _r6.max(_max);
110
111        var _suffix7 = _part7.mul(_suffix8);
112        var _r7 = _prefix7.slice(1, _zero).mul(_suffix7);
113        _max = _r7.max(_max);
114
115        var _prefix8 = _part8.mul(_prefix7);
116        var _r8 = _prefix8.slice(1, _zero).mul(_suffix8);
117        _max = _r8.max(_max);
118
119        var _suffix9 = _part9.mul(_suffixA);
120        var _r9 = _prefix9.slice(1, _zero).mul(_suffix9);
121        _max = _r9.max(_max);
122
123        var _prefixA = _partA.mul(_prefix9);
124        var _rA = _prefixA.slice(1, _zero).mul(_suffixA);
125        _max = _rA.max(_max);
126
```

```
127            _max = _prefixB.slice(1, _zero).mul(_partB).max(_max);
128        }
129
130      long maxValue = _max.reduceLanes(MAX);
131
132      return maxValue;
133    }
134  }
135
```

- Lines 29–52 load 12 vectors. Note the additional `fromArray` method argument—`indexMap`. Despite the apparent parallelism of the **gather** operation, it accesses memory that is essentially sequential.

- Lines 54–82 compute two cumulative products in parallel. The first two scan steps, in lines 54–68, are more compact than in the previous program, thanks to optimization through reuse of common subexpressions of the two cumulative products.

- Lines 84–127 multiply the elements of cumulative products.

Benchmarks

Table 13-1 and Table 13-2 compare the sliding sum algorithm implementations.

Table 13-1. *Single-core speedup on x86 platforms (higher is better)*

Variant	GL	Z2	IL	SR	Z5
baseline	1.00	1.00	1.00	1.00	1.00
gather	0.06	2.94	3.12	5.20	7.39
horizontal	0.04	2.56	6.88	5.19	9.50
online	0.02	1.77	2.70	1.84	3.59
sliding	4.37	4.44	4.93	3.97	5.11
vertical	0.04	3.04	7.34	5.69	9.60

The X86 benchmark results demonstrate a clear hierarchy of sliding sum implementations, with the vertical optimal scan achieving the best performance on modern processors. The sliding scalar optimization provides consistent 4–5× speedup across all platforms, making it a reliable fallback when vectorization overhead is too high. Interestingly, the gather-based universal algorithm underperforms the explicit pivot (vertical) by 20–30% on most platforms, confirming that indexed loads carry significant overhead compared to direct permutation operations.

Table 13-2. *Single-core speedup on ARM platforms (higher is better)*

Variant	M4	O6	CO	NV	G3
baseline	1.00	1.00	1.00	1.00	1.00
gather	0.05	0.07	0.06	0.05	5.51
horizontal	0.02	0.03	0.03	0.02	6.40
online	0.01	0.01	0.01	0.01	3.36
sliding	5.90	7.07	6.81	5.58	6.46
vertical	0.03	0.04	0.03	0.02	7.98

The ARM benchmark results reveal a dramatic divide between 128-bit and 256-bit SVE implementations for the sliding product algorithm. 128-bit platforms show catastrophic slowdowns of 0.01–0.07× for all vector variants, making them completely impractical, while G3 (Amazon Graviton 3) achieves excellent 5–7.98× speedups. This stark contrast indicates that the algorithm's 12-vector unrolling and complex pivot operations overwhelm the 128-bit vector pipelines but execute efficiently with G3's 256-bit SVE. The scalar sliding variant provides remarkable 5–7× speedups across all ARM platforms. G3's vertical scan achieves the best overall ARM result at 7.98×, slightly exceeding even its scalar sliding performance (6.46×), demonstrating that wider vectors can outperform algorithmic optimizations when properly supported.

What's Next

We now turn to a classic interview problem that appears deceptively simple: finding the maximum subarray sum. The next chapter shows how Kadane's algorithm can be reformulated using prefix sums and prefix minima, revealing a path to vectorization that combines multiple parallel scans in a single pass.

Maximum Subarray Sum

Given an array of integers, find the contiguous subarray with the largest sum and return that sum.

For example:

```
Input:  [-2, 1, -3, 4, -1, 2, 1, -5, 4]
Answer: 6
[4, -1, 2, 1] has maximum sum 6

Input:  [1]
Answer: 1

Input:  [5, 4, -1, 7, 8]
Answer: 23
The entire array [5, 4, -1, 7, 8]
```

In This Chapter

1. How to reformulate Kadane's algorithm using prefix sums and prefix minima

2. Combining multiple parallel scans in a single loop

3. Why conditional restarts resist direct vectorization

4. Lightweight algorithms for narrow vector widths

R. Snytsar, *Mastering SIMD with Java Vector API*, https://doi.org/10.1007/979-8-8688-2676-4_14

Kadane's Algorithm

Kadane's algorithm is a solid solution—equally effective in interviews and production code. The algorithm rests on one key observation:

At each position *i*, the maximum sum of a subarray ending at *i* equals either:

1. nums[i] (start a new subarray)

2. nums[i] + maximum sum ending at *i* − 1 (extend the previous one)

In other words:

$$maxEndingHere[i] = max\left(nums[i], maxEndingHere[i-1] + nums[i]\right)$$

If maxEndingHere[i-1] is negative, starting a new subarray from nums[i] yields a larger sum.

```
1    package com.nonpareilcoder.realleetcode;
2
3    public class MaximumSubarrayBaseline {
4      static public int compute(int[] input) {
5        int maxSoFar = input[0];
6        int maxEndingHere = input[0];
7
8        for (int i = 1; i < input.length; i++) {
9          // Either extend existing subarray or start new one
10         int v = input[i];
11         maxEndingHere = Math.max(v, maxEndingHere + v);
12
13         // Update global maximum
14         maxSoFar = Math.max(maxSoFar, maxEndingHere);
15       }
16
17       return maxSoFar;
18     }
19   }
20
```

Kadane's recurrence superficially resembles a prefix sum:

$$prefixSum[i] = prefixSum[i-1] + nums[i]$$

$$maxEndingHere[i] = max\big(nums[i], maxEndingHere[i-1] + nums[i]\big)$$

Prefix sums vectorize through parallel scan because addition is *associative*: $(a + b) + c = a + (b + c)$. We can partition the array into blocks, compute partial sums independently, then adjust the results. Kadane's algorithm works differently. The *max* operation introduces a *conditional restart*: when the accumulated sum turns negative, starting fresh becomes advantageous. These restart points cannot be determined ahead of time—they depend on all preceding values. However, the problem can be reformulated in terms amenable to parallel computation—using prefix sums and prefix minima.

Reformulating the Problem

We need to find the maximum

$$M = \mathop{\mathrm{MAX}}_{0 \le i \le j < n} S(i,j),$$

where

$$S(i,j) = \sum_{k=i}^{j-1} x_k$$

Using the definition of an exclusive prefix sum

$$P(i) = \sum_{k=0}^{i-1} x_k$$

we can express this using prefix sums as

$$M = \mathop{\mathrm{MAX}}_{0 \le i \le j < n} P(j) - P(i)$$

The key insight follows. For a fixed j, the maximum difference is achieved when $P(i)$ is minimized. Therefore,

$$M = \MAX_{0 \le j < n} P(j) - \MIN_{0 \le i < j} P(i)$$

The solution now decomposes into parallel steps:

- Compute prefix sums $P(i)$.

- Compute the prefix minimum of these sums.

- Perform a final max reduction.

Having identified the necessary computations, we can merge all three operations into a single loop, eliminating intermediate storage.

```
1    package com.nonpareilcoder.realleetcode;
2
3    public class MaximumSubarrayPrefix {
4      static public int compute(int[] input) {
5        int prefix_sum = 0, prefix_min = 0, max = 0;
6        for (int i = 0; i < input.length; i++) {
7          max = Math.max(max, prefix_sum - prefix_min);
8          prefix_min = Math.min(prefix_min, prefix_sum);
9          prefix_sum += input[i];
10       }
11       max = Math.max(max, prefix_sum - prefix_min);
12
13       return max;
14     }
15   }
16
```

- Note that the prefix sums are first used to compute the maximum and only then updated in the current iteration. This is a telltale sign of exclusive sums.

This scalar solution is already prepared for vectorization: all three operations (prefix sum, prefix minimum, maximum) are associative and thus amenable to parallel scan.

Vector Solution

We now have three operations, each of which vectorizes:

1. **Prefix sum**: Parallel scan with addition

2. **Prefix minimum**: Parallel scan with *min*

3. **Global maximum**: Reduction with *max*

The key idea: instead of three separate passes over the array, we combine all operations in a single loop, processing data in blocks of several vectors.

Using these building blocks, we construct a nested vector scan with unrolling. Since we must maintain both prefix sum vectors and prefix minimum vectors simultaneously, we unroll by eight vectors—a compromise between parallelism and register pressure.

```
1    package com.nonpareilcoder.realleetcode;
2
3    import jdk.incubator.vector.*;
4    import static jdk.incubator.vector.VectorOperators.*;
5
6    public class MaximumSubarrayPreferredX8 {
7      static final VectorSpecies<Integer> SP =
8          IntVector.SPECIES_PREFERRED;
9
10     static public int compute(int[] input) {
11       final int vl = SP.length();
12       final int arraySize = input.length;
13
14       final int longIterations = arraySize / (8 * vl);
15       final int longRemainder = arraySize % (8 * vl);
16
17       final var _zero = IntVector.zero(SP);
18       final var _top = IntVector.broadcast(SP, Integer.MAX_VALUE);
19
20       final var _uzp0 = VectorShuffle.makeUnzip(SP, 0);
21       final var _uzp1 = VectorShuffle.makeUnzip(SP, 1);
22
23       var _prev_sum = _zero;
```

```
24        var _prev_min = _top;
25        var _max = _zero;
26
27        int pos = 0;
28        for (int i = 0; i < longIterations; i++) {
29          var _sum0 = IntVector.fromArray(SP, input, pos + 0 * vl);
30          var _sum1 = IntVector.fromArray(SP, input, pos + 1 * vl);
31          var _sum2 = IntVector.fromArray(SP, input, pos + 2 * vl);
32          var _sum3 = IntVector.fromArray(SP, input, pos + 3 * vl);
33          var _sum4 = IntVector.fromArray(SP, input, pos + 4 * vl);
34          var _sum5 = IntVector.fromArray(SP, input, pos + 5 * vl);
35          var _sum6 = IntVector.fromArray(SP, input, pos + 6 * vl);
36          var _sum7 = IntVector.fromArray(SP, input, pos + 7 * vl);
37
38          var _t0 = _sum0;
39          _sum0 = _sum0.rearrange(_uzp0, _sum1);
40          _sum1 = _t0.rearrange(_uzp1, _sum1);
41          var _t1 = _sum2;
42          _sum2 = _sum2.rearrange(_uzp0, _sum3);
43          _sum3 = _t1.rearrange(_uzp1, _sum3);
44          var _t2 = _sum4;
45          _sum4 = _sum4.rearrange(_uzp0, _sum5);
46          _sum5 = _t2.rearrange(_uzp1, _sum5);
47          var _t3 = _sum6;
48          _sum6 = _sum6.rearrange(_uzp0, _sum7);
49          _sum7 = _t3.rearrange(_uzp1, _sum7);
50
51          _t0 = _sum0;
52          _sum0 = _sum0.rearrange(_uzp0, _sum2);
53          _t1 = _sum1;
54          _sum1 = _sum1.rearrange(_uzp0, _sum3);
55          _sum2 = _t0.rearrange(_uzp1, _sum2);
56          _sum3 = _t1.rearrange(_uzp1, _sum3);
57          _t2 = _sum4;
58          _sum4 = _sum4.rearrange(_uzp0, _sum6);
```

```
59        _t3 = _sum5;
60        _sum5 = _sum5.rearrange(_uzp0, _sum7);
61        _sum6 = _t2.rearrange(_uzp1, _sum6);
62        _sum7 = _t3.rearrange(_uzp1, _sum7);
63
64        _t0 = _sum0;
65        _sum0 = _sum0.rearrange(_uzp0, _sum4);
66        _t1 = _sum1;
67        _sum1 = _sum1.rearrange(_uzp0, _sum5);
68        _t2 = _sum2;
69        _sum2 = _sum2.rearrange(_uzp0, _sum6);
70        _t3 = _sum3;
71        _sum3 = _sum3.rearrange(_uzp0, _sum7);
72        _sum4 = _t0.rearrange(_uzp1, _sum4);
73        _sum5 = _t1.rearrange(_uzp1, _sum5);
74        _sum6 = _t2.rearrange(_uzp1, _sum6);
75        _sum7 = _t3.rearrange(_uzp1, _sum7);
76
77
78        _sum1 = _sum1.add(_sum0);
79        _sum3 = _sum3.add(_sum2);
80        _sum5 = _sum5.add(_sum4);
81        _sum7 = _sum7.add(_sum6);
82
83        _sum3 = _sum3.add(_sum1);
84        _sum7 = _sum7.add(_sum5);
85
86        _sum7 = _sum7.add(_sum3);
87
88      var _sumZ = _prev_sum.slice(vl - 1, _sum7);
89
90      for (int step = 1; step < vl; step <<= 1) {
91        var _shifted = _zero.slice(vl - step, _sumZ);
92        _sumZ = _sumZ.add(_shifted);
93      }
```

```
 94
 95            _sum0 = _sum0.add(_sumZ);
 96            _sum1 = _sum1.add(_sumZ);
 97            _sum3 = _sum3.add(_sumZ);
 98            _sum7 = _sum7.add(_sumZ);
 99
100            _sum5 = _sum5.add(_sum3);
101
102            _sum2 = _sum2.add(_sum1);
103            _sum4 = _sum4.add(_sum3);
104            _sum6 = _sum6.add(_sum5);
105
106
107            var _min7 = _sum6;
108            var _min6 = _sum5;
109            var _min5 = _sum4;
110            var _min4 = _sum3;
111            var _min3 = _sum2;
112            var _min2 = _sum1;
113            var _min1 = _sum0;
114            var _min0 = _prev_sum.slice(vl - 1, _sum7);
115
116            _prev_sum = _sum7;
117
118
119            _min1 = _min1.min(_min0);
120            _min3 = _min3.min(_min2);
121            _min5 = _min5.min(_min4);
122            _min7 = _min7.min(_min6);
123
124            _min3 = _min3.min(_min1);
125            _min7 = _min7.min(_min5);
126
127            _min7 = _min7.min(_min3);
128
```

```
129        var _minZ = _prev_min.slice(vl - 1, _min7);
130
131        for (int step = 1; step < vl; step <<= 1) {
132          var _shifted = _top.slice(vl - step, _minZ);
133          _minZ = _minZ.min(_shifted);
134        }
135
136      _min0 = _min0.min(_minZ);
137      _min1 = _min1.min(_minZ);
138      _min3 = _min3.min(_minZ);
139      _min7 = _min7.min(_minZ);
140
141      _min5 = _min5.min(_min3);
142
143      _min2 = _min2.min(_min1);
144      _min4 = _min4.min(_min3);
145      _min6 = _min6.min(_min5);
146
147      _prev_min = _min7;
148
149      _max = _sum0.sub(_min0).max(_max);
150      _max = _sum1.sub(_min1).max(_max);
151      _max = _sum2.sub(_min2).max(_max);
152      _max = _sum3.sub(_min3).max(_max);
153      _max = _sum4.sub(_min4).max(_max);
154      _max = _sum5.sub(_min5).max(_max);
155      _max = _sum6.sub(_min6).max(_max);
156      _max = _sum7.sub(_min7).max(_max);
157
158    pos += 8 * vl;
159    }
160
161    int prefix_sum = _prev_sum.lane(vl - 1);
162    int prefix_min = _prev_min.lane(vl - 1);
163    int max = _max.reduceLanes(MAX);
```

```
164
165        for (int i = 0; i < longRemainder; i++) {
166          prefix_min = Math.min(prefix_min, prefix_sum);
167          prefix_sum += input[pos++];
168          max = Math.max(max, prefix_sum - prefix_min);
169        }
170
171      return max;
172      }
173    }
174
```

- Lines 29–36 load eight vectors.

- Lines 38–75 unroll the eight vectors.

- Lines 78–104 compute the prefix sum.

- Lines 107–114 elegantly copy the still-unrolled prefix sum with a one-position shift.

- Lines 119–145 compute the prefix minimum.

- Lines 149–156 update the vector maximum.

- Line 163 performs horizontal max reduction.

- Lines 165–169 handle the short scalar tail of the algorithm.

Lightweight Algorithm

On platforms with 128-bit vectors (ARM NEON, for instance), the previous algorithm may be unnecessarily complex. Here is a simplified variant optimized for narrower vector widths.

```
1    package com.nonpareilcoder.realleetcode;
2
3    import jdk.incubator.vector.*;
4    import static jdk.incubator.vector.VectorOperators.*;
5
```

```
 6   public class MaximumSubarray128X8 {
 7     static final VectorSpecies<Integer> SP =
 8       IntVector.SPECIES_128;
 9     static final int vl = SP.length();
10
11     static final VectorShuffle<Integer> _zip0 =
12         VectorShuffle.makeZip(SP, 0);
13     static final VectorShuffle<Integer> _zip1 =
14         VectorShuffle.makeZip(SP, 1);
15
16     static public int compute(int[] input) {
17       final int arraySize = input.length;
18
19       final int longIterations = arraySize / (8 * vl);
20       final int longRemainder = arraySize % (8 * vl);
21
22       final var _zero = IntVector.zero(SP);
23       final var _top = IntVector.broadcast(SP, Integer.MAX_VALUE);
24
25       var _prev_sum = _zero;
26       var _prev_min = _top;
27       var _max = _zero;
28
29       int pos = 0;
30       for (int i = 0; i < longIterations; i++) {
31         var _sum0 = IntVector.fromArray(SP, input, pos + 0 * vl);
32         var _sum1 = IntVector.fromArray(SP, input, pos + 1 * vl);
33         var _sum2 = IntVector.fromArray(SP, input, pos + 2 * vl);
34         var _sum3 = IntVector.fromArray(SP, input, pos + 3 * vl);
35         var _sum4 = IntVector.fromArray(SP, input, pos + 4 * vl);
36         var _sum5 = IntVector.fromArray(SP, input, pos + 5 * vl);
37         var _sum6 = IntVector.fromArray(SP, input, pos + 6 * vl);
38         var _sum7 = IntVector.fromArray(SP, input, pos + 7 * vl);
39
40         var _t0 = _sum0;
```

```
41            _sum0 = _sum0.rearrange(_zip0, _sum4);
42            _sum4 = _t0.rearrange(_zip1, _sum4);
43            var _t1 = _sum1;
44            _sum1 = _sum1.rearrange(_zip0, _sum5);
45            _sum5 = _t1.rearrange(_zip1, _sum5);
46            var _t2 = _sum2;
47            _sum2 = _sum2.rearrange(_zip0, _sum6);
48            _sum6 = _t2.rearrange(_zip1, _sum6);
49            var _t3 = _sum3;
50            _sum3 = _sum3.rearrange(_zip0, _sum7);
51            _sum7 = _t3.rearrange(_zip1, _sum7);
52
53            _t0 = _sum0;
54            _t1 = _sum1;
55            _t2 = _sum4;
56            _t3 = _sum5;
57
58            _sum0 = _t0.rearrange(_zip0, _sum2);
59            _sum1 = _t0.rearrange(_zip1, _sum2);
60
61            _sum4 = _t1.rearrange(_zip0, _sum3);
62            _sum5 = _t1.rearrange(_zip1, _sum3);
63
64            _sum2 = _t2.rearrange(_zip0, _sum6);
65            _sum3 = _t2.rearrange(_zip1, _sum6);
66
67            _sum6 = _t3.rearrange(_zip0, _sum7);
68            _sum7 = _t3.rearrange(_zip1, _sum7);
69
70
71            _sum1 = _sum1.add(_sum0);
72            _sum3 = _sum3.add(_sum2);
73            _sum5 = _sum5.add(_sum4);
74            _sum7 = _sum7.add(_sum6);
75
```

```
76          _sum3 = _sum3.add(_sum1);
77          _sum7 = _sum7.add(_sum5);
78
79          _sum7 = _sum7.add(_sum3);
80
81          var _sumZ = _prev_sum.slice(3, _sum7);
82
83          var _shifted = _zero.slice(3, _sumZ);
84          _sumZ = _sumZ.add(_shifted);
85
86          _shifted = _zero.slice(2, _sumZ);
87          _sumZ = _sumZ.add(_shifted);
88
89          _sum0 = _sum0.add(_sumZ);
90          _sum1 = _sum1.add(_sumZ);
91          _sum3 = _sum3.add(_sumZ);
92          _sum7 = _sum7.add(_sumZ);
93
94          _sum5 = _sum5.add(_sum3);
95
96          _sum2 = _sum2.add(_sum1);
97          _sum4 = _sum4.add(_sum3);
98          _sum6 = _sum6.add(_sum5);
99
100
101         var _min7 = _sum6;
102         var _min6 = _sum5;
103         var _min5 = _sum4;
104         var _min4 = _sum3;
105         var _min3 = _sum2;
106         var _min2 = _sum1;
107         var _min1 = _sum0;
108         var _min0 = _prev_sum.slice(3, _sum7);
109
110         _prev_sum = _sum7;
```

```
111
112
113             _min1 = _min1.min(_min0);
114             _min3 = _min3.min(_min2);
115             _min5 = _min5.min(_min4);
116             _min7 = _min7.min(_min6);
117
118             _min3 = _min3.min(_min1);
119             _min7 = _min7.min(_min5);
120
121             _min7 = _min7.min(_min3);
122
123         var _minZ = _prev_min.slice(3, _min7);
124
125             _shifted = _top.slice(3, _minZ);
126             _minZ = _minZ.min(_shifted);
127
128             _shifted = _top.slice(2, _minZ);
129             _minZ = _minZ.min(_shifted);
130
131             _min0 = _min0.min(_minZ);
132             _min1 = _min1.min(_minZ);
133             _min3 = _min3.min(_minZ);
134             _min7 = _min7.min(_minZ);
135
136             _min5 = _min5.min(_min3);
137
138             _min2 = _min2.min(_min1);
139             _min4 = _min4.min(_min3);
140             _min6 = _min6.min(_min5);
141
142             _prev_min = _min7;
143
144             _max = _sum0.sub(_min0).max(_max);
145             _max = _sum1.sub(_min1).max(_max);
```

```
146          _max = _sum2.sub(_min2).max(_max);
147          _max = _sum3.sub(_min3).max(_max);
148          _max = _sum4.sub(_min4).max(_max);
149          _max = _sum5.sub(_min5).max(_max);
150          _max = _sum6.sub(_min6).max(_max);
151          _max = _sum7.sub(_min7).max(_max);
152
153        pos += 8 * vl;
154      }
155
156      int prefix_sum = _prev_sum.lane(vl - 1);
157      int prefix_min = _prev_min.lane(vl - 1);
158      int max = _max.reduceLanes(MAX);
159
160      for (int i = 0; i < longRemainder; i++) {
161        prefix_min = Math.min(prefix_min, prefix_sum);
162        prefix_sum += input[pos++];
163        max = Math.max(max, prefix_sum - prefix_min);
164      }
165
166      return max;
167    }
168  }
169
```

- Lines 40–68 unroll eight vectors "in the opposite direction" using the **zip** operation.

- Lines 81–87 contain the fully unrolled horizontal prefix scan loop.

- Lines 123–129 unroll the second scan in the same manner.

Benchmarks

Table 14-1 and Table 14-2 present the benchmark results.

Table 14-1. *Single-core speedup on x86 platforms (higher is better)*

Variant	GL	Z2	IL	SR	Z5
baseline	1.00	1.00	1.00	1.00	1.00
preferredX8	0.04	1.40	2.27	2.77	4.32
prefix	1.02	1.32	0.86	1.23	1.33
shortX8	0.06	1.24	1.59	1.73	2.61

The X86 benchmark results reveal a stark performance divide between processors with different vector capabilities. Z5 (AMD Turin) achieves the best performance with a 4.32× speedup for the preferredX8 variant, showcasing the benefits of modern AVX-512 implementations with excellent out-of-order execution.

The prefix variant delivers modest but consistent speedups of 1.23–1.33× on AVX-capable processors while actually causing a slight slowdown on IL (0.86×), suggesting that horizontal scan operations incur overhead on this architecture. The preferredX8 variant clearly benefits from wider vectors and aggressive unrolling, scaling from 1.40× on the AVX2-based Z2 (AMD Rome) to 4.32× on Z5. Overall, these results confirm that this algorithm benefits substantially from wide vector registers and modern execution pipelines.

Table 14-2. *Single-core speedup on ARM platforms (higher is better)*

Variant	M4	O6	CO	NV	G3
baseline	1.00	1.00	1.00	1.00	1.00
preferredX8	0.73	0.85	0.83	1.72	1.47
prefix	1.28	1.18	1.12	1.30	1.17
shortX8	0.96	1.08	1.06	2.40	1.11

The ARM benchmark results present a more challenging picture for vectorization, with several platforms showing slowdowns or marginal gains. The Apple M4 is a notable outlier with a 0.73× slowdown for preferredX8, indicating that its NEON implementation struggles with the complex scan operations required by this algorithm. NV (Nvidia Grace) achieves the best ARM performance, reaching 2.40× speedup for shortX8 and 1.72× for preferredX8, likely due to its advanced pipeline capable of executing multiple vector instructions simultaneously.

The prefix variant delivers the most consistent results across all ARM platforms, with speedups ranging from 1.12× to 1.30×, making it the safest choice for portable ARM code. Interestingly, the shortX8 variant—optimized for 128-bit vectors—achieves only modest gains on most platforms (0.96–1.11×) but excels on NV, suggesting that pipeline characteristics matter more than raw vector width for this algorithm. G3 (Amazon Graviton 3) with its 256-bit SVE shows moderate improvements (1.47× for preferredX8) but is outperformed by the narrower-vector NV.

Practical Applications

The maximum subarray sum algorithm finds use in a wide range of practical problems.

- **Financial analysis and trading**: Finding the optimal period with maximum cumulative return in a time series of prices

- **Signal processing**: Extracting segments with maximum energy in audio or video streams

- **Bioinformatics and genomics**: Detecting genome regions with maximum concentration of certain nucleotides

- **Logistics**: Optimizing routes or loads by identifying the most profitable consecutive operations

- **Text analysis and NLP**: Finding topically dense paragraphs or sentences

- **Network monitoring and traffic analysis**: Detecting periods of maximum channel utilization

- **Games and simulations**: Optimizing sequences of moves or actions with maximum cumulative utility

- **Machine learning**: Extracting key portions of time series for model input

- **Quality control and industrial analytics**: Identifying weak links in production chains through accumulated error or deviation

In all these cases, the key advantage of the vectorized solution is the ability to process large volumes of data in real time.

What's Next

Our final chapter tackles one of mathematics' most intriguing unsolved problems: the Collatz conjecture. We explore divergent execution, where different vector lanes follow radically different computational paths, and discover the surprising power of memoization combined (or not) with work piling: techniques that push vectorization to its limits.

CHAPTER 15

The Collatz Conjecture

Project Euler. Problem 14. This chapter explores one of the most intriguing unsolved problems in mathematics: the Collatz conjecture. The problem demonstrates that even simple algorithms can pose serious challenges for SIMD parallelism when different inputs require substantially different processing times.

In This Chapter

1. Divergent execution: handling vastly different iteration counts across vector lanes

2. The expand operation for loading new work into completed lanes

3. Multi-step lookahead using residue classes modulo powers of two

4. When memoization dominates vectorization and when work piling becomes over-optimization

Problem Statement

The Collatz conjecture (also known as the $3n + 1$ problem or the Syracuse problem) is formulated as follows:

Start with any positive integer n. Then, repeat the following process:

- If n is even: divide by 2 ($n \to n/2$).

- If n is odd: multiply by 3 and add 1 ($n \to 3n + 1$).

Conjecture: Regardless of the starting value n, this sequence (orbit) always reaches 1.

© Roman Snytsar 2026

R. Snytsar, *Mastering SIMD with Java Vector API*, https://doi.org/10.1007/979-8-8688-2676-4_15

Example Orbits

Example 1: $n = 13$

$$13 \rightarrow 40 \rightarrow 20 \rightarrow 10 \rightarrow 5 \rightarrow 16$$
$$\rightarrow 8 \rightarrow 4 \rightarrow 2 \rightarrow 1$$

Length: 10 steps

Example 2: $n = 6$

$$6 \rightarrow 3 \rightarrow 10 \rightarrow 5 \rightarrow 16$$
$$\rightarrow 8 \rightarrow 4 \rightarrow 2 \rightarrow 1$$

Length: 9 steps

Example 3: $n = 27$

$$27 \rightarrow 82 \rightarrow 41 \rightarrow 124 \rightarrow 62 \rightarrow 31$$
$$\rightarrow 94 \rightarrow 47 \rightarrow 142 \rightarrow 71 \rightarrow 214$$
$$\rightarrow 107 \rightarrow \ldots \rightarrow 4 \rightarrow 2 \rightarrow 1$$

Length: 112 steps (intermediate values reach 9232, far exceeding the starting value).

Despite its simple formulation, the Collatz conjecture remains *unproven* for over 80 years. It has been verified for all numbers up to 2^{68}, yet a mathematical proof is lacking.

Problem 14 of Project Euler offers practice in computing Collatz orbits:

Find the starting number under one million that produces the longest orbit.

Formally: For all $n < 1{,}000{,}000$, find n for which the Collatz orbit length is maximum.

Straightforward Solution

The simplest approach is to compute the orbit for each number according to the definition:

```
1   package com.nonpareilcoder.projecteuler;
2
3   public class CollatzConjectureScalar {
4     static public long longestOrbit(int problemSize) {
5       int max = 1, start = 1;
6
```

```
 7       for (int i = 2; i < problemSize; i++) {
 8         int orbit = 1;
 9         for (long val = i; val > 1; orbit++) {
10           if ((val & 1) == 1)
11             val = 3 * val + 1;
12           else
13             val >>= 1;
14         }
15
16         if (orbit > max) {
17           max = orbit;
18           start = i;
19         }
20       }
21
22     return start;
23   }
24 }
25
```

- The outer loop in lines 7–20 is deterministic and trivially parallel: there is no data dependency between iterations.

- The inner loop in lines 9–14 is non-deterministic. This is precisely the charm of the Collatz formula: neighboring orbit lengths can differ radically and are hard to predict. This property explains why the Collatz conjecture finds applications in cryptography; cryptographers have a fondness for computationally hard problems with unpredictable outcomes.

- The conditional in lines 10–13 is also weakly deterministic. The alternation of even and odd elements in an orbit is hard to predict. We will, however, attempt to challenge this claim below.

- Line 13 already applies an optimization: a bit shift replaces division by 2.

- Lines 16–19 select the maximum orbit.

Divergent Execution

The outer loop iterations are independent of each other. To speed up execution, we distribute the computation across multiple threads corresponding to individual iterations and run them in parallel across vector lanes. However, we face an obstacle: the conditional embedded in the loop resists parallelization by its very nature.

The issue is that vector code operating on multiple data streams simultaneously cannot "jump over" individual instruction blocks—it cannot, like sequential code, choose just one branch of an **if-else** statement and ignore the other. In the vector model, all lanes must move in lockstep, processing the same instructions on different data.

How do we escape this predicament? The solution is as follows:

- Compute both branches of the conditional in parallel.

- Apply a mask to select the correct values.

We thus bypass the limitation of vector execution: instead of selective code execution, we compute both branches simultaneously and then carefully "blend" the results according to the mask. This branchless technique preserves the logic of the conditional while fully exploiting the potential of parallel computation. It is worth verifying that the benefits of vectorization outweigh the overhead of computing both alternatives.

```
1    package com.nonpareilcoder.projecteuler;
2
3    import jdk.incubator.vector.*;
4    import static jdk.incubator.vector.VectorOperators.*;
5
6    public class CollatzConjectureVectorized {
7      static final VectorSpecies<Long> SP =
8        LongVector.SPECIES_PREFERRED;
9
10     static public long longestOrbit(int problemSize) {
11       final int vl = SP.length();
12       final LongVector _zero = LongVector.zero(SP);
13
14       LongVector _max = _zero;
15       LongVector _start = _zero;
16
```

```
17    LongVector _idx = VectorShuffle.iota(SP, 0, 1, false)
18        .toVector().reinterpretAsLongs();
19
20    for (int i = 2; i < problemSize; i += vl) {
21      var _inRange = SP.indexInRange(i, problemSize);
22
23      LongVector _val = _idx.add(i, _inRange);
24      LongVector _pos = _val;
25      LongVector _orbit = LongVector.broadcast(SP, 1);
26
27      for (; ; ) {
28        VectorMask<Long> _done = _val.compare(LE, 1);
29        if (_done.allTrue())
30          break;
31
32        var _odd = _val.and(1).compare(EQ, 1);
33
34        LongVector _valOdd = _val.mul(3).add(1);
35        LongVector _valEven = _val.lanewise(LSHR, 1);
36
37        _val = _valEven.blend(_valOdd, _odd).blend(1, _done);
38        _orbit = _orbit.add(1).blend(_orbit, _done);
39      }
40
41      var _less = _max.compare(LT, _orbit, _inRange);
42
43      _max = _max.blend(_orbit, _less);
44      _start = _start.blend(_pos, _less);
45    }
46
47    for (int step = 1; step < SP.length(); step <<= 1) {
48      LongVector _shiftedMax = _max.slice(step, _zero);
49      LongVector _shiftedStart = _start.slice(step, _zero);
50
51      var _less = _max.compare(LT, _shiftedMax);
52      _max = _max.blend(_shiftedMax, _less);
```

```
53              _start = _start.blend(_shiftedStart, _less);
54          }
55
56          long start = _start.lane(0);
57          return start;
58      }
59  }
60
```

- Line 32 forms the mask **_odd** that determines parity.

- Line 34 computes the "true" branch—for the case when the number is odd.

- Line 35 computes the "false" branch—for the case when the number is even.

- Line 37 combines both results according to the mask.

- Line 28 forms the mask **_done** that determines lane termination.

- Line 41 forms a third mask **_less** that governs the selection of the maximum orbit.

- The same mask is used in line 51 during the final reduction.

The vectorized algorithm works correctly, but we can speed it up by reducing the number of inner loop iterations.

Finding Patterns

Researchers studying the Collatz conjecture have noticed patterns that allow faster orbit computation.

- If n is odd, then $3n + 1$ is even, and we can immediately divide by 2 without additional checks.

- If n is even, meaning the least significant bit is zero, it pays to check subsequent bits (right to left, in order of increasing significance). This way we count trailing zero bits and shift n right by that many positions at once.

Both optimizations combine beautifully.

```java
1    package com.nonpareilcoder.projecteuler;
2
3    import jdk.incubator.vector.*;
4    import static jdk.incubator.vector.VectorOperators.*;
5
6    public class CollatzConjectureAccelerated {
7      static final VectorSpecies<Long> SP =
8        LongVector.SPECIES_PREFERRED;
9
10     static public long longestOrbit(int problemSize) {
11       final int vl = SP.length();
12
13       LongVector _max = LongVector.zero(SP);
14       LongVector _start = LongVector.zero(SP);
15
16       LongVector _idx = VectorShuffle.iota(SP, 0, 1, false)
17           .toVector().reinterpretAsLongs();
18
19       for (int i = 2; i < problemSize; i += vl) {
20         var _inRange = SP.indexInRange(i, problemSize);
21
22         LongVector _val = _idx.add(i, _inRange);
23         LongVector _pos = _val;
24         LongVector _orbit = LongVector.broadcast(SP, 1);
25
26         for (;;) {
27           var _ctz = _val.lanewise(TRAILING_ZEROS_COUNT);
28
29           _val = _val.lanewise(LSHR, _ctz);
30           _orbit = _orbit.add(_ctz);
31
32           var _active = _val.compare(GT, 1);
33           if (!_active.anyTrue())
34             break;
```

```
35
36              _val = _val.mul(3, _active).add(1, _active);
37              _val = _val.lanewise(LSHR, 1, _active);
38              _orbit = _orbit.add(2, _active);
39            }
40
41         var _less = _max.compare(LT, _orbit);
42
43         _max = _max.blend(_orbit, _less);
44         _start = _start.blend(_pos, _less);
45       }
46
47     LongVector _zero = LongVector.zero(SP);
48     for (int step = 1; step < SP.length(); step <<= 1) {
49       LongVector _shiftedMax = _max.slice(step, _zero);
50       LongVector _shiftedStart = _start.slice(step, _zero);
51
52       var _less = _max.compare(LT, _shiftedMax);
53       _max = _max.blend(_shiftedMax, _less);
54       _start = _start.blend(_shiftedStart, _less);
55     }
56
57     long start = _start.lane(0);
58     return start;
59   }
60 }
61
```

- Line 27 computes the number of trailing zeros of n.

- Line 29 shifts n by that count.

- Line 30 increases the orbit length by the same count.

- Now all vector elements are guaranteed to be odd. Lines 36–37 perform a two-step odd-even sequence: multiply by 3, add 1, divide by 2.

- Line 38 increases the orbit length by 2 at once.

Multi-step Lookahead

Consider the problem from a different perspective. Recall that two integers a and b are called **residues modulo n** (or congruent modulo n) if they yield the same remainder when divided by n. This is written as

$$a \equiv b \pmod{n}$$

The original formulation partitions all numbers into two residue classes modulo 2: even and odd. We push further along this path and partition all numbers into residue classes modulo 4. Represent all numbers as $4x + y$, where y is the remainder when divided by 4. For each residue class, trace the trajectory of its orbit.

Case **y=0:** $4x$ (even)

$$\rightarrow 2x \quad (\text{even})$$
$$\rightarrow x \quad (\text{undetermined})$$

As we already know, if the two least significant bits are zero, the number can be shifted right by two positions, and the orbit length can be increased by 2 at once. Nothing new so far.

Case **y=1:** $4x + 1$ (odd)

$$\rightarrow 12x + 4 \quad (\text{even})$$
$$\rightarrow 6x + 2 \quad (\text{even})$$
$$\rightarrow 3x + 1 \quad (\text{undetermined})$$

Now this is interesting: for residues congruent to one, we can predict the orbit three steps ahead.

Case **y=2:** $4x + 2$ (even)

$$\rightarrow 2x + 1 \quad (\text{odd})$$
$$\rightarrow 6x + 4 \quad (\text{even})$$
$$\rightarrow 3x + 2 \quad (\text{undetermined})$$

For residues congruent to two, we can also predict the orbit three steps ahead. This is also a trivial result following from previous optimizations: an even number shifts right, then the two-step sequence follows.

Case **y=3:** $4x + 3$ (odd)

$$\rightarrow 12x + 10 \quad (\text{even})$$
$$\rightarrow 6x + 5 \quad (\text{odd})$$
$$\rightarrow 18x + 16 \quad (\text{even})$$
$$\rightarrow 9x + 8 \quad (\text{undetermined})$$

For the residue congruent to three, we can predict the orbit four (!) steps ahead. This is a new and unexpected conclusion.

In general, a number of the form $4x + y$ transforms according to the formula $Ax + B$, and the orbit length increases by C. The values of A, B, and C are summarized in Table 15-1.

Table 15-1. *Collatz transformation coefficients for 2 trailing bits*

y	A	B	C	Sequence
0	1	0	2	$4x \rightarrow 2x \rightarrow x$
1	3	1	3	$4x + 1 \rightarrow 12x + 4 \rightarrow 6x + 2 \rightarrow 3x + 1$
2	3	2	3	$4x + 2 \rightarrow 2x + 1 \rightarrow 6x + 4 \rightarrow 3x + 2$
3	9	8	4	$4x + 3 \rightarrow 12x + 10 \rightarrow 6x + 5 \rightarrow 18x + 16 \rightarrow 9x + 8$

Even with 128-bit vectors, the columns A, B, and C fit into two vectors each, meaning the table lookup can be implemented as element permutation within vector registers without memory access. This is a key advantage: register operations are orders of magnitude faster than memory operations.

```java
1   package com.nonpareilcoder.projecteuler;
2
3   import jdk.incubator.vector.*;
4   import static jdk.incubator.vector.VectorOperators.*;
5
6   public class CollatzConjectureLookup {
7       static final VectorSpecies<Long> SP =
8         LongVector.SPECIES_PREFERRED;
9
10      static final long[] a4 = new long[]{1, 3, 3, 9};
11      static final long[] b4 = new long[]{0, 1, 2, 8};
```

```java
12     static final long[] c4 = new long[]{2, 3, 3, 4};
13
14     static public long longestOrbit(int problemSize) {
15       final int vl = SP.length();
16
17       long xShift = 2;
18       long yMask = ~(-1 << xShift);
19
20       var _load = SP.indexInRange(0, 4);
21       LongVector _a0 = LongVector.fromArray(SP, a4, 0, _load);
22       LongVector _b0 = LongVector.fromArray(SP, b4, 0, _load);
23       LongVector _c0 = LongVector.fromArray(SP, c4, 0, _load);
24
25       _load = SP.indexInRange(vl, 4);
26       LongVector _a1 = LongVector.fromArray(SP, a4, vl, _load);
27       LongVector _b1 = LongVector.fromArray(SP, b4, vl, _load);
28       LongVector _c1 = LongVector.fromArray(SP, c4, vl, _load);
29
30       final LongVector _zero = LongVector.zero(SP);
31
32       LongVector _max = _zero;
33       LongVector _start = _zero;
34
35       LongVector _idx = VectorShuffle.iota(SP, 0, 1, false)
36           .toVector().reinterpretAsLongs();
37
38       for (int i = 2; i < problemSize; i += vl) {
39         var _inRange = SP.indexInRange(i, problemSize);
40
41         LongVector _val = _idx.add(i, _inRange);
42         LongVector _pos = _val;
43         LongVector _orbit = _zero;
44
45         for (; ; ) {
46           VectorMask<Long> _done = _val.compare(LE, 2);
```

```
47              if (_done.allTrue())
48                break;
49
50              LongVector _x = _val.lanewise(LSHR, xShift);
51              LongVector _y = _val.and(yMask);
52
53              LongVector _aa = _y.selectFrom(_a0, _a1);
54              LongVector _bb = _y.selectFrom(_b0, _b1);
55              LongVector _cc = _y.selectFrom(_c0, _c1);
56
57              _val = _x.mul(_aa).add(_bb).blend(_val, _done);
58              _orbit = _orbit.add(_cc).blend(_orbit, _done);
59            }
60
61          _orbit = _orbit.add(_val);
62
63          var _less = _max.compare(LT, _orbit, _inRange);
64
65          _max = _max.blend(_orbit, _less);
66          _start = _start.blend(_pos, _less);
67        }
68
69        for (int step = 1; step < SP.length(); step <<= 1) {
70          LongVector _shiftedMax = _max.slice(step, _zero);
71          LongVector _shiftedStart = _start.slice(step, _zero);
72
73          var _less = _max.compare(LT, _shiftedMax);
74          _max = _max.blend(_shiftedMax, _less);
75          _start = _start.blend(_shiftedStart, _less);
76        }
77
78        long start = _start.lane(0);
79        return start;
80      }
81    }
82
```

Combined Approach

We now combine both previous approaches: removal of trailing zeros from the "Finding Patterns" section and the table method from the "Multi-step Lookahead" section.

- Begin each iteration by removing trailing zero bits.

- Now all intermediate values are guaranteed to be odd. Recalculate the tables A, B, and C accounting for this fact. In other words, without changing the table size, we can look one bit further ahead.

- Note also that both the y values and the A, B, and C values fit in the Short type range. This means the vector tables can pack four times as many numbers, utilizing two additional bits of the intermediate value.

We construct new tables (Table 15-2) by representing intermediate values as $n = 32x + 2y + 1$.

Table 15-2. *Collatz transformation coefficients for 6 trailing bits*

y	A	B	C	Sequence
0	27	2	8	$32x+1 \rightarrow 96x+4 \rightarrow 48x+2 \rightarrow 24x+1$ $\rightarrow 72x+4 \rightarrow 36x+2 \rightarrow 18x+1$ $\rightarrow 54x+4 \rightarrow 27x+2$
1	9	1	7	$32x+3 \rightarrow 96x+10 \rightarrow 48x+5 \rightarrow 144x+16$ $\rightarrow 72x+8 \rightarrow 36x+4 \rightarrow 18x+2$ $\rightarrow 9x+12$
2	9	2	7	$32x+5 \rightarrow 96x+16 \rightarrow 48x+8 \rightarrow 24x+4$ $\rightarrow 12x+2 \rightarrow 6x+1 \rightarrow 18x+4$ $\rightarrow 9x+2$

(continued)

Table 15-2. (_continued_)

y	A	B	C	Sequence
3	81	20	9	$32x+7 \rightarrow 96x+22 \rightarrow 48x+11 \rightarrow 144x+34$ $\rightarrow 72x+17 \rightarrow 216x+52 \rightarrow 108x+26$ $\rightarrow 54x+13 \rightarrow 162x+40 \rightarrow 81x+20$
4	81	26	9	$32x+9 \rightarrow 96x+28 \rightarrow 48x+14 \rightarrow 24x+7$ $\rightarrow 72x+22 \rightarrow 36x+11 \rightarrow 108x+34$ $\rightarrow 54x+17 \rightarrow 162x+52 \rightarrow 81x+26$
5	27	10	8	$32x+11 \rightarrow 96x+34 \rightarrow 48x+17 \rightarrow 144x+52$ $\rightarrow 72x+26 \rightarrow 36x+13 \rightarrow 108x+40$ $\rightarrow 54x+20 \rightarrow 27x+10$
6	9	4	7	$32x+13 \rightarrow 96x+40 \rightarrow 48x+20 \rightarrow 24x+10$ $\rightarrow 12x+5 \rightarrow 36x+16 \rightarrow 18x+8$ $\rightarrow 9x+4$
7	81	40	9	$32x+15 \rightarrow 96x+46 \rightarrow 48x+23 \rightarrow 144x+70$ $\rightarrow 72x+35 \rightarrow 216x+106 \rightarrow 108x+53$ $\rightarrow 324x+160 \rightarrow 162x+80 \rightarrow 81x+40$
8	9	5	7	$32x+17 \rightarrow 96x+52 \rightarrow 48x+26 \rightarrow 24x+13$ $\rightarrow 72x+40 \rightarrow 36x+20 \rightarrow 18x+10$ $\rightarrow 9x+5$
9	27	17	8	$32x+19 \rightarrow 96x+58 \rightarrow 48x+29 \rightarrow 144x+88$ $\rightarrow 72x+44 \rightarrow 36x+22 \rightarrow 18x+11$ $\rightarrow 54x+34 \rightarrow 27x+17$
10	3	2	6	$32x+21 \rightarrow 96x+64 \rightarrow 48x+32 \rightarrow 24x+16$ $\rightarrow 12x+8 \rightarrow 6x+4 \rightarrow 3x+2$

(_continued_)

Table 15-2. (*continued*)

y	A	B	C	Sequence
11	27	20	8	$32x+23 \rightarrow 96x+70 \rightarrow 48x+35 \rightarrow 144x+106$ $\rightarrow 72x+53 \rightarrow 216x+160 \rightarrow 108x+80$ $\rightarrow 54x+40 \rightarrow 27x+20$
12	27	22	8	$32x+25 \rightarrow 96x+76 \rightarrow 48x+38 \rightarrow 24x+19$ $\rightarrow 72x+58 \rightarrow 36x+29 \rightarrow 108x+88$ $\rightarrow 54x+44 \rightarrow 27x+22$
13	81	71	9	$32x+27 \rightarrow 96x+82 \rightarrow 48x+41 \rightarrow 144x+124$ $\rightarrow 72x+62 \rightarrow 36x+31 \rightarrow 108x+94$ $\rightarrow 54x+47 \rightarrow 162x+142 \rightarrow 81x+71$
14	27	26	8	$32x+29 \rightarrow 96x+88 \rightarrow 48x+44 \rightarrow 24x+22$ $\rightarrow 12x+11 \rightarrow 36x+34 \rightarrow 18x+17$ $\rightarrow 54x+52 \rightarrow 27x+26$
15	243	242	10	$32x+31 \rightarrow 96x+94 \rightarrow 48x+47 \rightarrow 144x+142$ $\rightarrow 72x+71 \rightarrow 216x+214$ $\rightarrow 108x+107 \rightarrow 324x+322$ $\rightarrow 162x+161 \rightarrow 486x+484$ $\rightarrow 243x+242$

The tables work correctly only when $x > 0$. For example, when $x = 0$ and $y = 2$, the sequence stops at $6x + 1$, reaching one prematurely. The case $x = 0$ must therefore be handled separately in the code.

Finally, if vectors are wider than 128 bits, the tables can be enlarged further. We omit the bulky derivations for numbers of the form $n = 64x + 2y + 1$ (256-bit tables) and $n = 128x + 2y + 1$ (512-bit tables), limiting ourselves to the result in code.

```
1    package com.nonpareilcoder.projecteuler;
2
3    import jdk.incubator.vector.*;
```

```
 4
 5    import static jdk.incubator.vector.VectorOperators.*;
 6
 7    public class CollatzConjectureCombined {
 8      static final VectorSpecies<Long> SL =
 9        LongVector.SPECIES_PREFERRED;
10      static final VectorSpecies<Short> SS =
11        ShortVector.SPECIES_PREFERRED;
12
13      static final short[] a128 = {
14        27, 9, 9, 81, 81, 27, 9, 81, 9, 27, 3, 27, 27, 81, 27, 243};
15      static final short[] b128 = {
16        2, 1, 2, 20, 26, 10, 4, 40, 5, 17, 2, 20, 22, 71, 26, 242};
17      static final short[] c128 = {
18        8, 7, 7, 9, 9, 8, 7, 9, 7, 8, 6, 8, 8, 9, 8, 10};
19
20      static final short[] a256 = {
21        27, 27, 9, 81, 81, 27, 9, 81, 27, 81, 3, 27, 27, 243, 27, 243,
22        81, 9, 27, 243, 243, 81, 27, 243, 9, 27, 9, 81, 81, 81, 81, 729};
23      static final short[] b256 = {
24        1, 2, 1, 10, 13, 5, 2, 20, 8, 26, 1, 10, 11, 107, 13, 121,
25        44, 5, 17, 152, 161, 56, 20, 182, 7, 22, 8, 71, 74, 76, 80, 728};
26      static final short[] c256 = {
27        9, 9, 8, 10, 10, 9, 8, 10, 9, 10, 7, 9, 9, 11, 9, 11,
28        10, 8, 9, 11, 11, 10, 9, 11, 8, 9, 8, 10, 10, 10, 10, 12};
29
30      static final short[] a512 = {
31        81, 27, 27, 81, 243, 81, 9, 81, 27, 81, 9, 27, 81, 729, 81,
32        729, 81, 27, 81, 243, 729, 81, 27, 243, 27, 27, 9, 243, 81, 81,
33        81, 729, 27, 81, 9, 243, 81, 27, 27, 243, 81, 243, 3, 81, 27,
34        243, 27, 243, 243, 9, 27, 729, 243, 243, 81, 729, 9, 81, 27, 81,
35        243, 243, 243, 2187};
36      static final short[] b512 = {
37        2, 1, 2, 5, 20, 8, 1, 10, 4, 13, 2, 5, 17, 161, 20, 182,
38        22, 8, 26, 76, 242, 28, 10, 91, 11, 11, 4, 107, 37, 38, 40,
```

```
39        364, 14, 44, 5, 137, 47, 16, 17, 152, 53, 161, 2, 56, 19, 175,
40        20, 182, 188, 7, 22, 593, 202, 206, 71, 638, 8, 74, 26, 76,
41        233, 236, 242, 2186};
42    static final short[] c512 = {
43        11, 10, 10, 11, 12, 11, 9, 11, 10, 11, 9, 10, 11, 13, 11, 13,
44        11, 10, 11, 12, 13, 11, 10, 12, 10, 10, 9, 12, 11, 11, 11, 13,
45        10, 11, 9, 12, 11, 10, 10, 12, 11, 12, 8, 11, 10, 12, 10, 12,
46        12, 9, 10, 13, 12, 12, 11, 13, 9, 11, 10, 11, 12, 12, 12, 14};
47
48    static final short[] d512 = {
49        1, 8, 6, 17, 20, 15, 10, 18, 13, 21, 8, 16, 24, 112, 19, 107,
50        27, 14, 22, 35, 110, 30, 17, 105, 25, 25, 12, 113, 33, 33, 20,
51        108, 28, 28, 15, 103, 116, 15, 23, 36, 23, 111, 10, 31, 31, 93,
52        18, 106, 119, 26, 26, 88, 39, 101, 114, 70, 13, 34, 21, 34, 96,
53        47, 109, 47};
54
55    static public long longestOrbit(int problemSize) {
56        final int vs = SS.length();
57
58        long xShift, yMask;
59        ShortVector _a0, _b0, _c0, _d0;
60        ShortVector _a1, _b1, _c1, _d1;
61
62        switch (vs) {
63          case 8:
64            xShift = 5;
65            yMask = ~(-1 << xShift);
66
67            _a0 = ShortVector.fromArray(SS, a128, 0);
68            _b0 = ShortVector.fromArray(SS, b128, 0);
69            _c0 = ShortVector.fromArray(SS, c128, 0);
70            _d0 = ShortVector.fromArray(SS, d512, 0);
71
72            _a1 = ShortVector.fromArray(SS, a128, vs);
73            _b1 = ShortVector.fromArray(SS, b128, vs);
```

```
 74              _c1 = ShortVector.fromArray(SS, c128, vs);
 75              _d1 = ShortVector.fromArray(SS, d512, vs);
 76            break;
 77
 78          case 16:
 79            xShift = 6;
 80            yMask = ~(-1 << xShift);
 81
 82              _a0 = ShortVector.fromArray(SS, a256, 0);
 83              _b0 = ShortVector.fromArray(SS, b256, 0);
 84              _c0 = ShortVector.fromArray(SS, c256, 0);
 85              _d0 = ShortVector.fromArray(SS, d512, 0);
 86
 87              _a1 = ShortVector.fromArray(SS, a256, vs);
 88              _b1 = ShortVector.fromArray(SS, b256, vs);
 89              _c1 = ShortVector.fromArray(SS, c256, vs);
 90              _d1 = ShortVector.fromArray(SS, d512, vs);
 91            break;
 92
 93          default:
 94            xShift = 7;
 95            yMask = ~(-1 << xShift);
 96
 97            var _load = SS.indexInRange(0, 64);
 98              _a0 = ShortVector.fromArray(SS, a512, 0, _load);
 99              _b0 = ShortVector.fromArray(SS, b512, 0, _load);
100              _c0 = ShortVector.fromArray(SS, c512, 0, _load);
101              _d0 = ShortVector.fromArray(SS, d512, 0, _load);
102
103            _load = SS.indexInRange(vs, 64);
104              _a1 = ShortVector.fromArray(SS, a512, vs, _load);
105              _b1 = ShortVector.fromArray(SS, b512, vs, _load);
106              _c1 = ShortVector.fromArray(SS, c512, vs, _load);
107              _d1 = ShortVector.fromArray(SS, d512, vs, _load);
108        }
```

```
109
110      final int vl = SL.length();
111      final long longMask = 0x0000000000000FFFFL;
112      final LongVector _zero = LongVector.zero(SL);
113
114    LongVector _max = _zero;
115    LongVector _start = _zero;
116
117    LongVector _idx = VectorShuffle.iota(SL, 0, 1, false)
118      .toVector().reinterpretAsLongs();
119
120    for (int i = 2; i < problemSize; i += vl) {
121      var _inRange = SL.indexInRange(i, problemSize);
122
123      LongVector _val = _idx.add(i, _inRange);
124      LongVector _pos = _val;
125      LongVector _orbit = _zero;
126
127      for (; ; ) {
128        LongVector _ctz = _val.lanewise(TRAILING_ZEROS_COUNT);
129
130        _val = _val.lanewise(LSHR, _ctz);
131        _orbit = _orbit.add(_ctz);
132
133        LongVector _x = _val.lanewise(LSHR, xShift);
134        var _y = _val.and(yMask).lanewise(LSHR, 1);
135        ShortVector _m = _y.reinterpretAsShorts();
136
137        VectorMask<Long> _done = _x.eq(0);
138
139        if (_done.allTrue()) {
140          var _dd = _m.selectFrom(_d0, _d1).reinterpretAsLongs();
141          _dd = _dd.and(longMask);
142
143          _orbit = _orbit.add(_dd);
```

```
144
145              VectorMask<Long> _less = _max.lt(_orbit);
146
147          _max = _max.blend(_orbit, _less);
148          _start = _start.blend(_pos, _less);
149
150          break;
151        } else {
152          var _aa = _m.selectFrom(_a0, _a1).reinterpretAsLongs();
153          var _bb = _m.selectFrom(_b0, _b1).reinterpretAsLongs();
154          var _cc = _m.selectFrom(_c0, _c1).reinterpretAsLongs();
155
156          _aa = _aa.and(longMask);
157          _bb = _bb.and(longMask);
158          _cc = _cc.and(longMask);
159
160          _val = _x.mul(_aa).add(_bb).blend(_val, _done);
161          _orbit = _orbit.add(_cc).blend(_orbit, _done);
162        }
163      }
164    }
165
166    for (int step = 1; step < SL.length(); step <<= 1) {
167      LongVector _shiftedMax = _max.slice(step, _zero);
168      LongVector _shiftedStart = _start.slice(step, _zero);
169
170      VectorMask<Long> _less = _max.lt(_shiftedMax);
171      _max = _max.blend(_shiftedMax, _less);
172      _start = _start.blend(_shiftedStart, _less);
173    }
174
175    long start = _start.lane(0);
176    return start;
177  }
178 }
179
316
```

- Lines 62–108 populate vectors with tables of maximum available size.

- Lines 128–131 process trailing zeros of the number.

- Lines 133–135 extract components x and y.

- Lines 152–161 perform table lookup for values A, B, and C and compute new intermediate values.

- Lines 139–150 execute the final iteration when $x = 0$.

- Lines 145–148 update the vector of maximum orbit length candidates.

- Lines 166–173 select the maximum orbit length via reduction.

Work Piling

One source of inefficiency remains in the algorithm: neighboring orbits have different lengths, so some vector lanes sit idle waiting for the longest orbit currently in flight to complete.

We compute the fill factor—the fraction of active lanes over the entire algorithm execution time (see Table 15-3).

Table 15-3. *Lane fill factor by vector length*

Algorithm	128	256	512
Vectorized	90.37%	77.58%	68.77%
Accelerated	88.95%	74.80%	65.39%
Multi-step	91.04%	78.94%	70.47%
Combined	88.27%	73.91%	63.76%

As Table 15-3 shows, the fill percentage drops substantially as vector length grows: the more lanes in a vector, the higher the probability that at least one of them gets stuck on a long orbit, delaying the others. Moreover, a more efficient algorithm advances several orbit steps per iteration, so short orbits complete faster, and the variance in completion times across lanes increases; the fill factor drops further still. We attempt to reduce lane idleness.

The simplest algorithm for increasing utilization is one we all learned in elementary school: whoever finishes early is immediately rewarded with extra work. In the literature, this technique goes by the name "work stealing"—a curious choice of words, as if I had somehow pilfered labor from an unsuspecting colleague. I can honestly say I have never stolen a piece of work in my life. I have, however, on countless occasions, found more work piled upon me than I could reasonably handle. In my humble opinion, "work piling" captures the reality far more accurately.

```
Terminology aside, the principle applies neatly to our problem: we pile
extra work onto idle vector lanes.
 1    package com.nonpareilcoder.projecteuler;
 2
 3    import jdk.incubator.vector.*;
 4    import static jdk.incubator.vector.VectorOperators.*;
 5    import static com.nonpareilcoder.projecteuler.
      CollatzConjectureCombined.*;
 6
 7    public class CollatzConjecturePiled {
 8      static final VectorSpecies<Long> SL =
 9        LongVector.SPECIES_PREFERRED;
10      static final VectorSpecies<Short> SS =
11        ShortVector.SPECIES_PREFERRED;
12
13
14      static public long longestOrbit(int problemSize) {
15        final int vs = SS.length();
16
17        long xShift, yMask;
18        ShortVector _a0, _b0, _c0, _d0;
19        ShortVector _a1, _b1, _c1, _d1;
20
21        switch (vs) {
22          case 8:
23              xShift = 5;
```

```
24        yMask = ~(-1 << xShift);
25
26        _a0 = ShortVector.fromArray(SS, a128, 0);
27        _b0 = ShortVector.fromArray(SS, b128, 0);
28        _c0 = ShortVector.fromArray(SS, c128, 0);
29        _d0 = ShortVector.fromArray(SS, d512, 0);
30
31        _a1 = ShortVector.fromArray(SS, a128, vs);
32        _b1 = ShortVector.fromArray(SS, b128, vs);
33        _c1 = ShortVector.fromArray(SS, c128, vs);
34        _d1 = ShortVector.fromArray(SS, d512, vs);
35        break;
36
37      case 16:
38        xShift = 6;
39        yMask = ~(-1 << xShift);
40
41        _a0 = ShortVector.fromArray(SS, a256, 0);
42        _b0 = ShortVector.fromArray(SS, b256, 0);
43        _c0 = ShortVector.fromArray(SS, c256, 0);
44        _d0 = ShortVector.fromArray(SS, d512, 0);
45
46        _a1 = ShortVector.fromArray(SS, a256, vs);
47        _b1 = ShortVector.fromArray(SS, b256, vs);
48        _c1 = ShortVector.fromArray(SS, c256, vs);
49        _d1 = ShortVector.fromArray(SS, d512, vs);
50        break;
51
52      default:
53        xShift = 7;
54        yMask = ~(-1 << xShift);
55
56        var _load = SS.indexInRange(0, 64);
57        _a0 = ShortVector.fromArray(SS, a512, 0, _load);
58        _b0 = ShortVector.fromArray(SS, b512, 0, _load);
```

```
59           _c0 = ShortVector.fromArray(SS, c512, 0, _load);
60           _d0 = ShortVector.fromArray(SS, d512, 0, _load);
61
62           _load = SS.indexInRange(vs, 64);
63           _a1 = ShortVector.fromArray(SS, a512, vs, _load);
64           _b1 = ShortVector.fromArray(SS, b512, vs, _load);
65           _c1 = ShortVector.fromArray(SS, c512, vs, _load);
66           _d1 = ShortVector.fromArray(SS, d512, vs, _load);
67         }
68
69       final int vl = SL.length();
70       final long longMask = 0x000000000000FFFFL;
71       final LongVector _zero = LongVector.zero(SL);
72
73       LongVector _max = _zero;
74       LongVector _start = _zero;
75
76       LongVector _idx = VectorShuffle.iota(SL, 0, 1, false)
77           .toVector().reinterpretAsLongs();
78
79       int i = 2;
80
81       var _inRange = SL.indexInRange(i, problemSize);
82
83       LongVector _val = _idx.add(i, _inRange);
84       LongVector _pos = _val;
85       LongVector _orbit = _zero;
86
87       i += vl;
88
89       while (i < problemSize) {
90         LongVector _ctz = _val.lanewise(TRAILING_ZEROS_COUNT);
91
92         _val = _val.lanewise(LSHR, _ctz);
93         _orbit = _orbit.add(_ctz);
```

```
 94
 95        LongVector _x = _val.lanewise(LSHR, xShift);
 96        LongVector _y = _val.and(yMask).lanewise(LSHR, 1);
 97        ShortVector _m = _y.reinterpretAsShorts();
 98
 99        VectorMask<Long> _done = _x.eq(0);
100
101        if (_done.anyTrue()) {
102          var _dd = _m.selectFrom(_d0, _d1).reinterpretAsLongs();
103          _dd = _dd.and(longMask);
104
105          LongVector _result = _orbit.add(_dd);
106
107          VectorMask<Long> _less = _max.lt(_result).and(_done);
108
109          _max = _max.blend(_result, _less);
110          _start = _start.blend(_pos, _less);
111
112          _inRange = SL.indexInRange(i, problemSize);
113          var _new = _zero.blend(_idx.add(i), _inRange).expand(_done);
114
115          _val = _val.blend(_new, _done);
116          _pos = _pos.blend(_new, _done);
117          _orbit = _orbit.blend(_zero, _done);
118
119          i += _done.trueCount();
120        } else {
121          var _aa = _m.selectFrom(_a0, _a1).reinterpretAsLongs();
122          var _bb = _m.selectFrom(_b0, _b1).reinterpretAsLongs();
123          var _cc = _m.selectFrom(_c0, _c1).reinterpretAsLongs();
124
125          _aa = _aa.and(longMask);
126          _bb = _bb.and(longMask);
127          _cc = _cc.and(longMask);
128
```

```
129          _val = _x.mul(_aa).add(_bb).blend(_val, _done);
130          _orbit = _orbit.add(_cc).blend(_orbit, _done);
131        }
132      }
133
134      for (;;) {
135        LongVector _ctz = _val.lanewise(TRAILING_ZEROS_COUNT);
136
137        _val = _val.lanewise(LSHR, _ctz);
138        _orbit = _orbit.add(_ctz);
139
140        LongVector _x = _val.lanewise(LSHR, xShift);
141        LongVector _y = _val.and(yMask).lanewise(LSHR, 1);
142        VectorShuffle<Short> _m = _y.reinterpretAsShorts().toShuffle();
143
144        VectorMask<Long> _done = _x.eq(0);
145
146        if (_done.allTrue()) {
147          LongVector _dd = _d0.rearrange(_m, _d1).reinterpretAsLongs();
148          _dd = _dd.and(longMask);
149
150          LongVector _result = _orbit.add(_dd);
151
152          VectorMask<Long> _valid = _zero.lt(_pos);
153          VectorMask<Long> _less = _max.lt(_result).and(_valid);
154
155          _max = _max.blend(_result, _less);
156          _start = _start.blend(_pos, _less);
157
158          break;
159        } else {
160          LongVector _aa = _a0.rearrange(_m, _a1).reinterpretAsLongs();
161          LongVector _bb = _b0.rearrange(_m, _b1).reinterpretAsLongs();
162          LongVector _cc = _c0.rearrange(_m, _c1).reinterpretAsLongs();
163
```

```
164              _aa = _aa.and(longMask);
165              _bb = _bb.and(longMask);
166              _cc = _cc.and(longMask);
167
168              _val = _x.mul(_aa).add(_bb).blend(_val, _done);
169              _orbit = _orbit.add(_cc).blend(_orbit, _done);
170            }
171          }
172
173          for (int step = 1; step < SL.length(); step <<= 1) {
174            LongVector _shiftedMax = _max.slice(step, _zero);
175            LongVector _shiftedStart = _start.slice(step, _zero);
176
177            VectorMask<Long> _less = _max.lt(_shiftedMax);
178            _max = _max.blend(_shiftedMax, _less);
179            _start = _start.blend(_shiftedStart, _less);
180          }
181
182          long start = _start.lane(0);
183          return start;
184        }
185     }
186
```

- Lines 105–110 update the maximum orbit length candidate vector from completed orbits.

- Lines 112–119 load new tasks in place of completed ones.

- Once the pool of new tasks is exhausted, we fall back to the previous algorithm in lines 134–171.

In line 113, we use the **expand** operation for the first time. It is the inverse of **compress**.

```
vector = input.expand(mask);
```

is equivalent to

```
for(int i = 0, j = 0; i < SP.length(); i++) {
  if(mask[i]) {
    vector[i] = input[j++];
  }
}
```

This operation is precisely what allows us to quickly place new tasks where old ones finished.

Memoization

Until now, we have been accelerating the computation of each orbit individually. Now we try to reuse the results of previous computations.

We store already-computed orbit lengths. If the Collatz conjecture holds, sooner or later, the intermediate value of each new orbit enters the range of previously computed starting values. From that point, the remaining orbit length can be looked up in previous results, and computation can terminate early. For our problem, we need to store up to one million previous values—quite reasonable memory requirements—and the Collatz conjecture has been thoroughly verified in this range.

```
1    package com.nonpareilcoder.projecteuler;
2
3    import jdk.incubator.vector.*;
4
5    import static jdk.incubator.vector.VectorOperators.*;
6    import static com.nonpareilcoder.projecteuler.
     CollatzConjectureCombined.*;
7
8    public class CollatzConjectureMemoized {
9      static final VectorSpecies<Long> SL =
10       LongVector.SPECIES_PREFERRED;
11     static final VectorSpecies<Short> SS =
12       ShortVector.SPECIES_PREFERRED;
13
```

```
14   static final long[] d = {
15     0, 1, 2, 8, 3, 6, 9, 17, 4, 20, 7, 15, 10, 10, 18, 18,
16     5, 13, 21, 21, 8, 8, 16, 16, 11, 24, 11, 112,
17     19, 19, 19, 107,
18     6, 27, 14, 14, 22, 22, 22, 35, 9, 110, 9, 30, 17, 17, 17, 105,
19     12, 25, 25, 25, 12, 12, 113, 113, 20, 33, 20, 33,
20     20, 20, 108, 108,
21     7, 28, 28, 28, 15, 15, 15, 103, 23, 116, 23, 15, 23, 23, 36, 36,
22     10, 23, 111, 111, 10, 10, 31, 31, 18, 31, 18, 93,
23     18, 18, 106, 106,
24     13, 119, 26, 26, 26, 26, 26, 88, 13, 39, 13, 101,
25     114, 114, 114, 70,
26     21, 13, 34, 34, 21, 21, 34, 34, 21, 96, 21, 47,
27     109, 109, 109, 47};
28
29   static public long longestOrbit(int problemSize) {
30     long[] orbits = new long[problemSize];
31     final int vs = SS.length();
32
33     long xShift, yMask;
34     ShortVector _a0, _b0, _c0;
35     ShortVector _a1, _b1, _c1;
36
37     switch (vs) {
38       case 8:
39         xShift = 5;
40         yMask = ~(-1 << xShift);
41
42         _a0 = ShortVector.fromArray(SS, a128, 0);
43         _b0 = ShortVector.fromArray(SS, b128, 0);
44         _c0 = ShortVector.fromArray(SS, c128, 0);
45
46         _a1 = ShortVector.fromArray(SS, a128, vs);
47         _b1 = ShortVector.fromArray(SS, b128, vs);
48         _c1 = ShortVector.fromArray(SS, c128, vs);
```

```
49            break;
50
51        case 16:
52          xShift = 6;
53          yMask = ~(-1 << xShift);
54
55          _a0 = ShortVector.fromArray(SS, a256, 0);
56          _b0 = ShortVector.fromArray(SS, b256, 0);
57          _c0 = ShortVector.fromArray(SS, c256, 0);
58
59          _a1 = ShortVector.fromArray(SS, a256, vs);
60          _b1 = ShortVector.fromArray(SS, b256, vs);
61          _c1 = ShortVector.fromArray(SS, c256, vs);
62          break;
63
64        default:
65          xShift = 7;
66          yMask = ~(-1 << xShift);
67
68          var _load = SS.indexInRange(0, 64);
69          _a0 = ShortVector.fromArray(SS, a512, 0, _load);
70          _b0 = ShortVector.fromArray(SS, b512, 0, _load);
71          _c0 = ShortVector.fromArray(SS, c512, 0, _load);
72
73          _load = SS.indexInRange(vs, 64);
74          _a1 = ShortVector.fromArray(SS, a512, vs, _load);
75          _b1 = ShortVector.fromArray(SS, b512, vs, _load);
76          _c1 = ShortVector.fromArray(SS, c512, vs, _load);
77      }
78
79    final int vl = SL.length();
80    final int cacheSize = Math.min(128, problemSize);
81    final long longMask = 0x000000000000FFFFL;
82    final LongVector _zero = LongVector.zero(SL);
83
```

```
 84        LongVector _max = _zero;
 85        LongVector _start = _zero;
 86
 87        LongVector _idx = VectorShuffle.iota(SL, 0, 1, false)
 88          .toVector().reinterpretAsLongs();
 89
 90        for (int i = 0; i < cacheSize; i += vl) {
 91          var _inRange = SL.indexInRange(i, problemSize);
 92
 93          LongVector _pos = _idx.add(i, _inRange);
 94          LongVector _orbit = LongVector.fromArray(SL, d, i, _inRange);
 95
 96          VectorMask<Long> _less = _max.lt(_orbit);
 97
 98          _max = _max.blend(_orbit, _less);
 99          _start = _start.blend(_pos, _less);
100
101          _orbit.intoArray(orbits, i, _inRange);
102        }
103
104        for (int i = cacheSize; i < problemSize; i += vl) {
105          var _inRange = SL.indexInRange(i, problemSize);
106
107          LongVector _val = _idx.add(i, _inRange);
108          LongVector _pos = _val;
109          LongVector _orbit = _zero;
110
111          int[] gather = new int[2 * vl];
112
113          for (; ; ) {
114            LongVector _ctz = _val.lanewise(TRAILING_ZEROS_COUNT);
115
116            _val = _val.lanewise(LSHR, _ctz);
117            _orbit = _orbit.add(_ctz);
118
```

```
119                    VectorMask<Long> _done = _val.lt(i);
120
121             if (_done.allTrue()) {
122               ((IntVector) _val.convert(L2I, 0)).intoArray(gather, 0);
123               var _v = LongVector.fromArray(SL, orbits, 0, gather, 0);
124
125               _orbit = _orbit.add(_v);
126
127               _orbit.intoArray(orbits, i, _inRange);
128
129               VectorMask<Long> _less = _max.lt(_orbit);
130
131               _max = _max.blend(_orbit, _less);
132               _start = _start.blend(_pos, _less);
133
134               break;
135             } else {
136               var _x = _val.lanewise(LSHR, xShift);
137               var _y = _val.and(yMask).lanewise(LSHR, 1);
138               var _m = _y.reinterpretAsShorts();
139
140               var _aa = _m.selectFrom(_a0, _a1).reinterpretAsLongs();
141               var _bb = _m.selectFrom(_b0, _b1).reinterpretAsLongs();
142               var _cc = _m.selectFrom(_c0, _c1).reinterpretAsLongs();
143
144               _aa = _aa.and(longMask);
145               _bb = _bb.and(longMask);
146               _cc = _cc.and(longMask);
147
148               _val = _x.mul(_aa).add(_bb).blend(_val, _done);
149               _orbit = _orbit.add(_cc).blend(_orbit, _done);
150             }
151           }
152         }
153
```

```
154        for (int step = 1; step < SL.length(); step <<= 1) {
155          LongVector _shiftedMax = _max.slice(step, _zero);
156          LongVector _shiftedStart = _start.slice(step, _zero);
157
158          VectorMask<Long> _less = _max.compare(LT, _shiftedMax);
159          _max = _max.blend(_shiftedMax, _less);
160          _start = _start.blend(_shiftedStart, _less);
161        }
162
163      long start = _start.lane(0);
164      return start;
165    }
166  }
167
```

- The termination condition changes in line 119. Now we check whether the intermediate value has fallen into the range of previously computed orbits.

- Lines 122–123 load previously computed values using the **gather** operation.

- Line 127 stores newly computed orbit values sequentially to memory.

Over-optimization

We supplement our lane fill table with data from the memoizing algorithm (Table 15-4).

Table 15-4. *Memoization lane fill factor*

Algorithm	128	256	512
Memoization	50.00%	37.56%	29.12%

As shown in Table 15-4, between half and two-thirds of resources sit uselessly idle. We pile work onto them.

```
 1    package com.nonpareilcoder.projecteuler;
 2
 3    import jdk.incubator.vector.*;
 4    import static jdk.incubator.vector.VectorOperators.*;
 5    import static com.nonpareilcoder.projecteuler.
      CollatzConjectureCombined.*;
 6    import static com.nonpareilcoder.projecteuler.
      CollatzConjectureMemoized.d;
 7
 8    public class CollatzConjectureComprehensive {
 9      static final VectorSpecies<Long> SL =
10        LongVector.SPECIES_PREFERRED;
11      static final VectorSpecies<Short> SS =
12        ShortVector.SPECIES_PREFERRED;
13
14      static public long longestOrbit(int problemSize) {
15        long[] orbits = new long[problemSize];
16        final int vs = SS.length();
17
18        long xShift, yMask;
19        ShortVector _a0, _b0, _c0;
20        ShortVector _a1, _b1, _c1;
21
22        switch (vs) {
23          case 8:
24            xShift = 5;
25            yMask = ~(-1 << xShift);
26
27            _a0 = ShortVector.fromArray(SS, a128, 0);
28            _b0 = ShortVector.fromArray(SS, b128, 0);
29            _c0 = ShortVector.fromArray(SS, c128, 0);
30
31            _a1 = ShortVector.fromArray(SS, a128, vs);
```

```
32          _b1 = ShortVector.fromArray(SS, b128, vs);
33          _c1 = ShortVector.fromArray(SS, c128, vs);
34          break;
35
36      case 16:
37          xShift = 6;
38          yMask = ~(-1 << xShift);
39
40          _a0 = ShortVector.fromArray(SS, a256, 0);
41          _b0 = ShortVector.fromArray(SS, b256, 0);
42          _c0 = ShortVector.fromArray(SS, c256, 0);
43
44          _a1 = ShortVector.fromArray(SS, a256, vs);
45          _b1 = ShortVector.fromArray(SS, b256, vs);
46          _c1 = ShortVector.fromArray(SS, c256, vs);
47          break;
48
49      default:
50          xShift = 7;
51          yMask = ~(-1 << xShift);
52
53          var _load = SS.indexInRange(0, 64);
54          _a0 = ShortVector.fromArray(SS, a512, 0, _load);
55          _b0 = ShortVector.fromArray(SS, b512, 0, _load);
56          _c0 = ShortVector.fromArray(SS, c512, 0, _load);
57
58          _load = SS.indexInRange(vs, 64);
59          _a1 = ShortVector.fromArray(SS, a512, vs, _load);
60          _b1 = ShortVector.fromArray(SS, b512, vs, _load);
61          _c1 = ShortVector.fromArray(SS, c512, vs, _load);
62      }
63
64      final int vl = SL.length();
65      final int cacheSize = Math.min(128, problemSize);
66      final long longMask = 0x000000000000FFFFL;
```

```
67        final LongVector _zero = LongVector.zero(SL);
68
69        LongVector _max = _zero;
70        LongVector _start = _zero;
71
72        LongVector _idx = VectorShuffle.iota(SL, 0, 1, false)
73            .toVector().reinterpretAsLongs();
74
75    double used = 0.0;
76
77    for (int i0 = 0; i0 < cacheSize; i0 += vl) {
78      var _inRange = SL.indexInRange(i0, problemSize);
79
80      LongVector _pos = _idx.add(i0, _inRange);
81      LongVector _orbit = LongVector.fromArray(SL, d, i0, _inRange);
82
83      VectorMask<Long> _less = _max.lt(_orbit);
84
85      _max = _max.blend(_orbit, _less);
86      _start = _start.blend(_pos, _less);
87
88      _orbit.intoArray(orbits, i0, _inRange);
89    }
90
91    int i0 = cacheSize, i1 = cacheSize;
92
93    VectorMask<Long> _inRange = SL.indexInRange(i0, problemSize);
94
95    LongVector _v0 = _idx.add(i0, _inRange);
96    LongVector _p0 = _v0;
97    LongVector _o0 = _zero;
98
99    i0 += vl;
100
101    int[] gather = new int[2 * vl];
```

```
102        int[] scatter = new int[2 * vl];
103
104    while (i0 < problemSize) {
105      LongVector _ctz = _v0.lanewise(TRAILING_ZEROS_COUNT);
106
107      _v0 = _v0.lanewise(LSHR, _ctz);
108      _o0 = _o0.add(_ctz);
109
110      VectorMask<Long> _done = _v0.lt(i1);
111
112      if (_done.anyTrue()) {
113        VectorMask<Long> _active = _done.not();
114        LongVector _v1 = _v0.blend(0, _active);
115
116        ((IntVector) _v1.convert(L2I, 0)).intoArray(gather, 0);
117        var _result = LongVector.fromArray(SL, orbits, 0, gather,
          0, _done);
118
119        _result = _result.add(_o0, _done);
120
121        ((IntVector) _p0.convert(L2I, 0)).intoArray(scatter, 0);
122        _result.intoArray(orbits, 0, scatter, 0, _done);
123
124        used += 2;
125
126        VectorMask<Long> _less = _max.compare(LT, _result, _done);
127
128        _max = _max.blend(_result, _less);
129        _start = _start.blend(_p0, _less);
130
131        _v0 = _v0.compress(_active);
132        _p0 = _p0.compress(_active);
133        _o0 = _o0.compress(_active);
134
135        VectorMask<Long> _insert = _active.compress().not();
```

```
136
137            _inRange = SL.indexInRange(i0, problemSize);
138            var _new = _zero.blend(_idx.add(i0), _inRange).expand
               (_insert);
139
140            _v0 = _v0.blend(_new, _insert);
141            _p0 = _p0.blend(_new, _insert);
142
143            i0 += _done.trueCount();
144            i1 = (int) _p0.lane(0);
145          } else {
146            LongVector _x = _v0.lanewise(LSHR, xShift);
147            LongVector _y = _v0.and(yMask).lanewise(LSHR, 1);
148            var _m = _y.reinterpretAsShorts();
149
150            var _aa = _m.selectFrom(_a0, _a1).reinterpretAsLongs();
151            var _bb = _m.selectFrom(_b0, _b1).reinterpretAsLongs();
152            var _cc = _m.selectFrom(_c0, _c1).reinterpretAsLongs();
153
154            _aa = _aa.and(longMask);
155            _bb = _bb.and(longMask);
156            _cc = _cc.and(longMask);
157
158            _v0 = _x.mul(_aa).add(_bb).blend(_v0, _done);
159            _o0 = _o0.add(_cc).blend(_o0, _done);
160          }
161        }
162
163        for (; ; ) {
164          LongVector _ctz = _v0.lanewise(TRAILING_ZEROS_COUNT);
165
166          _v0 = _v0.lanewise(LSHR, _ctz);
167          _o0 = _o0.add(_ctz);
168
169          VectorMask<Long> _done = _v0.lt(i1);
```

```
170
171        if (_done.allTrue()) {
172          LongVector _v1 = _zero.blend(_v0, _done);
173
174          ((IntVector) _v1.convert(L2I, 0)).intoArray(gather, 0);
175          var _result = LongVector.fromArray(SL, orbits, 0, gather,
             0, _done);
176
177          _result = _result.add(_o0, _done);
178
179          ((IntVector) _p0.convert(L2I, 0)).intoArray(gather, 0);
180          _result.intoArray(orbits, 0, gather, 0, _done);
181
182          VectorMask<Long> _less = _max.compare(LT, _result, _done);
183
184          _max = _max.blend(_result, _less);
185          _start = _start.blend(_p0, _less);
186
187          break;
188        }
189        else {
190          LongVector _x = _v0.lanewise(LSHR, xShift);
191          LongVector _y = _v0.and(yMask).lanewise(LSHR, 1);
192          var _m = _y.reinterpretAsShorts();
193
194          var _aa = _m.selectFrom(_a0, _a1).reinterpretAsLongs();
195          var _bb = _m.selectFrom(_b0, _b1).reinterpretAsLongs();
196          var _cc = _m.selectFrom(_c0, _c1).reinterpretAsLongs();
197
198          _aa = _aa.and(longMask);
199          _bb = _bb.and(longMask);
200          _cc = _cc.and(longMask);
201
202          _v0 = _x.mul(_aa).add(_bb).blend(_v0, _done);
203          _o0 = _o0.add(_cc).blend(_o0, _done);
```

```
204              }
205            }
206
207        for (int step = 1; step < SL.length(); step <<= 1) {
208          LongVector _shiftedMax = _max.slice(step, _zero);
209          LongVector _shiftedStart = _start.slice(step, _zero);
210
211          VectorMask<Long> _less = _max.compare(LT, _shiftedMax);
212          _max = _max.blend(_shiftedMax, _less);
213          _start = _start.blend(_shiftedStart, _less);
214        }
215
216        long start = _start.lane(0);
217        return start;
218      }
219    }
220
```

- Lines 110–114 extract intermediate values that have fallen into the range of previously computed orbits.

- Lines 116–117 load previously computed orbits for these values using the **gather** operation.

- Lines 121–122 store newly computed orbit values to memory using the **scatter** operation.

- We need to track not only the index of the next new task but also the boundary of the orbit range fully covered by previous computations. For this reason, indices of orbits currently in flight are maintained in sorted order. Lines 131–133 therefore compact working vectors using the **compress** operation.

- Lines 135–143 load new tasks into freed positions at the end of working vectors using the **expand** operation.

- Once the pool of new tasks is exhausted, we fall back to the previous algorithm in lines 163–205.

Since we must maintain working vectors in sorted order, loading new tasks has become more complex. Furthermore, each load follows a slow **gather** operation with an equally slow **scatter** operation.

We count the number of slow memory accesses (Table 15-5).

Table 15-5. *Memory access count comparison*

Algorithm	128	256	512
Memoization	499936	249968	124984
Work piling	1713258	1202332	728040

As Table 15-5 reveals, the work-piling algorithm requires 3–6 times more memory accesses than simple memoization. Each new task load entails a pair of **gather/scatter** operations, and this overhead more than negates the gain from the higher lane fill factor. The inefficiency grows with increasing vector length: the ratio of memory accesses is 3.4 for 128-bit vectors, 4.8 for 256-bit, and 5.8 for 512-bit. This is a classic example of over-optimization: the attempt to eliminate one source of inefficiency spawned another, even more costly one.

Result

The answer to Project Euler problem 14: the starting number **837799** produces an orbit of length **525** steps, the maximum among all numbers under one million.

Benchmarks

Table 15-6 and Table 15-7 compare the Collatz orbit computation strategies.

Table 15-6. *Single-core speedup on x86 platforms (higher is better)*

Variant	GL	Z2	IL	SR	Z5
accelerated	0.06	1.76	3.57	3.16	3.01
combined	0.11	3.48	11.31	10.34	9.09
comprehensive	0.24	3.76	14.23	17.37	13.41
lookup	0.02	1.60	3.45	3.25	2.94
memoized	0.55	13.07	28.57	33.53	30.48
piled	0.11	3.83	11.45	10.85	8.48
scalar	1.00	1.00	1.00	1.00	1.00
vectorized	0.02	1.31	2.07	1.68	2.23

The X86 benchmark results reveal that memoization dominates all other Collatz optimization strategies by a substantial margin. The memoized variant achieves extraordinary speedups of 28.57–33.53× on AVX-512 platforms. The comprehensive variant (combining memoization with work piling) achieves strong results (14.23–17.37× on AVX-512) but trails simple memoization by 2×, validating the chapter's observation about over-optimization introducing costly gather/scatter operations.

Table 15-7. *Single-core speedup on ARM platforms (higher is better)*

Variant	M4	06	CO	NV	G3
accelerated	0.33	0.98	0.74	0.76	1.32
combined	0.74	1.74	1.24	1.21	2.89
comprehensive	1.78	8.41	6.47	7.55	3.65
lookup	0.43	0.81	0.67	0.67	1.09
memoized	5.91	10.52	8.30	12.16	13.32
piled	0.72	1.63	1.26	1.23	1.93
scalar	1.00	1.00	1.00	1.00	1.00
vectorized	0.30	0.65	0.56	0.59	1.01

The ARM benchmark results confirm memoization as the dominant strategy for the Collatz problem, though with more modest speedups than X86. G3 (Amazon Graviton 3) achieves the best memoized performance at 13.32×, followed closely by NV (Nvidia Grace) at 12.16×, demonstrating that wider SVE vectors and efficient gather operations benefit this cache-heavy workload. The results illustrate another contrarian pattern: when the algorithm is compute bound, optimization via memory access is the most effective strategy.

Conclusion

We have reached the end of our exploration of SIMD programming. Along the way, we did not just study SIMD techniques and algorithms—we learned to think differently: to reason in terms of data-level and instruction-level parallelism. Just as an artist learns to see colors they never noticed before, we learned to see the potential for parallel computation where we once saw only sequential operations.

The future of SIMD technologies is promising. The evolution of processor architectures, the emergence of new instruction sets, and ongoing compiler improvements create new opportunities for software optimization. In this rapidly changing landscape, mastery of SIMD programming principles becomes not merely an advantage but a necessary skill for every developer striving to create truly efficient programs.

We hope this book has provided useful knowledge and encouraged further exploration of SIMD programming. Perhaps some of you will venture beyond high-level languages to explore the depths of system libraries and machine code, where each step reveals new opportunities for optimization.

We trust the knowledge you have gained will prove useful in your future work with parallel programming.

We wish you success in your endeavors.

Index

A

Advanced Vector Extensions (AVX), 1
AI, *see* Artificial intelligence (AI)
Apple M4, 85
Arithmetic operations, 20
ARM's vector architecture, 3
Array of structures, 115
Artificial intelligence (AI), 219
Associativity, 98
Asymmetric loop, 244–248
AVX, *see* Advanced Vector
        Extensions (AVX)
AVX2, 1
AVX-512, 2, 136, 202

B

BigInteger, 208, 224
Billionaire algorithm, 223–227
Binary search, 249
Bit manipulation techniques, 107
Bitonic sorting, 236–240, 247
Blend operation, 60

C

Cache-oblivious, 24
Collatz conjecture
    ARM platforms
        dominant strategy, 339
        single-core speedup, 338
    combined approach, 309–317
    computation, 337
    divergent execution, 300–302
    example orbits, 298
    finding patterns, 302–304
    lane fill factor, 317
    memoization, 324–329
    multi-step lookahead, 305–308
    over-optimization, 329–337
    problem statement, 297
    SIMD parallelism, 297
    straightforward solution, 298, 299
    transformation coefficients for 2
            trailing bits, 306
    transformation coefficients for 6
            trailing bits, 309–311
    work piling, 317–324
    x86 platforms
        single-core speedup, 338
Commutative property, 15
Commutativity, 98
Compress operation, 78, 79, 336
Congruent modulo n, 305
Convergents of e
    ARM platforms
        hardware capabilities, 232
        single-core speedup, 231
    Billionaire algorithm, 223–227
    computation, 230
    example, 205
    horizontal vector solution, 209–212
    infinite continued fraction, 205
    Karatsuba algorithm, 219–223

Convergents of *e* (*cont.*)
    scalar solution, 206–209
    short vectors, 227–230
    Strassen algorithm, 215–219
    vertical vector solution, 213–215
    x86 platforms
        digit extraction, 231
        single-core speedup, 231
Cryptography, 299
Cumulative sum, 87, 140, 178

D

Data-level parallelism, 12, 341
Digit-level parallelism, 231
Divide and conquer
      principle, 263
Downsweep, 149, 158
Duplicate removal approaches
    ARM platforms
        NEON and SVE
          implementations, 85
        single-core speedup, 84
    compress-based, 84
    extra memory access, 82–84
    two-pointer method, 77, 78
    vector compression, 78–82
    x86 platforms
        single-core speedup, 84

E

Element-wise vector
      algorithm, 260–262
Exclusive OR (XOR)
    scalar solution, 98
    vector solution, 99
Expand operation, 336

F

Fibonacci numbers, 208
    ARM platforms
        scalar leap optimization, 120
        single-core speedup, 120
    computation approaches, 119
    scalar algorithm, 111, 112
    scalar hopping, 116, 117
    vector algorithm, 113–116
    vector hopping, 117, 119
    x86 platforms
        scalar leap optimization, 120
        single-core speedup, 120
fromArray method, 276

G

G3 (Amazon Graviton 3), 39, 108, 203,
      253, 277, 295
Gather operation, 336
Gigenary system, 223
GL (Intel Gemini Lake), 37
Global maximum, 283

H

Hankel matrices, 219, 220
Hardware-oriented terminology, 12
Hull–Dobell theorem, 124
Hyperthreading, 244

I

Ice Lake processor, 42
Identity element, 98
IEEE 754 standard, 20
IL (Intel Ice Lake), 37, 84, 136, 202, 252
Inclusion-exclusion principle, 73

Infinite continued fraction, 205
Instruction-level parallelism, 12, 103, 148, 213, 248, 253, 341
intoArray method, 251

J

Java Microbenchmark Harness (JMH), 8
Java Vector API, 3
Java Virtual Machine (JVM), 42
JIT, *see* Just-In-Time (JIT)
JMH, *see* Java Microbenchmark Harness (JMH)
Just-In-Time (JIT), 3
JVM, *see* Java Virtual Machine (JVM)

K

Kadane's algorithm, 280, 281
Kahan's algorithm, 18–21, 26, 33, 38
Karatsuba algorithm, 219–223, 226

L

Lanewise, 11
LCG, *see* Linear congruential generator (LCG)
Least significant bit, 125
Lemire's method, 124
Lemire's test, 58
Linear congruential generator (LCG), 124

M

Mask-based computation, 103
Maximum subarray sum
    ARM platforms
        single-core speedup, 294
        slowdowns/marginal gains, 295
    example, 279
    Kadane's algorithm, 280, 281
    lightweight algorithm, 288–293
    practical applications, 295, 296
    problem reformulation, 281, 282
    results, 294
    vector solution, 283–288
    x86 platforms
        preferredX8 variant, 294
        single-core speedup, 294
        vector capabilities, 294
Mean *vs.* standard deviation algorithms, 28
Memoization, 177–190, 202, 203, 324–329, 338
Memory access count comparison, 337
Memory-bound workload, 36
Merge path method, 235–236
Merging arrays
    algorithms, 252
    ARM platforms
        implementations, 253
        single-core speedup, 253
    asymmetric loop, 244–248
    bitonic sorting, 236–240
    merge path method, 235, 236
    ranking elements, 248–252
    two-pointer method, 233–235
    unrolled loop, 240–243
    x86 platforms
        single-core speedup, 252
        vectorization, 252
Mini algorithm, 190–201
Modular bias, 126
Multiples of 3 or 5
    algorithmic optimization, 75
    arithmetic progression, 73–75
    ARM platforms

Multiples of 3 or 5 (*cont.*)
    single-core speedup, 76
  problem statement, 41
  scalar solution
    assembly listing, 48–50
    bytecode interpretation, 42
    C1 and C2 output, 55, 56
    compiled method, 42–48, 51–55
    exception and deoptimization
      handlers, 58
    idiv instructions, 50
    implementation, 41
    JVM's machinery, 42
    loop epilogue, 57
    method exit, 58
    multiplication, 56
    safepoint polling, 57
    unrolled main loop, 56, 57
  vector loop
    AVX-SSE transition, 72
    compiler's optimization, 58, 60
    constant pool, 69
    divisibility test, 58
    dynamic masking, 71
    first vector iteration, 70
    horizontal reduction, 71, 72
    initialization code, 69, 70
    machine code, 60–68
    masked operations, 60
    method exit, 72
    method header and
      statistics, 69
    safepoint polling, 71
    scalar epilogue, 71
    stack frame setup, 69
    uncommon traps, 72
    unrolled main loop, 70
  x86 platforms
    algorithmic optimization, 75
    single-core speedup, 75
    vectorization, 75

N

Naive algorithm, 256–258
Neural network hyperparameters, 125
nextFloat method, 125
nextInt method, 126
Normalization, 17
NV (Nvidia Grace), 39, 85, 108, 339

O

O6 (CIX CD8180), 85
Object-oriented paradigm, 115

P, Q

Pairwise addition, 13–15
Parallelization scheme, 113
Performance testing
  ARM processors, 8
  Intel and AMD, 7, 8
Prediction, 103
Prefix minimum, 283
Prefix sum, 87, 178, 283
  ARM platforms
    single-core speedup, 96
    vectorization, 96
  challenges, 94
  inclusive *vs.* exclusive sums, 89
  scalar solution, 88, 89
  vector solution, 89–94
  x86 platforms
    single-core speedup, 95
    trends, 95

R

Rainwater trapping
 accelerating optimal scan, 158–177
 ARM platforms
  single-core speedup, 203
 elevation bars, 139
 implementations, 202, 203
 interview solution, 140, 141
 memoization, 177–190
 mini algorithm, 190–201
 optimal vector scan, 148–157
 unrolled vector scan, 144–148
 vector scan, 141–144
 x86 platforms
  optimal scan implementations, 202
  single-core speedup, 202
  transposedX16 variant, 202
Random number generation
 ARM platforms
  performance characteristics, 137
  single-core speedup, 137
 implementations, 136, 137
 java.util.Random, 124–128
 method, 123
 practical applications, 135
 vector acceleration, 128–135
 x86 platforms
  single-core speedup, 136
reduceLanes method, 30, 31
reduce operation, 13
Rejection sampling, 126
Remainder distribution, 126
Remainder probabilities, 126
Residues modulo n, 305
RISC-V architecture, 3
RISC-V vector extension (RVV), 3
RVV, *see* RISC-V vector extension (RVV)

S

Scalable Vector Extension (SVE), 3
Scatter, 251, 252
Scatter operation, 336
Self-inverse, 98
Sequential addition, 10–12
Sequential data dependency, 12
Serial summation, 12
SIMD, *see* Single-Instruction-
  Multiple-Data (SIMD)
Single-Instruction-Multiple-Data
  (SIMD), 9, 341
Single-pass algorithm, 25–29
Slice operation, 79, 80, 82, 83
Sliding algorithm, 258–260
Sliding sum, 257, 276, 277
Spectral test, 125
SR (Intel Sapphire Rapids), 36
Statistical processing
 ARM platforms
  catastrophic performance
   degradation, 38
  execution timing, 38
  single-core speedup, 38, 39
 single-pass algorithm, 25–29
 two-pass algorithm, 23–24
 vector approach, 29–35
 x86 platforms
  execution timing, 35, 36
  single-core speedup, 37
  singlePass variant, 36
  vectorized statistics
   computation, 36
Strassen algorithm, 215–219
Streaming SIMD Extensions (SSE
  architecture), 1
Structure of arrays, 116

Suffix maximum computation, 157
Suffix sum, 87, 94, 178, 261
SVE, *see* Scalable Vector Extension (SVE)
Syracuse problem, *see* Collatz conjecture

T

Triples
    low-level optimizations, 104, 105
    problem, 103
    rules, 104
    state transitions, 104
    ternary digit (trit), 104
    vector solution, 105–107
    XOR, 103
Two-pass algorithm, 23–24
Two-pointer method, 77, 78, 233–235
Two-scan algorithm, 263–267
Two unique elements
    problem, 100, 101
    vector solution, 101–103

U

Universal algorithm, 272–277
Universal rearrange instruction, 151
Unzip0 operation, 151
Unzip1 operation, 151
Upsweep, 149, 158

V

Vector acceleration
    random number generation, 128–135
Vector addition
    algorithm comparison, 21
    Kahan's algorithm, 18–21
    pairwise addition, 13–15
    rounding, 15–18
    sequential addition, 10–12
    source data, 9
Vector approach
    accuracy comparison, 33
    element-wise operations, 30
    horizontal operation, 30
    loop implementation, 29
    mechanism, 33
    principles, 31
    reasons, 35
    types, 30
Vector compression, 78–82
Vector length
    approaches, 4–6
    ARM ecosystem, 6
    benefits, 4
    decision table, 6
    JIT compiler, 4
    predefined constants, 3
    VLA approach, 7
Vector-length-agnosticism (VLA), 7,
    29, 35, 157
Vector pivot, 157
Vector programming, 60
Vector reduction algorithm, 90
Vector scan, 89–91, 94, 96, 113, 141–144
Vector transposition, 150
Vertical algorithm, 267–271
VLA, *see* Vector-length-
    agnosticism (VLA)

W

Work piling, 317–324
Work stealing, 318

X, Y

x86 architecture, 1, 2
x86 vector extensions, 2
XOR, *see* Exclusive OR (XOR)
XOR-based *vs.* trit-based algorithms, 108

Z

Z5 (AMD Turin), 36, 202
Zip operation, 201, 237, 293
Zip0 operation, 150
Zip1 operation, 150, 151

GPSR Compliance
The European Union's (EU) General Product Safety Regulation (GPSR) is a set
of rules that requires consumer products to be safe and our obligations to
ensure this.

If you have any concerns about our products, you can contact us on

ProductSafety@springernature.com

In case Publisher is established outside the EU, the EU authorized
representative is:

Springer Nature Customer Service Center GmbH
Europaplatz 3
69115 Heidelberg, Germany